Daniel R. Fesenmaier,
Joseph T. O'Leary,
Muzaffer Uysal
Editors

Recent Advances in Tourism Marketing Research

Pre-publication
REVIEWS,
COMMENTARIES,
EVALUATIONS . . .

"**T**his volume identifies and strongly establishes the need for improved research methods in the worldwide tourism industry. It poses questions that are vital to scientists and practitioners alike. There are clearly written examples of issues and methods that can be employed by all levels of tourism professionals.

The book's major strength is that it raises questions and provides answers that will prove to be valuable to anyone charged with advancing tourism."

Russell A. Bell, PhD
Associate Professor
Marketing & Tourism
Cornell School
of Hotel Administration

More pre-publication
REVIEWS, COMMENTARIES, EVALUATIONS . . .

"Understanding the behavior of tourists today, will help us to better understand the human being tomorrow. (Socio-economic development is said to offer us greater disposable income, more leisure time and greater freedom to choose between satisfying pursuits– throughout our lifespan. This is a characteristic of the short periods when we are tourists.) Apart from the practical value of the findings, this is what makes tourism research particularly important.

Recent Advances in Tourism Marketing Research includes papers presenting new or improved research methodologies that will help readers to better understand the complex character of tourism, and will assist practitioners to develop adequate marketing strategies. One interesting section of the book covers the use of models to understand tourists' choice of destination, while various papers present the use of the experience sampling method involving tourists in research. Other papers discuss cases of importance-performance analysis, and a new approach to conversion research. An excellent summary by Gordon D. Taylor outlines the present state of tourism research and its future prospects. As a whole, this work is to be greatly welcomed."

Márton Lengyel, PhD, MA
Professor
Chief of the Tourism
Research Centre, Budapest University
of Economic Sciences, and President
of the Hungarian Tourism Society

"This text offers a great resource to tourism educators, researchers and graduate students. The collection of articles highlights a wide range of topics ranging from psychology based studies to business oriented decisions. These articles collectively provide an effective literature review of research techniques for current tourism topics and will serve as a model for other aspiring research. This effort will also assist to advance tourism research and its credibility as a field of social science."

Robert M. O'Halloran, PhD
Associate Professor
School of Hotel, Restaurant
& Tourism Management Daniels
College of Business
University of Denver

More pre-publication
REVIEWS, COMMENTARIES, EVALUATIONS . . .

"**F**esenmaier, O'Leary and Uysal's new edited volume on *Recent Advances in Tourism Marketing Research* nicely reflects the current issues of major concern in this domain. A good deal of progress has been achieved in travel behavior modeling conceptually and in refining the empirical measurement procedures. Tourism research nowadays does no longer replicate the exercises demonstrated in consumer research. It has evolved to become a mature field of study starting to pay back what it has borrowed from the behavioral sciences. The contributions collected in this volume have originality, methodological solidity, and practical relevance. Several articles center on vacation destination choice. There is a balanced mixture of approaches relying on established methodology such as multiple regression, conjoint, or discrete (logic) choice models, and others exploring less routinized tools such as feedforward neural networks with back-propagation learning. The volume contains micro models seeking explanation on the disaggregate level and econometric models including marketing variables on the aggregate level as well. The reader intrigued by the recent controvery about the usefulness and implications of service quality research in tourism will also find some stimulating material on importance and performance measurement. This volume is particularly helpful for research-minded practitioners and for graduate students. It may be recommended to readers who want to familiarize themselves with a representative range of tourism research topics without having to scan databases of numerous journals and conference proceedings."

Josef A. Mazanec
Professor
Director of the Institute for Tourism & Leisure Studies
Vienna University of Economics & Business Administration
Wien, Austria

Recent Advances
in Tourism Marketing
Research

Recent Advances in Tourism Marketing Research

Daniel R. Fesenmaier
Joseph T. O'Leary
Muzaffer Uysal
Editors

The Haworth Press, Inc.
New York • London

Recent Advances in Tourism Marketing Research has also been published as *Journal of Travel & Tourism Marketing*, Volume 5, Numbers 1/2 & 3 1996.

The development, preparation, and publication of this work has been undertaken with great care. However, the publisher, employees, editors, and agents of The Haworth Press and all imprints of The Haworth Press, Inc., including The Haworth Medical Press and Pharmaceutical Products Press, are not responsible for any errors contained herein or for consequences that may ensue from use of materials or information contained in this work. Opinions expressed by the author(s) are not necessarily those of The Haworth Press, Inc.

The Haworth Press, Inc., 10 Alice Street, Binghamton, NY 13904-1580 USA

Library of Congress Cataloging-in-Publication Data

Recent advances in tourism marketing research / Daniel R. Fesenmaier, Joseph T. O'Leary, Muzaffer Uysal.

p. cm.

"Recent advances in tourism marketing research has also been published as 'Journal of travel & tourism marketing', volume 5, numbers 1/2 & 3 1996"

Includes bibliographical references (p.) and index.

ISBN 1-56024-836-X (alk. paper)

1. Tourist trade–Marketing–Research. I. Fesenmaier, Daniel R. II. O'Leary, Joesph T. III. Uysal, Muzaffer. IV. Journal of travel & tourism marketing.

G155.A1R42 1996   96-32039

338.4'791–dc20   CIP

INDEXING & ABSTRACTING

Contributions to this publication are selectively indexed or abstracted in print, electronic, online, or CD-ROM version(s) of the reference tools and information services listed below. This list is current as of the copyright date of this publication. See the end of this section for additional notes.

- *ABSCAN, Inc.,* P. O. Box 2384, Monroe, LA 71207-2384

- *Cabell's Directory of Publishing Opportunities in Business & Economics (comprehensive & descriptive bibliographic listing with editorial criteria and publication production data for selected business & economics journals),* Cabell Publishing Company, Box 5428, Tobe Hahn Station, Beaumont, TX 77726-5428

- *Centre des Hautes Etudes Touristiques (CHET),* IMMEUBLE EUROFFICE, 38 av. de l'Europe B.P. 661, 13094 Aix-en-Provence Cedex 2, France

- *CNPIEC Reference Guide: Chinese National Directory of Foreign Periodicals,* P.O. Box 88, Beijing, Peoples Republic of China

- *IBZ International Bibliography of Periodical Literature,* Zeller Verlag GmbH & Co., P.O.B. 1949 Osnabruck, Germany

- *International Hospitality and Tourism Database, The,* John Wiley & Sons, Inc., 605 Third Avenue, New York, NY 10158-0012

- *International Hospitality and Tourism Database: The Guide to Industry and Academic Sources,* Cornell University, Stouffer Hotel Library, Statler Hall, Ithaca, NY 14853-6902

- *INTERNET ACCESS (& additional networks) Bulletin Board for Libraries ("Bubl"), coverage of information resources on INTERNET, JANET, and other networks.*
  - JANET X.29: UK.AC.BATH.BUBL or 00006012101300
  - TELNET: BUBL.BATH.AC.UK or 138.38.32.45 login 'bubl'
  - Gopher: BUBL.BATH.AC.UK (138.32.32.45). Port 7070
  - World Wide Web: http: / / www.bubl.bath.ac.uk./BUBL/ home.html
  - NISSWAIS: telnetniss.ac.uk (for the NISS gateway)
  The Andersonian Library, Curran Building, 101 St. James Road, Glasgow G4 ONS, Scotland

(continued)

- ***Journal of Health Care Marketing (abstracts section)***, Georgia Tech-School of Management, Ivan Allen College-225 North Avenue NW, Atlanta, GA 30332

- ***Leisure, Recreation & Tourism Abstracts, c/o CAB International/CAB ACCESS . . . available in print, diskettes updated weekly, and on INTERNET. Providing full bibliographic listings, author affiliation, augmented keyword searching,*** CAB International, P.O. Box 100, Wallingford Oxon 0X10 8DE, United Kingdom

- ***Lodging & Restaurant Index***, Purdue University, Stone Hall Room 220, West Lafayette, IN 47907-1002

- ***Management & Marketing Abstracts***, Pira International, Randalls Road, Leatherhead, Surrey KT22 7RU, England

- ***Sage Urban Studies Abstracts (SUSA)***, Sage Publications, Inc., 2455 Teller Road, Newbury Park, CA 91320

- ***Social Planning/Policy & Development Abstracts (SOPODA)***, Sociological Abstracts, Inc., P. O. Box 22206, San Diego, CA 92192-0206

- ***Sociological Abstracts (SA)***, Sociological Abstracts, Inc., P. O. Box 22206, San Diego, CA 92192-0206

- ***Sport Database/Discus***, Sport Information Resource Center, 1600 James Naismith Drive, Suite 107, Gloucester, Ontario K1B 5N4, Canada

- ***Urban Affairs Abstracts***, National League of Cities, 1301 Pennsylvania Avenue NW, Washington, DC 20004

- ***Worldwide Hospitality & Tourism Trends Database ("WHATT" Database)***, William F. Harrah College of Hotel Administration, Box 456023, 4505 Maryland Parkway, Las Vegas, NV 89154-6023

(continued)

SPECIAL BIBLIOGRAPHIC NOTES

related to special journal issues (separates)
and indexing/abstracting

☐ indexing/abstracting services in this list will also cover material in any "separate" that is co-published simultaneously with Haworth's special thematic journal issue or DocuSerial. Indexing/abstracting usually covers material at the article/chapter level.

☐ monographic co-editions are intended for either non-subscribers or libraries which intend to purchase a second copy for their circulating collections.

☐ monographic co-editions are reported to all jobbers/wholesalers/approval plans. The source journal is listed as the "series" to assist the prevention of duplicate purchasing in the same manner utilized for books-in-series.

☐ to facilitate user/access services all indexing/abstracting services are encouraged to utilize the co-indexing entry note indicated at the bottom of the first page of each article/chapter/contribution.

☐ this is intended to assist a library user of any reference tool (whether print, electronic, online, or CD-ROM) to locate the monographic version if the library has purchased this version but not a subscription to the source journal.

☐ individual articles/chapters in any Haworth publication are also available through the Haworth Document Delivery Services (HDDS).

Recent Advances in Tourism Marketing Research

CONTENTS

ABOUT THE EDITORS

Daniel R. Fesenmaier, PhD, is Associate Professor of Tourism in the Department of Leisure Studies at the University of Illinois at Urbana-Champaign. He has served as chair of the Committee for Marketing Models, Canadian Taskforce for Tourism Data and as a consultant to several tourism marketing and development projects in the United States, Canada, Korea, and Africa. Dr. Fesenmaier is the author of a number of research articles dealing with the economics and marketing of tourism and a monograph on community tourism development entitled *Developing and Marketing Tourism Resources*. He is also the co-editor of *Recreation Planning and Management* and *Communication Systems in Tourism Marketing*.

Joseph T. O'Leary, PhD, is Professor of Outdoor Recreation in the Department of Forestry and Natural Resources at Purdue University. He also holds an appointment in the Department of Restaurant, Hotel, Institutional and Tourism Management. Previously, he was Co-coordinator and Marine Advisory Services Leader for the Illinois-Indiana Sea Grant Program. Dr. O'Leary has published research articles in various journals including the *Journal of Forestry*, the *Journal of Leisure Research*, *Leisure Sciences*, *Tourism Management*, and the *Journal of Travel Research*. His research interests include the social behavior and travel patterns of domestic and international recreation consumers, secondary analysis of major national travel, and recreation related data.

Muzaffer Uysal, PhD, is Professor of Tourism in the Department of Hotel, Restaurant and Institutional Management at the Virginia Polytechnic Institute and State University in Blacksburg. Dr. Uysal has extensive experience in the travel and tourism fields and has authored or co-authored research articles and several book chapters related to different aspects of tourism marketing, demand/supply interaction, and international tourism. He is Associate Editor for *Leisure Sciences* for tourism related areas and methods. He also serves on the editorial boards of four international tourism and marketing journals and on the Education Advisory Council of the National Tour Foundation.

Preface–
The Year 2000:
Issues and Challenges

INTRODUCTION

Since the industrial revolution and throughout the last century, and indeed through the two World Wars, we have measured the wealth of nations almost entirely on the development of tangible goods: mining and manufacturing, agriculture and livestock and on the construction of infra- structure: highways and dams and oceanliners, railroads, and other vehicles which transport people and tangible assets from place to place around the world.

In recent years, scientific and technological discoveries have overwhelmed many of our older industries. A bright new world of innovation has already flooded mankind with services . . . consumer services–from tele- phones to facsimiles to a new century of computers, from cameras and movies to radio and television, from satellites to the universe of telecom- munications. In this expanding new world of technological devices and services we have founded one grand new service which is hardly recog- nized as a serious industry at all: an activity known today as tourism; an industry which encompasses many of these innovations, making startling changes in the world's economy, transforming the globe throughout more than a hundred developed and developing nations. How we market tour- ism in an ever changing world will be a major challenge for the travel and tourism industry.

To better understand and accept this industry's ability to market and promote global tourism in the future will depend on solid market research. Often such research must be conducted in a chaotic world, hammering out new innovative and creative approaches which may be different from traditional guidelines for marketing research. In brief, tourism marketing

[Haworth indexing entry note]: "Preface–The Year 2000: Issues and Challenges." Edgell, David L., Sr. Published in *Recent Advances in Tourism Marketing Research* (ed: Daniel R. Fesenmaier, Joseph T. O'Leary, and Muzaffer Uysal). The Haworth Press, Inc., 1996, pp. xiii-xvii. Single or multiple copies of this article are available from The Haworth Document Delivery Service [1-800-342-9678, 9:00 a.m. - 5:00 p.m. (EST). E-mail address: getinfo@haworth.com].

xiii

methodology must be flexible and resilient enough to foster the development of new tourism products and services in a rapidly changing world. The result may be to revolutionize the way we manage and market the tourism industry.

This introduction to the special volume will position international tourism within the broader context of the worldwide services economy. This article will focus on the significance of changing tourism issues and trends which will drive future marketing strategies.

THE NEW TOURISM HORIZON

Tourism has the potential to engage and change the economic, political and ecological dimensions of future lifestyles. In this perception, the highest purpose of the principles of tourism market research will be to integrate the economic, political, cultural, intellectual and environmental benefits of tourism for people, destinations and countries towards a higher quality of life. Such research will likely change our traditional travel and tourism marketing strategies.

As we approach the millennial threshold, the dynamic progress that has been made in international tourism will continue to accelerate. The last half of the twentieth century has already witnessed tremendous changes in transportation and communication technology, the twin engines which have propelled enormous changes in worldwide tourism. What has been clear in the past will also be true in the future, that peace and prosperity are the keys which best open the door to tourism growth.

A look at travel and tourism within this context mandates that marketing executives must understand the need for developing wide-ranging strategies which can be adjusted as worldwide conditions mature. They must be knowledgeable about market trends and flexible enough to adjust marketing plans in the face of rapidly changing market forces. In summary, marketing within the new tourism horizon must fully comprehend the complex nature of tourism and the immense mechanics of its implementation.

WORLDWIDE IMPORTANCE OF TOURISM

The twentieth century has seen a giant leap in leisure time for millions of people in both the developed and developing countries. Shorter working hours, greater individual prosperity, faster and cheaper travel and the impact of advanced technology have all helped to make the leisure and travel industry the fastest growing industry in the world. The significance of tourism as a source of income and employment, and as a major factor in the balance of payments for many countries, has been attracting increasing attention on the part of governments, regional and local authorities, and others with an interest in economic development.

New research by the World Travel and Tourism Council indicated that tourism in 1995 already generated direct and indirect employment for approximately 212 million people worldwide, or about one in every nine workers. According to the report, global tourism (both domestic and international) is a $3.4 trillion industry that will continue to grow in the future. Equally important, is the fact that tourism, as an export, is of critical importance to both industrialized and developing destinations. As an economic factor, tourism is growing faster than the rest of the world economy in terms of export output, value added, capital investment, and employment.

While tourism has been growing rapidly since World War II, and will likely continue its dynamic growth in the foreseeable future; this does not mean the industry will necessarily grow smoothly. There is reason to believe that there will be occasional structural, economic, political, and philosophical impediments in the path of progress. Also, in past years, there has been inadequate public understanding of the economic and social importance of tourism. Recently, however, the "worldwide importance of tourism" has been better understood, which is increasing the pressure for greater tourism market research to support new marketing strategies.

IN THE GLOBAL TOURISM CONTEXT

As part of the overall growth of services, tourism is finally beginning to be recognized as an important sector in the global economy. Key multilateral governmental organizations such as the World Tourism Organization (Madrid, Spain), Organization for Economic Cooperation and Development (Paris, France), Organization of American States (Washington, D.C.), Asia-Pacific Economic Cooperation (Singapore) and others are providing important research and data to the tourism industry with one of the goals being to link tourism to other sectors of the worldwide economy. The European Community, North America Free Trade Agreement and other regional economic instruments are seeking to break down traditional barriers to conducting tourism services across borders which will ultimately aid international tourism marketing. The World Travel and Tourism Council, Pacific Asia Travel Association and other groups representing private and public interests are already building a higher level of cooperation and coalition-building for tackling broad policy and marketing issues. This is indicative of progress made in this industry over the past twenty-five years.

The importance of what happened globally in the tourism policy arena in 1994 was manifested by the movement of the world toward implementing the General Agreement on Trade in Services (GATS) as part of the Multilateral Trade Negotiations of the Uruguay Round of the General Agreement on Tariffs and Trade (GATT). These efforts to improve freedom of fair trade (including trade in tourism) will have positive effects on international tourism marketing. The prognosis in early 1996 for implementing the GATS in the categories of: "Tourism and Related Services" and "Recreational, Cultural and Supporting Services" is very promising.

As the world increasingly becomes a "global village" most governments will seek to encourage greater travel to their respective destinations. Most developed and developing countries conduct their national tourism promotion under the aegis of a government tourism policy covering research, marketing, coordination, development and training. Often this is in conjunction with associations of private sector tourism interests, joint public-private consultative bodies, and international and intergovernmental organizations. This kind of cooperation and coordination will become an integral part of national tourism marketing strategies as each country strives to increase the size of its slice of the tourism pie.

TOURISM COMPETITION

The international competition for tourism revenues is formidable. Between 1980 and 1990 tourism arrivals around the world expanded more than 150%. The tourism customers of the 1990s are different from their predecessors in ways that challenge traditional approaches to tourism marketing.

In the eyes of the consumer there are many objectives. Tourists are people, energized by personal wants and needs. Their common denominator is that they are mobile and that by definition they are motivated to leave the place where they reside, to travel to another place or several other places which they would like to visit because of business or pleasure. Collectively, pleasure travelers' desires are endless: sunny hideaways, panoramic vistas, exotic cultures, wilderness adventures, historic sites, and a tremendous variety of indoor events and activities as well: all of these things, each with infinite variations.

While the opportunities for worldwide growth in tourism are prodigious, increased competition between governments and amongst the private sector is unpredictable. Increasing awareness of the relationship of tourism to political, economic, sociocultural, and environmental factors will emphasize the need for increased professionalism in tourism policy, planning, development and marketing strategies. In order to respond to the dynamic changes taking place in the competitive world of tourism, marketing programs will need to be constantly adjusted and updated to take account of new market research.

CONCLUSION

In summary, tourism today is seen and recognized as the largest service industry in the world. In fact, it has become one of the most productive components in the universe of trade, among all nations. The question is about tomorrow's tourism and what the future of the travel and tourism industry will become.

The tourism industry can be expected to face many challenges. It will need to develop effective plans to deal with political violence and environmental disruptions to the tourism market. New and better technological innovations as well as improved responses to environmental disasters or better approaches in adjusting to currency fluctuations will all have an impact on the growth of tourism. The way in which the industry responds to these challenges as new ones arise will determine the direction and maturity of this giant industry.

This special volume documents the new paradigms for tourism marketing. It recognizes a world that changes rapidly and a tourism product that challenges our traditional ways of conducting tourism business. Ultimately it is the quality of the tourism research input, and the environment in which the tourism industry operates, which will shape future strategies for marketing the tourism product in an ever-changing world.

David L. Edgell, Sr.

Introduction

Interest in tourism has increased dramatically over the past few years and is reflected by a tremendous increase in the use of tourism as a vehicle for economic development throughout the world. Travel and the resulting industry has also been considered an important vehicle for cultural expression and therefore, has received substantial attention from scholars in a number of disciplines. Research in travel and tourism marketing has also improved dramatically in quality and depth, reflecting the growing maturity of the field and the contributions of a diverse field of scholars and professionals.

The articles included in this volume reflect the explosion in high quality tourism marketing research. The authors come from a number of disciplines and perspectives, ranging from the more traditional programs in Hotel, Restaurant and Tourism Management and Leisure Studies to geography, urban and regional planning and sociology. The variety of perspectives is reflected in the issues addressed by the research included in this volume. Qualitative methods in marketing research have grown substantially over the past few years and are now recognized as offering viable alternatives to more traditional quantitative methodologies. Discrete choice/travel demand modeling methods have evolved and matured and now offer several mainstream tools with which to better understand existing and potential markets. Importance-performance analysis, a long standing tool for strategies marketing analysis, has been the focus of much research and now is an even better tool for tourism marketers.

Importantly, research in travel and tourism continues to grow . . . the material presented in this volume reflects only a small portion of the diversity and richness of this effort. The growth in tourism research has produced a number of opportunities for tourism marketers. As suggested by John Naisbitt in *Global Paradox*, recent developments in technology and in society have transformed the fundamental nature of tourism mar-

---

[Haworth co-indexing entry note]: "Introduction." Fesenmaier, Daniel R., Joseph T. O'Leary, and Muzaffer Uysal. Co-published simultaneously in *Journal of Travel & Tourism Marketing* (The Haworth Press, Inc.) Vol. 5, No. 1/2, 1996, pp. 1-2; and *Recent Advances in Tourism Marketing Research* (ed: Daniel R. Fesenmaier, Joseph T. O'Leary, and Muzaffer Uysal) The Haworth Press, Inc., 1996, pp. 1-2. Single or multiple copies of this article are available from The Haworth Document Delivery Service [1-800-342-9678, 9:00 a.m. - 5:00 p.m. (EST). E-mail address: getinfo@haworth.com].

1

keting. The smallest players are now empowered to compete effectively with those that "dominate" the industry. The arrival of "mega" databases on consumer behavior (including travelers) enable tourism researchers to develop all new and personalized products for the "total journey." New communication channels are emerging which modify substantially the way travelers can learn about available opportunities and offer the potential for building "relationships" with prospective consumers. This growth also presents a number of new and exciting challenges to tourism researchers that will have broad impacts on our world.

We hope readers enjoy the articles in this volume. We believe they represent well the quality and depth of market research currently being conducted in tourism.

Daniel R. Fesenmaier
Joseph T. O'Leary
Muzaffer Uysal

Capturing the Moments:
Concerns of *In Situ* Leisure Research

William P. Stewart
R. Bruce Hull IV

SUMMARY. *In situ* assessments are part of a general diversification from traditional research methods within the social sciences. The need for *in situ* sampling methods in leisure, recreation, and tourism exists because: (1) they distinguish between questions about situations and questions about persons; and (2) their minimum reliance on information associated with the inaccuracies of human memory and cognitive processing. Because of their focus on the present moment, *in situ* designs provide information about recreational situations largely inaccessible with traditional methods. Such information addresses traditional questions from a new perspective and allows exploration of new questions. The limitations of *in situ* designs are discussed regarding: (1) self-report and the alteration of experience; (2) repeated self-report and the alteration of experience; and (3) lack of compliance with the self-administration of self-report. *[Article copies available from The Haworth Document Delivery Service: 1-800-342-9678. E-mail address: getinfo@haworth.com]*

Over the past decade or so, there has been a general diversification from traditional research methods within the social sciences. This paper reviews

William P. Stewart is Associate Professor, Department of Recreation, Park and Tourism Sciences, Texas A&M University, College Station, TX 77843-2261. R. Bruce Hull IV is Associate Professor, Department of Forestry, Virginia Polytechnic Institute and State University, Blacksburg, VA 24061.

[Haworth co-indexing entry note]: "Capturing the Moments: Concerns of *In Situ* Leisure Research." Stewart, William P., and R. Bruce Hull IV. Co-published simultaneously in *Journal of Travel & Tourism Marketing* (The Haworth Press, Inc.) Vol. 5, No. 1/2, 1996, pp. 3-20; and *Recent Advances in Tourism Marketing Research* (ed: Daniel R. Fesenmaier, Joseph T. O'Leary, and Muzaffer Uysal) The Haworth Press, Inc., 1996, pp. 3-20. Single or multiple copies of this article are available from The Haworth Document Delivery Service [1-800-342-9678, 9:00 a.m. - 5:00 p.m. (EST). E-mail address: getinfo@haworth.com].

recent developments in methods, and in particular, focuses on the adaptation of *in situ* sampling methods to leisure, recreation, and tourism research problems. Since conceptual issues are at the crux of most methodological problems, this essay first discusses the need for *in situ* methods. More specifically, the ability of *in situ* designs to address new and arguably more precise questions about leisure, recreation, and tourism is discussed. Secondly, procedures for the adaptation of *in situ* designs to leisure, recreation and tourism problems are discussed, followed by a critique of potential limitations of *in situ* research.

DEVELOPMENT OF RESEARCH QUESTIONS

Time, setting, and person interrelate in complex ways to define recreational situations. As one of the parent disciplines, psychology has provided leisure researchers with several world views in which to understand the relationships between time, setting, and person (Ittelson, 1973; Pervin & Lewis, 1977). The interactional approach, which has been the dominant perspective in contemporary psychology (cf. Mannell, 1980), treats time, setting, and person as independent entities with particular characteristics. The focus of investigations is usually on the direct and interactive effects of environmental factors on behavior and psychological processes. To describe the interactional approach, Altman and Rogoff provide the following analogy:

> . . . interactional world views treat psychological phenomena like Newtonian particles or like billiard balls. Each particle or ball exists separately from the others and has its own independent qualities. The balls or particles interact as one ball bangs into another ball, thereby altering their locations. The goal of interactional research is to study the impact of certain particles and balls (environmental and situational qualities) on other particles and balls (psychological processes and behaviors). (1987, p. 15)

The transactional approach is another perspective from psychology, used to study the confluence of time, setting, and person. Transactional analysis typically de-emphasizes the cause-effect relationships between factors and directs attention to the ways in which time, setting, and person "jointly define one another and contribute to the meaning and nature of a holistic event" (Altman and Rogoff, 1987, p. 24). To explain the transactional approach, Ittelson argues:

Man is never concretely encountered independent of the situation through which he acts, nor is the environment ever encountered independent of the encountering individual. It is meaningless to speak of either as existing apart from the situation in which it is encountered. (Ittelson, 1973, p. 19)

Although both the interactional and transactional perspectives have been associated with various types of empirical investigations, one could argue that *in situ* methods would be compatible, if not a direct fit, with either of these world views. Both of these perspectives embrace the notion of the person as being part of, or embedded in, an environment. In this sense, both interactional and transactional perspectives, along with *in situ* methods, are focused on the relationships among time, setting, and person.

One could argue that a majority of literature in leisure, recreation, and tourism could be traced to understanding the relationships among time, setting, and persons. More succinctly, two fundamental research questions could characterize much of leisure, recreation, and tourism studies: (1) questions about situations; and (2) questions about person. Although time, setting, and person are intertwined in both of these questions, the former question directs a search for leisure as situationally-derived, and the latter directs a search for leisure as a function of personal characteristics.

The power of *in situ* methods is in their ability to analytically discriminate between questions about situations and questions about persons using the same data set (Larson & Delespaul, 1990). From the perspective of framing research questions, it is important not to conflate questions about situations with those about persons. One could confuse a momentary satisfied feeling about one's trip, with a trip that was continually satisfactory; or a present set of experiential outcomes with an enduring set of experiential outcomes. Compared to traditional methods, *in situ* designs improve one's ability to provide insight, and perhaps disentangle, the complex interactions of time, setting, and person. The following analysis of research questions is adapted from Larson and Delespaul (1990; see also Samdahl, 1989) for application to leisure, recreation, and tourism research.

Questions About Situations

Clawson and Knetsch's (1966) pioneering work segmented recreation behavior into five phases, known as the "recreation experience continuum." The five phases are chronologically ordered and each phase typically is associated with a different set of situations: (1) The "anticipation" phase generally would be associated with one's home and work situations;

(2) The "travel to the destination" phase would generally be associated with transportation-related situations (i.e., walking, bicycling, inside of cars, airplanes, motels); (3) The "on-site" phase would be associated with the attractions, activities, lodging, facilities, and visitors and staff encountered at the tourist destination(s); (4) The "return travel" phase would be associated with similar types of situations as the "travel to the destination" phase; and (5) The "recollection" phase would be associated with a variety of situations and extend indeterminately into the future.

The five phases of recreation and tourism behavior suggest a dynamic and evolving experience. Several researchers have provided both theory and evidence to support a recreation experience continuum with at least five distinct phases and therefore five distinct sets of situations (Driver and Tocher, 1974; Hammitt, 1980). The independent variables for questions about recreation and tourist situations would include setting attributes, type of service provided at the destination, and other contextual variables. Questions about situations relevant to leisure, recreation, and tourism include:

- What kind of environmental attributes influence positive and negative feelings?
- How is the social setting related to individual experience?
- How does quality-of-service influence users' feelings of satisfaction?
- How are decisions to return influenced by on-site situations?
- How do tourism impacts influence individual experience?
- In what situations are visitors most sensitive to crowding?

Responding to these questions requires comparisons between settings *within individuals*. Patterns of individual experience that systematically differ between situations need to be identified and explained. A comparison between groups of people (who provided a response set at just one point in time) will not allow these patterns to emerge; such a comparison is unable to distinguish whether the responses were properties of the situation or properties of the person.

Questions About Persons

Recreation researchers have a history of inquiry regarding questions about persons. Independent variables typically include demographic characteristics (race, sex), typology frameworks (specialization, involvement, wilderness purism), and personality traits (social responsibility, experience use history). Such questions include:

- Do repeat visitors differ from novices in their leisure experience?
- Do visitors who were highly involved in the destination choice process have a high sense of fulfillment?
- What types of persons frequently participate in leisure activities?
- Are women different than men in their response to visitor services?
- Do visitors who stop at travel information centers have different travel experiences than those who do not stop?
- Are individuals who score high on a social-responsibility scale affected by environmental impacts?

These questions entail comparisons between groups of people in the same situation. In particular, obtaining responses in several situations allows for comparisons between groups of subjects regarding intra-subject difference between situations. If dispositional effects of persons exist, then distinct experience patterns will emerge for each group (i.e., groups distinguished by differences in intra- group variation between situations).

Confusing Questions

Sometimes the direction of research is ambiguous, and it is difficult to untangle whether the issue is about situations, persons, or their interaction:

- Is experiencing solitude associated with travel to remote areas? (Is this question about situations that afford solitude or about persons who seek solitude?)
- Is being relaxed related to recreation places? (Is this question about recreation places that relax or about relaxed persons who visit recreation places?)
- Is feeling crowded correlated with high encounter levels? (Is this question about situations which make one feel crowded or about persons who feel crowded?)
- Is high-involvement related to stopping at a visitor center for information? (Is this question about high-involvement situations or high-involvement persons?)

If the questions are about situations, then the following revisions would clarify the research questions:

- Does travel to remote areas afford better opportunities for solitude than non-remote destinations?
- Do recreation places provide relaxation more than other types of environments?

- Is one most likely to feel crowded at high-encounter levels than at low-encounter levels?
- Is involvement high at visitor centers relative to other en-route travel situations?

If the questions are about persons then the following revisions would clarify the research questions:

- What type of travel destinations are chosen by people who seek solitude?
- Do persons visit recreation places when they are relaxed?
- Are some persons more likely to feel crowded?
- Compared to other types of travelers, are highly-involved persons more likely to stop at visitor centers for information?

These two sets of questions illustrate the differences between questions of situations and questions of persons. Importantly, different questions require different methods. Questions about situations require analyses that examine intra-subject variation across situations; whereas questions about persons would require a search for inter-subject (between group) differences within situations.

In contrast to *in situ* designs, methods that obtain information at just one point in time (i.e., one response per person) have difficulty discerning effects of situations from those of persons. *In situ* procedures are not unique in this ability, however. Experimental or quasi-experimental designs (e.g., Cook and Campbell, 1979; Mannell, 1980) also can compare differences among situations and differences among persons through experimental control. For example, the situation can be controlled by manipulating a treatment variable (such as litter, crowding, or level of service) or by the assignment of subjects to various treatments. *In situ* procedures facilitate comparison among situations, by obtaining repeated observations of the same person within and across situations. In doing so, it allows for intra-subject differences (i.e., individual change) which require explanation. In other words, intra-subject differences are viewed as variance in need of partitioning. Many traditional methods that obtain one response per person do not control factors such as intra-subject differences and therefore must rely on correlational (i.e., cross-sectional) designs to infer causality.

Several examples of *in situ* applications to leisure, recreation, and tourism research serve to illustrate their utility. In their investigations of everyday life situations, Kubey and Csikszentmihalyi (1990) examined feelings during various activities and found that feelings of challenge, use of skills, and positive moods (e.g., alert, cheerful, active) were highest during leisure activities and lowest during TV viewing. Hull et al. (1992) examined day hikers' moods at 12 different points along a trail. Their results indicate that recreationists' experiences (moods) could be differentiated by the effects of situations (i.e., stage of hike, environmental attributes). They further suggested that the nature of recreation may entail distinctive patterns of situationally-derived experiences, in contrast to traditional methods associated with static conceptions of expected benefits or outcomes. In a related study, Stewart and Hull (1992) found a small and decreasing relationship between the on-site and various recollection phases of a recreation experience. They found that hikers' images of their recreation experiences evolved over nine months "separately and distinctively from the present moments of the on-site experience" (p. 207). That is, not only was the on-site experience different from post-activity recollections, but post-activity recollections changed over time. The possibility of situational reinterpretation implies that one's experiences cannot be fully understood by a one-time assessment. In addition, Lee et al. (1994) provide evidence of "experience transformation" and argue that humans have the ability to reinterpret situations "in accordance with what is important to them at the time of interpretation" (p. 208). Such findings converge with the speculation of Mannell that "the recollected (on-site) experience may take on new meaning and emotional tone–in fact, it may be reconstructed and remembered very differently" (1980, p. 85).

Thus, with the application of research designs that explicitly recognize the dynamic nature of leisure, recreation, and tourism experiences, questions can be asked that recognize its dynamic and situationally-dependent nature. Such questions include: What on-site situations have the most enduring influence? What on-site situations have an effect on future choice behavior? What types of persons are sensitive to on-site setting attributes? Are "high" points in the trip more likely to influence future trip decisions compared to "low" points in the trip? How does one identify high and low points of a leisure experience? These and many related questions have implications for the investment and management of the destination and to off-site investments regarding destination-image management. On balance, *in situ* designs facilitate and/or promote the asking of a different class of (arguably more precise) research questions. However, there are other reasons for considering *in situ* methods besides their analytical potential.

LIMITATIONS OF HUMAN COGNITIVE PROCESSES

Researchers have explored various concepts associated with recreation and tourism experiences and destination choice processes. Popular concepts have included: motivations, expectations, satisfaction appraisals, crowding, and substitution. The study of such concepts often assumes the ability for extensive cognitive processing and accurate recall. Theoretical frameworks, associated with the above concepts typically characterize travelers as being rational consumers of information, with efficiency as a behavioral objective. Such frameworks have included: importance-performance analysis, discrepancy theory, theory of reasoned action, multiple-satisfactions approach, and cost-benefit trade-off frameworks.

Imposed Need to Reconstruct

Within the leisure, recreation, and tourism literature, many theoretical frameworks depict leisure as a state of mind. Yet it is not unusual for such studies to employ a survey design (i.e., one-time post-activity assessment), and thus require respondents to reconstruct previous states of mind. As an example, the application of expectancy theory coupled with a survey design *requires extensive cognitive processing capabilities* on the part of sampled recreationists. The basic tenet of expectancy theory is that one's expected and desired psychological benefits will be one's actual psychological benefits. It assumes that humans are knowledgeable about the consequences of their behavior and that the desire for certain psychological benefits motivates the search for an activity/environment that will provide such benefits. The expectancy theory framework indicates that one's expectations for various outcomes concur with one's actual outcome. For instance, if one wants solitude through a recreation activity, then expectancy theory's framework suggests that one will find the setting that provides for solitude. In a survey design typical of most recreation studies, if one reports having experienced solitude, it is thought that one must have been motivated to recreate by the desire for solitude in one's pre-trip decision-making process. Such framework and application explicitly characterizes the human mind as having memory and computational abilities similar to the processing of a computer.

Like the application of several frameworks in leisure, recreation, and tourism studies, the above illustration of expectancy theory depicts tourists as consumers who are unaffected by an (implied) static touristic experience. In contrast, leisure, recreation, and tourism theorists have developed several perspectives that depict leisure as a psychologically dynamic and creative endeavor (e.g., Brightbill, 1961; DeGrazia, 1962; Mannell, 1980; Kelly, 1987). Following from this contrasting perspective, some important and related questions emerge: (1) Can the "re-created" person provide valid reports (i.e., reconstructions) of previous states-of-mind regarding decision-making criteria, motivations, experiences, perceptions, and so on? (2) Given its evolving nature, what methods are most suitable for capturing a leisure-travel experience? (3) What degree of cognitive processing is implied in each alternative method, and would such a degree be expected to provide valid self-reports? A growing body of literature has begun to investigate the dynamic nature of the leisure, recreation, and tourism experience, and consequent questions regarding the required degree of cognitive processing implicit in research methods. Some studies have indicated that the on-site experience may influence the post-activity report of experiential outcomes (e.g., Peterson & Lime, 1973; Manfredo, 1984; Ewert, 1993). In addition, empirical studies have been undertaken to document the experiential differences between pre-activity, on-site, and post-activity phases (Hammitt, 1980).

Limitations on the Ability to Reconstruct

A theoretical framework which has provided insight to the limitations of human mental processing is cognitive dissonance theory. The major tenet being that individuals react to social and environmental circumstances in terms of psychological adjustments. Individuals strive to maintain cognitive consistency; when confronted with situations which are different than expected, individuals change themselves (e.g., their expectations, desired outcomes) rather than changing their environmental circumstance. Rationalization, as a coping mechanism, allows subjects to accommodate the environment thereby maintaining psychological consistency. Recognition of cognitive dissonance theory has a long, albeit not well-integrated, history of development in recreation and tourism literature (Ewert, 1993; Stewart, 1992; Manning, 1985; Heberlein & Shelby, 1977).

In depicting individuals as being psychologically flexible and accommodating of external situations, dissonance theory casts a shadow on the traditional method of recreation and tourism research: the post hoc survey design.[1] If expectations, motives, satisfactions, and other such appraisals are fluid, then assessing such constructs in a post hoc fashion may not provide valid information regarding antecedent states, and would not be representative of the total recreation experience and decision-making process. Using the self-initiated-tape-recording-method, Lee et al. (1994) provide insight to the transitory potential of leisure experience, and concomitant limitations of human cognitive processing when describing the consequences of a leisure experience. When comparing subjects' retrospections with immediate recollections of a leisure experience, subjects exhibited varying degrees of transformations. Perhaps the extreme was a subject whose immediate recall of the experience indicated distraction and disengagement, yet three months later the experience was reported as being relaxed and fun (p. 206). In addition, Mannell and Iso-Ahola (1987) have doubted the human ability to access high-order cognitive processes related to leisure. In their critique of various perspectives of leisure, they questioned the ability for individuals to be aware of their needs, to be able to report their needs, and to judge the fulfillment of their needs.

The accommodating nature of human cognitive processes has come to light in a number of different arenas in the social science literature. There has been an accumulation of studies that have provided argument and evidence regarding the limited ability for individuals to recall previous mental states and behavior. In their often cited review, Nisbett and Wilson (1977) concluded that humans are often inaccurate regarding the report of stimuli that influenced their decisions and inaccurate about the stability of their own attitude or behavior (i.e., unaware of their own responses to stimuli). In a subsequent review of human cognitive processes, Ericsson and Simon (1980) also provided argument and evidence regarding the inaccuracy of human memory, and consequent reliance on misleading inferences; their discussion concludes that *reports of current mental states are among the most valid* and that researchers needing experiential data should direct their designs at the assessment of current states (see also Fiske, 1980; Mischel, 1981: Bernard, Killworth, Kronenfeld, & Sailer, 1984; Bradburn, Rips, & Shevell, 1987). This is the intent of *in situ* research.

IN SITU PROCEDURES

There are various ways to assess individual experience. The experience sampling method (ESM) requires a signalling device (or beeper) that randomly indicates when subjects should complete a questionnaire (Larson & Csikszentmihalyi, 1983). The questions usually are directed at obtaining information regarding the subject's momentary situation and psychological state. A brief self-report questionnaire is designed to assess the subjects' situation and state in less than three minutes. Respondents typically carry a sufficient number of forms in a booklet. The general purpose of the ESM is to study the subjective experience of persons in their natural (or *in situ*) situation. Conceptually, the objective of the ESM is to expose patterns in the characteristics of a person's psychological state and the systematic effects of different settings on these states (Csikszentmihalyi & Larson, 1987). Numerous studies by Csikszentmihalyi and colleagues further developed and refined the method in their studies of leisure, flow, and everyday life experiences (Kubey & Csikszentmihalyi, 1990; Larson & Csikszentmihalyi, 1983). ESM is not new to recreation and leisure research, and most recently has been employed by Samdahl (1991) to compare theoretical and connotative meanings of leisure.

Other *in situ* procedures are closely related to ESM. One adaptation of the ESM has been employed by Hull et al. (1992) who used markers along a trail instead of beepers. Each subject encountered the same set of markers which allowed the researchers to assess the effects of the sampled settings (i.e., the environment around the markers) across the sampled subjects. The advantage of this adaptation is that it provided control over the situation being sampled and it allowed the experimenters to describe and measure aspects of the situation. With the original procedures of ESM, subjects do not necessarily share the same environments (upon being beeped), so the assessment of the effects of situational attributes is problematic for two reasons: (1) assessment of within subject effects of situational attributes may be limited due to reliance on self-report to provide information about attributes; and (2) assessment of between subject differences regarding effects of situational attributes is limited due to subjects being in different situations upon being "beeped." The major difference between the basic ESM and the adaptation by Hull et al. is that all subjects respond within the context of nearly the same situational attributes. Such an adaptation may be useful in the study of research *questions about situations.*

Within their adaptation of ESM, the specific procedures of Hull et al. (1992) were as follows: Twelve environments (or views) along a day-hiking trail were marked by a temporary post, topped with a 20 cm. square placard. A number with an arrow pointing toward the landscape to be evaluated was painted on each placard. Hikers were instructed to stand behind each placard, face in the direction of the arrow, and complete one of the self-report questionnaire forms (see Appendix) that was contained in a booklet that was issued to them at the beginning of their hike. Potential subjects were recruited at the trailhead and asked whether they would be willing to participate in a research project. Persons were screened to insure their intent was to hike the full length of the trail associated with the study. Before describing the instructions in detail, the magnitude of the task was explained and potential subjects were told they would be rewarded with a candy bar at the beginning and end of their hikes and $25 after they completed the full requirements of the study. If subjects agreed to participate, they were given a questionnaire booklet and detailed instructions on its use (about a 5 minute task). At each step in the process of subject recruitment, subjects were given the chance to decline to participate. Less than half of the subjects did so.

Other *in situ* designs also have been successfully employed. In pre-test/post-test studies, Ewert (1993) used agency personnel at trailhead stations to administer questionnaires; Stewart (1992; see also, Manfredo, 1984) collected *in situ* data through on-trail interviews. Shaw's (1986) methods were tied to time-diary designs and required subjects to complete a series of questions at researcher-specified junctures in their time or behavior. Lee et al. (1994) issued a tape-recorder to each subject and required them to respond orally to a series of questions immediately following leisure activity.

In situ designs usually involve repeated measures; however, the number of repeated measures (i.e., situational assessments) vary widely. For practical reasons, there is typically an inverse relationship between number of repeated measures and number of subjects. As an example, if 10 subjects are called upon 10 times to complete 10 items, the researcher has 1000 data points with which to work; if 20 subjects complete 20 items 20 times, the researcher has 8000 data points. Other than pre-test/post-test designs, in situ research usually yields large amounts of data on a comparatively small number of individual subjects.

There is not a standard accepted method for the analysis of data collected through *in situ* designs. Because *in situ* methods typically collect many data on any given subject, it allows for extended analyses of individual cases as well as for useful aggregation over cases (Hormuth, 1986; Epstein, 1983; see also Petrinovich and Widamen, 1984, for the use of these designs in habituation studies). Thus, *in situ* designs potentially allow for the combination of two contrasting methodological approaches: the idiographic and the nomothetic. The idiographic approach would focus interpretation on individual change across various situations, whereas nomothetic analyses would search for similarities (in individual change) for aggregation purposes (Runyan, 1983; Samdahl, 1989).

In short, *in situ* designs provide a powerful framework to investigate questions about situations, persons, and their interaction. *In situ* methods explicitly recognize the varying influence of situations on individuals. However, any single method can not fully capture a phenomenon; and *in situ* designs are not without their limitations. The following discussion suggests some boundaries.

CRITICISMS OF IN SITU DESIGNS

Criticism 1. Self-report and the alteration of experience. Methods based on self-report can potentially alter the nature of the experience and the perception of the situation. Responding to questions about one's own mental state may affect that mental state. A question may serve as a prompt or stimulus that influences subjects' reports, and possibly affects reports to subsequent questions asked.

This criticism is not only directed at *in situ* designs, but also to most other methods in leisure, recreation, and tourism. One could argue that invasiveness to the on-site experience is higher with *in situ* compared to traditional methods (i.e., mail-back questionnaire) and hence, more likely to alter experience. However, due to the *ex situ* nature of traditional methods, one also could argue that the degree of invasiveness during the off-site recall of the on-site experience (i.e., recalling the on-site experience for the purposes of completing a questionnaire) is higher compared to *in situ* methods and hence, more likely to alter the experience. The point is that the potential for alteration of experience is a threat associated with any method that requires subjects to respond to questions. As a discipline, leisure, recreation, and tourism scholars have been tolerant of this threat. If self-report is required, then the threat of altering the leisure experience exists regardless of the timing of the asking of the question.

Criticism 2. Repeated self-reports and the alteration of experience. Repeatedly asking questions may enhance self-focused attention and make subjects abnormally self-aware. In doing so, it could promote conformity with perceived norms and alter the context and experience of the situation being studied (Wicklund, 1975; Hormuth, 1982). However, some researchers have argued that increased self-awareness is welcome because it improves the accuracy of self-reports (Hormuth, 1986; Brandstatter, 1983). Evidence from the self-awareness literature indicates that experimental inducement of self-awareness actually increases the validity of self-reported information (Franzoi & Brewer, 1984; Gibbons, 1983; Pryor et al., 1977). In a review of this literature, Hormuth concluded that the influence of periodic interruptions of ESM "does not seem to be strong enough to change the situation nor increase the accuracy of perception" (1986, p. 286). In their preliminary examination of self-awareness and leisure experience, Samdahl and Kleiber (1989) suggest that the intensity of self-awareness is not relevant to the quality of one's leisure experience; however, their approach to "self-awareness" was directed at "public self-awareness" rather than cognizance of internal states (pp. 8-9). One could argue that the nature of some leisure experiences demands total involvement of perceptual faculties (cf. Csikszentmihalyi, 1975) and hence, periodic interruptions and their potential for increased self-awareness would significantly alter the experience and concomitantly affect self-report. To the extent that this argument is valid would be a limitation of the application of *in situ* designs.

Criticism 3. Lack of compliance with the self-administration of self-report. The procedures for *in situ* designs, particularly ESM-related designs, usually require subjects to carry a packet of self-report questionnaire forms, and at specified signals, subjects are required to write down information about their momentary situation and psychological state (Csikszentmihalyi & Larson, 1987). In the application of ESM to leisure, recreation, and tourism, researchers may require subjects to provide self-reports at particular locations in order to address questions about situations (and allow for the assessment of responses to researcher-selected situational attributes).

For conclusions of *in situ* studies to be valid, subjects need to comply with the demands of the method. Compliance covers two issues: (1) whether subjects responded to the questionnaires when asked; and (2) whether subjects answered each item on the questionnaire. Results from various validity studies of ESM, which were directed primarily at the former issue, indicate that compliance varies across populations. Although more than 95% of subjects respond to signals, the proportion doing so within 5 minutes of being "beeped" was reported 80% in one population and 60% in another (Hormuth, 1986). In addition, in a study which lasted eight days and randomly signalled on a 24 hour basis, only one-fourth of the sample was able to respond to 95% or more of the signals (Hormuth, 1986). However, as suggested by Csikszentmihalyi and Larson (1987), shortening the duration of the total sampling period, and signalling only during daylight hours, dramatically improves compliance. For example, in her application of ESM, Samdahl (1991) recruited 18 subjects for seven days each and "beeped" them at seven randomly selected time periods each day between 7:30 a.m. and 11:00 p.m. She reported an 82% response rate and indicated that the primary cause of non-response was due to subjects being away from their beeper and unaware of being "beeped." Regarding compliance of subjects completing each item on the questionnaire, Hull et al. (1992) found less than 2% of items on completed questionnaires were missing data.

Comparing the results of ESM with those of time-use diaries provides a test of convergent validity. Both of these methods have been used to describe the time allocated to various activities and the experiences associated with such activities. Researchers have reported considerable convergence between results of ESM and time-use diaries (Kubey & Csikszentmihalyi, 1990; Csikszentmihalyi & Larson, 1987; Robinson, 1985).

CONCLUDING REMARK

Leisure, recreation, and tourism research has been heavily influenced by the dynamics of the basic social sciences. In some instances, traditional methods may limit a researcher's ability to disentangle questions about situations from those of persons, and force a reliance on information associated with the inaccuracies of cognitive processing. Such problems have fueled a movement toward *in situ* designs and focus on current states, and correspond with a growing interest in ESM-related methods. Exploring the application of *in situ* designs is not peculiar to small groups of leisure, recreation, and/or tourism researchers, but is part of a much larger academic movement. Although there are problems with any theoretical framework or methodological perspective, the potential for *in situ* designs to address unanswered questions in leisure, recreation, and tourism research appears promising.

NOTE

1. Riddick, DeSchriver, & Weissinger, 1984, 1991, have indicated that more than 90% of recreation research published in the early 1980s is based upon the post hoc survery design; the percentage in the late 1980s is about 75%.

REFERENCES

Altman, I. & Rogoff, B. (1987). World views in psychology: Trait, interactional, organismic, and transactional perspectives. In D. Stokols & I. Altman (Eds.), *Handbook of Environmental Psychology Vol.1* (pp. 7-40). New York: Wiley.

Bernard, H., Killworth, P., Kronenfeld, D., & Sailer, L. (1984). On the validity of retrospective data: The problem of informant accuracy. *Annual Review of Anthropology, 13,* 495-517.

Bradburn, N., Rips, R., & Shevell, S. (1987). Answering autobiographical questions: The impact of memory and inference on surveys. *Science, 236,* 157-161.

Brandstatter, H. (1983). Emotional responses to other persons in everyday lifesituations. *Journal of Personality and Social Psychology, 45(4),* 871-883.

Brightbill, C.K. (1961). *Man and Leisure.* Westport, CT: Greenwood.

Cook, T. & Campbell, D. (1979). *Quasi-Experimentation: Design and Analysis Issues for Field Settings.* Boston: Houghton Mifflin.

Clawson, M. & Knetsch, J.L. (1966). *Economics of Outdoor Recreation.* Baltimore, MD: Johns Hopkins University.

Csikszentmihalyi, M. (1975). *Beyond boredom and anxiety.* San Francisco: Jossey-Bass.

Csikszentmihalyi, M. & Larson, R. (1987). Validity and reliability of the experience-sampling method. *Journal of Nervous and Mental Disease, 175(9),* 526-536.

De Grazia, S. (1962). *Of Time Work and Leisure.* New York: The Twentieth Century Fund.

Driver, B. & Tocher, S. (1974). Toward a behavioral interpretation of recreational engagements, with implications for planning. In B. Driver (Ed.), *Elements in Outdoor Recreation Planning* (pp. 9-31). Ann Arbor: University of Michigan.

Epstein, S. (1983). Aggregation and beyond: Some basic issues on the prediction of behavior. *Journal of Personality, 51*, 36-392.

Ericsson, K. & Simon, H. (1980). Verbal reports as data. *Psychological Review, 87*, 215-251.

Ewert, A. (1993). Differences in the level of motive importance based on trip outcome, experience level and group type. *Journal of Leisure Research, 25(4)*, 335-349.

Fiske, D. (1980). When are verbal reports veridical? In R. Shroeder (Ed.), *Fallible Judgments in Behavioral Research* (pp. 59-66). San Francisco: Jossey-Bass.

Franzoi, S.L. & Brewer, L.C. (1984). The experience of self-awareness and its relation to level of self-consciousness: An experiential sampling study. *Journal of Research in Personality, 18*, 522-540.

Gibbons, F.X. (1983). Self-attention and self-report: The "veridicality" hypothesis. *Journal of Personality, 51*, 517-542.

Hammitt, W. (1980). Outdoor recreation: Is it a multiphase experience? *Journal of Leisure Research, 19(1)*, 115-130.

Heberlein, T.A., & Shelby, B. (1977). Carrying capacity, values, and the satisfaction model: A reply to Greist. *Journal of Leisure Research, 9(2)*, 142-148.

Hormuth, S. (1982). Self-focused attention and the adherence to personal standards. In K. Obuchowski & A. Kossakowski (Eds.), *Progress in psychology of personality* (pp. 95-105). Berlin: VEB Deutscher Verlay der Wissenschaften.

Hormuth, S. (1986). The sampling of experiences *in situ. Journal of Personality, 54(1)*, 262-293.

Hull, R., Stewart, W., & Yi, Y. (1992). Experience patterns: capturing the dynamic nature of a recreation experience. *Journal of Leisure Research, 24(3)*, 240-252.

Ittelson, W. (1973). Environment perception and contemporary conceptual theory. In W. Ittelson (Ed.), *Environment and Cognition* (pp. 1-19). New York: Seminar.

Kelly, J.R. (1987). *Freedom to Be: A New Sociology of Leisure.* New York: MacMillan.

Kubey, R. & Csikszentmihalyi, M. (1990). *Television and the quality of life: How viewing shapes everyday experience.* Hillsdale, NJ: Lawrence Erlbaum.

Larson, R. & Csikszentmihalyi, M. (1983). The experience sampling method. In H. Reis (Ed.), *New Directions for naturalistic methods in the behavioral sciences* (pp. 41-56). San Francisco: Jossey-Bass.

Larson, R. & P. Delespaul. (1990). Analyzing experience sampling data: a guidebook for the perplexed. In M. de Vries (Ed.), *The Experience of Psychopathology*, Cambridge, U.K.: Cambridge University.

Lee, Y., Dattilo, J., & Howard, D. (1994). The complex and dynamic nature of leisure experience. *Journal of Leisure Research, 26(3)*, 195-211.

Manfredo, M. (1984). The comparability of onsite and offsite measures of recreation needs. *Journal of Leisure Research, 16*, 245-249.

Mannell, R. (1980). Social psychological techniques and strategies for studying leisure experiences. In S. Iso-Ahola (Ed.) *Social Psychological Perspectives on Leisure and Recreation* (pp. 62- 88). Springfield, IL: Charles Thomas.

Mannell, R. & Iso-Ahola, S. (1987). Psychological nature of leisure and tourism experience. *Annals of Tourism Research, 14*, 314-331.

Manning, R.E. (1986). *Studies in Outdoor Recreation.* Corvallis, OR: Oregon State University.

Mischel, W. (1981). A cognitive-social learning approach to assessment. In T. Merluzzi, C. Glass, & M. Genest (Ed.), *Cognitive Assessment.* New York: Guilford.

Nisbett, R. & Wilson, T. (1977). Telling more than we can know: Verbal reports on mental processes. *Psychological Review, 84*, 231-259.

Pervin, L. & Lewis, M. (Eds.) (1977). *Perspectives in Interactional Psychology.* New York: Plenum.

Peterson, G. & Lime, D. (1973). Two sources of bias in the measurement of human response to the wilderness environment. *Journal of Leisure Research, 5*, 66-73.

Petrinovich, L. & Widaman, K. (1984). An evaluation of statistical strategies to analyze repeated-measures data. In H. Peeke & L. Petrinovich (Eds.) *Habituation, Sensitization, and Behavior.* Orlando: Academic.

Pryor, J.B., Gibbons, F.X., Wicklund, R.A., Fazio, R., & Hood, R. (1977). Self-focused attention and self-report validity. *Journal of Personality, 45*, 513-527.

Riddick, C., DeSchriver, M., & Weissinger, E. (1984). A methodological review of research in Journal of Leisure Research from 1978 to 1982. *Journal of Leisure Research, 14*, 311-321.

Riddick, C., DeSchriver, M., & Weissinger, E. (1991). A methodological review of research in *Journal of Leisure Research* from 1983 through 1987. Paper presented at the National Recreation and Park Association, Leisure Research Symposium, Baltimore, M.D. October, 17-20.

Robinson, J. (1985). The validity and reliability of diaries versus alternative time use measures. In F.T. Juster & F.P. Stafford (Eds.) *Time, goods, and well-being.* Ann Arbor: University of Michigan.

Runyan, W.M. (1983). Idiographic goals and methods in the study of lives. *Journal of Personality, 51*, 413-437.

Samdahl, D. (1989). Analyzing "beeper" data: Statistical considerations for experience sampling studies. *Therapeutic Recreation Journal, 23*(4), 47-61.

Samdahl, D. (1991). Issues in the measurement of leisure: A comparison of theoretical and connotative meanings. *Leisure Sciences, 13 (1)*, 33-49.

Samdahl, D. & Kleiber, D. (1989). Self-awareness and leisure experiences. *Leisure Sciences, 11*(1), 1-10.

Shaw, S. (1986). Leisure, recreation or free time? Measuring time usage. *Journal of Leisure Research, 18*(3), 177-189.

Stewart, W. (1992). Influence of the onsite experience on recreation experience preference judgments. *Journal of Leisure Research, 24(2)*, 185-198.

Stewart, W. P. & Hull, R. B. (1992). Satisfaction of what? Post hoc versus real-time construct validity. *Leisure Sciences, 14*, 195-209.

Wicklund, R. A. (1975). Objective self-awareness. In L. Berkowitz (Ed.), *Advances in Experimental Social Psychology (Vol. 8).* New York: Academic.

APPENDIX. Self-Report Questionnaire Form used by Hull et al. (1992). The same form was used across all twelve markers; only the marker number was changed.

Please stand in front of marker 1, facing in the direction the arrow points, before answering the following questions.

1. Use these word-pairs to describe, as best you can, how you feel right now.

	Not at all						*Very Much*
calm	1	2	3	4	5	6	7
rushed	1	2	3	4	5	6	7
exhilarated	1	2	3	4	5	6	7
important	1	2	3	4	5	6	7
hectic	1	2	3	4	5	6	7
stimulated	1	2	3	4	5	6	7
dull	1	2	3	4	5	6	7
in control	1	2	3	4	5	6	7
bored	1	2	3	4	5	6	7
peaceful	1	2	3	4	5	6	7
insignificant	1	2	3	4	5	6	7
excited	1	2	3	4	5	6	7
restful	1	2	3	4	5	6	7
unstimulated	1	2	3	4	5	6	7
overwhelmed	1	2	3	4	5	6	7

2. How does the scenic beauty of this view compare *to others you have seen along this trail?*

low scenic beauty 1   2   3   4   5   6   7   high scenic beauty

3. How does the scenic beauty of this view compare *to the most beautiful view you can remember?*

low scenic beauty 1   2   3   4   5   6   7   high scenic beauty

4. I would like to see more views like this one.

strongly disagree 1   2   3   4   5   6   7   strongly agree

5. How satisfied are you with your experience right now?

not at all   1   2   3   4   5   6   7   very much

6. Would you rather be some place else right now (home, car, camp, movies, restaurant, etc.)?

not at all   1   2   3   4   5   6   7   very much

Revealing
Socially Constructed Knowledge Through Quasi-Structured Interviews and Grounded Theory Analysis

Roger Riley

SUMMARY. Socially constructed knowledge pertains to the everyday understandings that mediate our lives. Much of how we act, our social relationships and how we perceive different phenomena are tempered by this knowledge. Even though this knowledge is important for living within the social world, it is considered to be taken-for-granted and commonsensical. This paper outlines the qualitative techniques of quasi-structured interviewing and grounded theory analysis that can reveal these personally held understandings and meanings. Included with these techniques are trustworthiness strategies aimed at increasing the methodological rigor for this type of qualitative research. *[Article copies available from The Haworth Document Delivery Service: 1-800-342-9678. E-mail address: getinfo@haworth.com]*

INTRODUCTION

Socially constructed knowledge pertains to the everyday understandings that mediate our lives. Much of the way people act, their relationships

Dr. Roger W. Riley is Assistant Professor, Department of Health, Physical Education, Recreation & Dance, Recreation and Park Administration Program, 101 McCormick Hall, Illinois State University, Normal, IL 61790-5121. His research interests include "elite" leisure travel and movie-induced tourism.

[Haworth co-indexing entry note]: "Revealing Socially Constructed Knowledge Through Quasi-Structured Interviews and Grounded Theory Analysis." Riley, Roger. Co-published simultaneously in *Journal of Travel & Tourism Marketing* (The Haworth Press, Inc.) Vol. 5, No. 1/2, 1996, pp. 21-40; and *Recent Advances in Tourism Marketing Research* (ed: Daniel R. Fesenmaier, Joseph T. O'Leary, and Muzaffer Uysal) The Haworth Press, Inc., 1996, pp. 21-40. Single or multiple copies of this article are available from The Haworth Document Delivery Service [1-800-342-9678, 9:00 a.m. - 5:00 p.m. (EST). E-mail address: getinfo@haworth.com].

with other people, and how they perceive different phenomena are tempered by this knowledge. Socially constructed knowledge is acquired through a process of socialization—never formally taught but gathered and made sense of by personal observation, social interaction, experience and inference. Although it encompasses the universally held understandings of a society, it is rarely acknowledged or discussed in social settings, and is taken-for-granted and considered commonsensical (Berger & Luckman, 1966). The universality of this knowledge is what makes a community (Seung, 1982; Taylor, 1985). Even though every member of a society is different, the commonly held meanings and references allow community members to interact and understand on the same plane of social existence (Taylor, 1985).

When attempting to gain access to socially constructed knowledge, the researcher is presented with a unique challenge. It is difficult to ask subjects to reflect upon knowledge that subconsciously guides their world because they rarely acknowledge or reflect upon it themselves. In these situations, the knowledge must be revealed by observing the subjects while they live their lives. This knowledge may also be gathered when subjects "tell" their life world through recollections of particular situations (Strauss & Corbin, 1990). From several stories focusing on similar situations, the universal understandings of particular socially constructed knowledge may be interpreted (Seung, 1982). An appropriate methodology for gathering and analyzing these life world stories is that of a qualitative nature (Denzin & Lincoln, 1994) because it allows for personal interaction with the subjects.

Tourism marketing investigators know little about the understandings or meanings that people gain from observing or participating in touristic experiences. While the sociology and anthropology arms of tourism research are less subject to this lack, the majority of tourism marketing research has relied on structured surveys and quantification. Although these approaches have provided the benefits of objectivity, the findings have been largely limited to predictions of macro tendency. As Havitz notes, this dependence has limited researchers from getting to know their subjects beyond their choices on closed response surveys. Moreover, the five point Likert Scale has minimal use when capturing the essence of a touristic experience (Havitz, 1994).

In contrast, qualitative researchers have pursued emic and interpretive approaches when exploring the understandings and meanings that people hold about different travel phenomena. While qualitative research can bring investigators closer to their subjects, many of these projects have been criticized for their lack of methodological rigor (Cohen, 1988). Qualitative research methods have also been criticized because they violate the long standing canons of positivist goodness (McCracken, 1988). However, there are qualitative approaches that have attempted an equivalency of positivist standards and research rigor while attempting to maintain a closeness to the subject and an interpretation of personal understanding and meaning (Denzin & Lincoln, 1994).

The purpose of this paper is to describe a qualitative methodology that seeks a middle ground between the competing issues of qualitative and quantitative research. It outlines an approach that emulates the positivist standards of objectivity while incorporating an emic and interpretive mode of inquiry for revealing socially constructed knowledge. The method is flexible enough to accommodate individual nuances while incorporating benchmarks of rigor for data gathering and analysis. This qualitative methodology employs quasi-structured interviewing for gathering data (Douglas, 1985; Kvale, 1983; McCracken, 1988) and an adaptation of grounded theory (Strauss & Glaser, 1967) for analysis of the data. An important addition to this methodology are the trustworthiness procedures instituted to ensure systematic and rigorous research throughout the research act (Lincoln & Guba, 1985). The approach has been categorized as a postpositivist method because it attempts to incorporate the value of internal and external validity while engaging in the actions of interpretation and being close to the subject (Denzin & Lincoln, 1994).

THE USE OF GROUNDED THEORY RESEARCH

The development of grounded theory originated from a perceived research need within the medical sociology and nursing field (Glaser & Strauss, 1964, 1968). In part, it was a response to "legitimate careful qualitative research, as by the 1960's this had sunk to a low status among an increasing number of sociologists because it was not believed capable of verification" (Strauss & Corbin, 1994, p. 275). The goals were to develop a method that addressed these perceived shortcomings by offering a research approach that could build stand-alone theory, and, to present an approach that could incorporate both quantitative and qualitative data (Strauss & Corbin, 1994). Recently, other areas of research endeavor have embraced the analytical flexibility that grounded theory offers with such topics as remarriage after divorce, home-building negotiations and domestic violence (Cauhape, 1983; Glaser, 1972; Lempert, 1992).

The flexibility of grounded theory lies in the systematic analysis of many data forms such as interviews, observations and written documents. Additional flexibility is found in the formulation and reformulation of theory to accept all variations of analyzed data. The underlying theme of grounded theory is that concept or theory generation is based on the context and perceptions of a chosen social scene (Crabtree & Miller, 1992) to reflect the "daily realities" of that which is actually going on (Strauss & Corbin, 1994). In this sense, any theory or concept development is bound to the parameters of the chosen context rather than enjoying wider generalizability.

The inductive process of grounded theory seeks to find patterns within data upon which theory can be developed (Henderson, 1991). With each analytical contribution, conceptual categories emerge. These categories are continually adjusted through "constant comparison" (Glaser & Strauss, 1967) so that new findings are accommodated into the emerging theory. When the theory repeatedly encompasses successive analytical findings, the theory is complete within the context for which it was conceived. Due to the adjustable nature of this approach, the findings may be far different than the original questions and ideas upon which the research question was founded.

Although qualitative research has enjoyed a long tradition within the area of tourism inquiry (Boorstin, 1964; Cohen, 1973; MacCannell, 1973, 1976; Turner, 1973, 1974), only one known use of grounded theory appears in tourism literature. This study searched for common dimensions that signified a perception of prestigious leisure travel. In the study, interview data was combined with other literature to find the basic components that made leisure travel prestigious. From informants' stories of prestigious leisure travel, it was found that perceived exclusivity was a key component. The other component was manifest in two forms of desirability. Prestigious travel could be personally desired by the observer or the desire could be based on an empathic understanding of the traveler's desire (Riley, in press).

Within marketing research, particularly within the context of consumer behavior, there has been a ground swell of qualitative work within the last twenty years. Early proponents have moved beyond the systematization and rigor issues of grounded theory (Denzin & Lincoln, 1994) and have embraced more evolved qualitative methods such as naturalistic inquiry (Belk, Sherry & Wallendorf, 1988; Hirschman, 1986; Holbrook, 1987; Kassarjian, 1987) and existential phenomenology (Thompson, Locander & Pollio, 1989). As the latter of these titles states, they are attempting to put the "consumer experience back into consumer research" (Thompson, Locander & Pollio, 1989, p. 133).

SOCIALLY CONSTRUCTED KNOWLEDGE

The concept of socially constructed knowledge originated from the socio-economic philosophy of Marx (Hirschman & Holbrook, 1992). Marx's philosophy was underpinned by a notion that the "beliefs people have are systematically related to their actual and material conditions of existence" (Wolff, 1975, p. 50) and that human thinking was determined by what transpired in the historical and social contexts of life (Hekman, 1986). Knowledge acquisition stemmed from the idea that all social relations were structured around social, political, and economic activities. Marx also believed that the knowledge accumulated by laborers was the only "correct" knowledge while those who were not involved in manual labor (intellectuals, economic elite) had "false" manifestations of knowledge (Hirschman & Holbrook, 1992). Mannheim redefined Marxian socio-economic knowledge theory by suggesting the existence of several knowledge structures rather than one "correct" knowledge structure. He proposed that the socio-economic conditions of many groups led to differently constructed social knowledge depending on their underlying influences (Berger & Luckman, 1966). With these differences there was a hint that knowledge was relative to the prevailing conditions of a person's existence. Later, ethnomethodolgists such as Schutz (1964) and Garfinkel (1967) suggested an underlying socially constructed knowledge that was common to all members of the same culture [in its widest sense]. This knowledge was held to be objectively truthful by that culture and governed the way people acted, even their consumer behavior. While perspectival differences existed within the culture, the underlying commonalties allowed for people to interpret the same phenomena similarly. The attraction of underlying social knowledge constructions was that ethnomethodologists could study macro-phenomena through a few people at the important level of everyday life. Contributions to a conception of socially constructed knowledge were also enhanced by Lucien Goldmann (1980). Through examining the consumptive culture of people, Goldmann believed that investigators could understand the common knowledge constructions of societies.

The Social Construction of Reality (Berger & Luckman, 1966) explained how people acquired socially constructed knowledge. Socially constructed knowledge was a taken-for-granted and commonsensical understanding and it was held objectively "truthful" for members in a particular society, regardless of its validity. Individuals continually internalized events that surrounded them and therefore individual consciousness was socially determined by what that society held relevant. The knowledge internalization process was an ongoing sequence that started at birth with the "immediate apprehension or interpretation of an objective event" (Berger & Luckman, 1966, p. 119). This knowledge was initially interpreted from, and attributed to, other people ("them") who already lived within the social world. When knowledge was internalized and attributed to an "us" or "we," the individual had become a member of that society (Berger & Luckman, 1966).

According to Berger and Luckman, two types of socialization contributed to social constructions of knowledge. Primary socialization occurred when individuals acquired knowledge common to everyone. Secondary socialization occurred when individuals were inducted into the knowledge possessed by specific groups or by the demands of particular roles or experiences. Each individual developed schema for integrating this more specific knowledge into their primary knowledge constructions. Primary socialized knowledge pertained to the understandings of everyday life. It was never formally taught but acquired through life-world experiences. Secondary socialized knowledge pertained to the particular instances of knowledge induction that were experienced by individuals within particular situations (Berger & Luckman, 1966).

In a study where the interviews and grounded theory are used, the investigator can get close to subjects so they share their perspective of their life-world. While each individual will tell their own "story" of the world, the commonsensical understandings of primary knowledge should emerge from the patterns and themes that are revealed during grounded theory analysis. It is Seung's (1982) contention that investigators who share the same social world can also interpret the data gathered from the respondents.

DATA GATHERING OF SOCIALLY CONSTRUCTED KNOWLEDGE

Interview Procedures

While commonsensical knowledge and the types of topics engendered by tourism research are unlikely to be threatening, it is important that investigators minimize bias when engaging in data gathering. In this sense, qualitative research scholars have been more prolific when explaining systematic and rigorous techniques for gathering socially constructed knowledge through interviews (Douglas, 1985; Kvale, 1983; Lofland, 1971; McCracken, 1988; Spradley, 1979; Wax, 1960) than for analyzing interview data (Strauss & Corbin, 1990; Miles & Huberman, 1993).

When adhering to the tenets of grounded theory through data gathering, investigators should minimize personal influence while trying to maximize the richness of information shared by respondents. A topic focus should be provided by the interviewer but the direction of conversation and subject matter must remain the domain of respondents (Kvale, 1983). The greater the structure imposed by the interviewer, the less respondents can offer their constructed knowledge. Therefore, respondents are considered to be the experts of their own reality and are forthwith labeled "informants" rather than respondents. "Respondent" implies dependence on the interviewer's agenda rather than speaking to agendas of their own (Lofland & Lofland, 1984). Good sampling techniques, the development of informants' trust and unobtrusive prompting for deeper descriptions are important issues for this type of interviewing.

Selection of Informants

The ultimate purpose of the quasi-structured interview method is to gain understanding and meaning rather than generalizing findings to a specific population. Therefore, the external validity measures of random selection and sufficiency of numbers are less relevant than one might find in positivist research (Henderson, 1991, p. 32). Nevertheless, interviews should be continued until all conceptual possibilities are exhausted [see theoretical saturation discussed below]. This may require interviewing a few people or many people, and will undoubtedly require additional interviews of the same people (Lincoln & Guba, 1985).

The techniques of theoretical sampling (Denzin 1989; Glaser & Strauss 1967; Strauss, 1987; Strauss & Corbin, 1990) and purposive sampling (Lincoln & Guba, 1985; Miles & Huberman, 1984) contribute to the selection of informants. Sampling should be designed to gain enough information to achieve "theoretical saturation" (Glaser & Strauss, 1967). That is, when the ongoing analysis of each interview reveals that findings are conceptually similar and repetitive, sampling is suspended (McCracken, 1988). Theoretical saturation is established when concepts have a pervasive presence in the findings. These concepts will occur regularly within conversations, they are the key ideas around which conversations are formed, and, they are often first issues that arise in conversations. The primacy of "first issues" may be interpreted to imply saliency for the informant.

Purposive sampling may be undertaken by using three "sampling rules of thumb" proposed by McCracken (1988). First, to minimize the effect of shared and mutual understandings, informants should not be acquainted with the investigator or the research project. These types of informants would be more likely to converse about matters that would be favorably received and would more likely communicate about mutually understood ideas. Second, informants should be avoided if they are conversant with the type of data gathering method or the topic, as they would be predisposed to answer with knowledge that was formally learned rather than socially constructed. Finally, to facilitate the "rule" of information variety and to maximize theoretical saturation, informants need to be deliberately chosen for contrast. Some informant variations that should be considered are age, gender, race, ethnicity, income, occupation, education, lifestyle and geographical location.

With each interview, diversity characteristics need to be reviewed and additional informants should be selected to fill known voids in the sample. McCracken states that most studies achieve saturation between 8-24 interviews depending on the topic focus (1988). If the study or phenomenon is conceptually small the sample size may be minimal; if the phenomenon is expansive, however, many informants may need to be interviewed before saturation is achieved.

Initial Contact with Informants

Engaging in acceptance and trust strategies is imperative for reducing the likelihood that informants will exaggerate, minimize, or distort their responses (Henderson, 1991). Therefore, engagement in full disclosure strategies through stated intentions, purpose and topic must be undertaken to place informants at ease. Acceptance and trust can be further enhanced by the mutual signing of an informed consent agreement. The agreement should guarantee anonymity, the ability to terminate interviews at any time and the promise of evidence restoration if desired by the informant (McCracken, 1988). To assist in the process of acceptance and trust, informants can be recruited through mutual acquaintance intermediaries. These intermediaries provide common bonds through which interactive trust can be established (Lincoln & Guba, 1985). An introduction by a trusted acquaintance will quell fears of meeting an unknown individual and will also reduce social intercourse barriers.

After initial contact between the two parties, techniques should be employed to develop interest and rapport because informants may view investigators as experts. If this should happen, informants would present themselves differently when compared to meeting an equal. This perception may lead to a reluctance to offer opinions and personal perspectives. Self-exposure procedures can be undertaken by the interviewer to reduce the expert/informant power differential (Douglas, 1985, Lincoln & Guba, 1985; Thompson, Locander & Pollio, 1989). These techniques can include a mutual sharing of knowledge about the intermediary, the sharing of personal background information and "idle chatter." Another rapport building technique entails the asking of simple descriptive questions so that informants develop comfortability drawing from personal experiences. Initial conversations should begin with general descriptive questions which the informant can easily answer. Questions of background and personal travel experiences may suffice in this situation. The grace period of easy-to-answer questions also allows informants to become comfortable with the recording technology. A final technique to promote detailed conversation is that the investigator should act in a "benign," yet "accepting" and "curious" manner. This technique implicitly transfers expertise from the investigator to the informant (Henderson, 1991; McCracken, 1988).

Influencing informants through an investigator's appearance and mannerisms has been debated in the literature without general agreement. If informants already know the interview purpose and intent, dressing and speaking at the informant's level may be considered patronizing. With this in mind, interviewers should present themselves in a manner befitting their position. The investigator should also conduct interviews in places specified by the prospective informant thereby reducing the additional anxiety of meeting on unfamiliar ground (Douglas, 1985; Fontana, 1977; Spradley, 1979; Wax, 1960).

Questioning Techniques

When eliciting socially constructed knowledge, formally structured questions should be minimized. Any subsequent interventions should be placed in the form of prompts and probes, based on the words of the informant. After informants speak about intermediaries, their life and travel exploits, they can be introduced to the topic area in question. The question should be of an orienting nature and should avoid specifics so the informant can speak about what is important to them. Typically, there is an immediate call for greater specification of the topic which should be met with phrases and gestures implying that informants should provide their own parameters.

As informants speak about the phenomenon in question, "floating prompts" and "planned prompts" (McCracken, 1988) can be employed to extend or deepen conversations. Floating prompts are injected when conversations have pertinence to the research question but embellishment is desired. Floating prompts are verbal and non-verbal requests for deeper descriptions. These requests use everyday communication techniques such as a questioned "oh," eyebrow flashes, or grunts of affirmation to imply interest. The repetition of key words or phrases in a questioning tone has the same effect. Techniques such as this allow for an investigator's intervention while keeping the focus on informants' stories (McCracken, 1988). Planned prompts are posed at the end of responses to encourage further discussion. Deliberately playing dumb (Henderson, 1991) and "silence" (Lincoln & Guba, 1985) can be employed for this purpose and will generally revitalize discussion in preference to continued silence. Other planned prompts include requests for deeper descriptions about the phenomenon, requests for embellishment of instances already discussed (Lincoln & Guba, 1985), and clarification of previous discussion (Kvale, 1983). Greater depth can also be gained through requests for contrasting incidents (McCracken, 1988).

When conversing about taken-for-granted and commonsensical knowledge, introspection is not usually undertaken by informants and "why" questions may encourage forced responses (Patton, 1980). Therefore, during interviews an investigator should avoid the temptation of asking "why?". These types of questions may imply that informants should analyze their answers for cause and effect relationships. It may also engender informant defensiveness as the question could be interpreted as judgmental (Thompson, Locander & Pollio, 1989).

Data Recording

While many forms of recording have been used for research purposes, audio taping is a preferred method for accurate recording of conversations. The benefits of audio taping accrue from the technological display that interviews are serious enough to warrant exact reproduction (Henderson, 1991). Audio taping also minimizes distractions that would be experienced if investigators record notes by hand. Informants gain cues from selected note taking and these cues may bias their conversations to what they believe investigators want. Handwritten note taking can only be selective when transcribing conversations and studies have found written records to be incomplete (Douglas, 1985). Additionally, it is impossible for investigators to realize the importance of information until it is analyzed (Fontana & Frey, 1994). Therefore, complete audio reproductions are preferred for the later transcription of conversations. Any reluctance to be tape recorded can be quelled by the prior disclosure of the leisure travel topic and by assurances that informants can have their tape recording if subsequent analysis is not desired. By engaging the record button during introductory conversation, the obtrusiveness of the machine can be diminished by the time the research question is asked.

All transcripts should be typed to mirror the conversations of the informant and the interviewer. This typing should include pauses, sighs, grunts, and all prompts and probes.

ANALYSIS OF SOCIALLY CONSTRUCTED KNOWLEDGE

Grounded Theory Analysis

Grounded theory analysis provides a systematic structure that allows the richness of socially constructed knowledge to emerge. It also avoids "total methodological anarchism" where any interpretation is allowable (Kvale, 1983). Grounded theory methods are designed to develop theories and concepts from many types of systematically collected data whether they be interviews, observations or documents. The key to grounded theory is that analysis and data collection are concurrent activities. The theories or concepts are built through constantly comparing past analyses with newly analyzed data. The theory or concepts are built to saturation through an iterative analytical process (Strauss & Corbin, 1994). Concepts are initially built by a splitting of the interview data into components parts. The subsequent iterative process requires a collapsing of the data under conceptually inclusive categories. As category headings become more abstracted from the original data, they are subsumed under more overarching conceptual categories. The categorical headings of the last iteration can be considered to be the underlying concepts desired in the study. The analysis process is divided into five stages (Figure 1).

Stage One—Familiarization

Familiarization is the most applicable phrase for characterizing the first stage of the analytical process. Kvale (1983) suggests that this stage is an acquaintanceship with the informant's "life world" and their knowledge. An informant profile is developed from each typed transcript and any personal information that is gained in the rapport building stage of interviews. Analysis also focuses on metaphorical, cultural and individual peculiarities of speech (McCracken, 1988). For example, if an informant uses the word "bombed," they may be referring to explosions, being drunk, or failing to achieve something. Intended connotations are important for analyses because they allow better understanding of the surrounding data pieces. Returning to the recorded conversation may also be needed where voice emphases and inflections are important to the meaning of a sentence.

FIGURE 1. Analysis Procedures

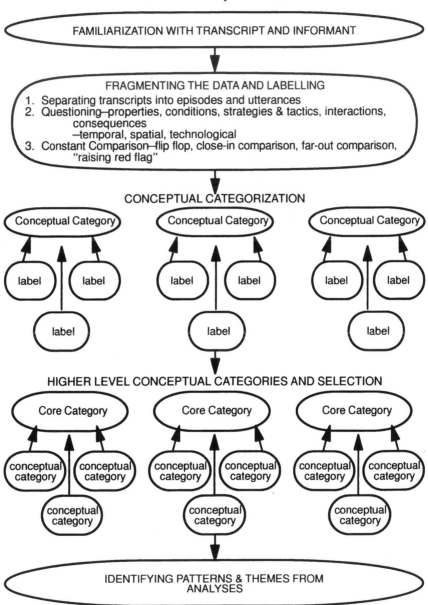

(Adapted from McCracken 1988; Strauss and Corbin 1990).

Stage Two—Fragmenting the Data

In stage two, the raw data is split into clusters, described, compared, and categorized by a label. Two processes are required to complete the second stage. The first process involves a division of the transcript into "utterances." Utterances are considered to be phrases, sentences, or paragraphs that encompass one characteristic of a travel episode or phenomenon (McCracken, 1988).

The second process in stage two requires the use of "questioning" and "constant comparisons" between the utterances of the transcript and previously analyzed data (Glaser & Strauss, 1967). The following questions are adapted from Strauss and Corbin (1990) and assist in describing the phenomenon in a semi-chronological sequence.

1. Properties	What actually happened? What describes this phenomenon? Can this phenomenon occur at any point on a continuum of like occurrences, or just at one point?
2. Causal Conditions	What circumstances precede this phenomenon? Indicating words such as, "because," "since," "as," and, "on account of," tend to signpost antecedent events.
3. Consequences	What happens as a result of this phenomenon? Indicating words such as, "as a result," "because of," "the result was," "the consequence was" tend to signpost some consequences.
4. Strategies and Tactics	What happened in reaction to the phenomenon, for the enhancement of the phenomenon, to circumvent the phenomenon, or to promote the phenomenon?
5. Interactions	What sort of interpersonal relations were involved in the phenomenon under discussion?

Spatial questions also assist in describing the geographical dispersion and placement of the phenomenon while technological questions can be employed to determine the assistance or constraining capacities of technology. Utterances are further described by asking questions of a temporal nature. Temporal questions are concerned with issues such as:

  i. the frequency of the phenomenon's occurrence;
 ii. the duration of the phenomenon;
iii. the rate (repetitively quick or slow); and,
iv. particular times the phenomenon occurred.

(Adapted from Strauss & Corbin, 1990).

Constant comparison techniques are then used to compare among analyzed utterances and to gain further meaning of each utterance. The constant comparison technique is also used to compare utterances with hypothetical occurrences outside the interview context. The four types of constant comparison techniques are:

1. The "Flip Flop" technique requires the phenomenon in each utterance to be compared with an extreme opposite case. The intent is to illuminate meaning by contrast;
2. "Close-In" comparisons require a search for similarities and differences between utterances so they can be grouped or separated;
3. "Far Out" comparisons places the phenomenon in situations that are absurdly different than stated. The aim is to interpret whether situational changes will affect the phenomenon; and,
4. "Waving The Red Flag" alerts the investigator to words of an absolutist sense. "Never," "always," "no way," "everyone knows" tended to indicate that the phenomenon was being taken-for-granted by the informant. Understanding is achieved by placing the red flag situations in contexts where they are not taken- for-granted.

(Adapted from Strauss & Corbin, 1990).

During coding, each segment of the analysis is assigned a label based on interpretation from the questions and comparisons. Similarly labeled utterances are then grouped. While Strauss and Corbin employ a letters and numbers coding system for their analysis [see Strauss & Corbin, 1990], the coding system preferred by this investigator is a file and mapping system. Each complete transcript is placed in a file folder while another copy is divided into separate utterances. Attached to each of the utterances are all the questions and comparison techniques. Beside them are gaps for their subsequent interpretations. After labeling, each utterance and an accompanying description is charted on the wall of a large room. The label utterances are then conceptually grouped through subsequent iterations of the analysis process.

Some utterances will receive similar labels because informants tend to be repetitive when speaking. Repetitions are collapsed under one label when the descriptions of the utterances are compared for commonalties. These labels and short descriptions are then posted on the wall for ease of comparison among interviews.

Stage Three–Conceptual Categorization

In stage three, the emphasis of the analysis moves from the fragmented utterances to the coded labels established in stage two. The two steps of stage three involve grouping labels into sets of relationships. Labels from stage two are subsumed under conceptually similar categories when they assist in describing and contributing to that category. The term "axial" category has been used by Strauss because "analysis revolves around the conceptual axis of the category" (Strauss 1987, p. 64).

The second step of stage three aligns conceptual categories into story-like groups related to their temporal place in a generic travel episode.

1. "Causal Conditions" describe the antecedent events that give rise to a phenomenon.
2. "Phenomenon Contexts" are the properties that describe the existence of the phenomenon.
3. "Intervening Conditions" are those features that enhance or restrain the phenomenon from happening. Examples may be timing, space, economic ability, socio-cultural interests, technology, personality, and historical factors (Strauss & Corbin, 1990).
4. "Strategies and Tactics" are the actions undertaken for the purpose of continuing or terminating the phenomenon.
5. "Consequences" relate to changes in people, places, and things. These changes are reactions that follow the occurrence of a phenomenon.

A generic story is then developed from all of the conceptual categories. The associated labels are listed underneath each category on the conceptual wall map.

Stage Four–Higher Level Conceptual Categories

Stage Four is roughly equivalent to the previous stage except analysis continues at a higher conceptual level. The conceptual categories are called "core categories" because the stage three categories are subsumed under them (Strauss & Corbin, 1990). For inclusion as a core category, they need to fulfill the following requirements:

   i. be related to as many lower level categories as possible;
   ii. have a pervasive presence in the data;
   iii. relate easily to subcategories; and,
   iv. be broad enough to allow variations within the categories subsumed under the core category.

   (Strauss, 1987).

A second step of stage four requires referencing back to the key research question. Core categories are selected out if not related to the research question. The remaining categories constitute the conceptual core of the interview conversation.

Stage Five—Comparing Across Analysis

The fifth stage compares the remaining core categories across all interviews. The aim is to identify common themes or patterns across the interviews. The themes and patterns need to occur across all interviews to be considered as core concepts and the remaining categories are considered to comprise the core concepts of the research question.

TRUSTWORTHINESS OF DATA GATHERING AND ANALYSIS

Although it has been less true as alternative ways of knowing evolve, qualitative researchers are sometimes confronted with having their analytic procedures judged by quantitative rules (McCracken, 1988). When conducting quasi-structured interviews and grounded theory analysis, this problem can be further addressed by using a set of techniques that established the trustworthiness of qualitative methods. The interpreted truth and relevancy of qualitative analyses can be established by the standards of credibility, transferability, dependability and confirmability (Lincoln & Guba, 1985). Although Lincoln and Guba were loath to make links with positivistic ideals, these concepts have roles roughly analogous to internal validity, external validity, reliability, and objectivity (1985).

When establishing the credibility of analysis, the tradition of the investigator-as-expert is reversed. This process is called "member checking" and is an invited assessment of the investigator's interpreted meaning (Belk, Sherry & Wallendorf, 1988; Hirschman & Holbrook, 1992; Lincoln & Guba, 1985). Informants can be invited to assess whether the early analyses are accurate reflections of their conversations. Member checks are most relevant after the axial coding stage because higher level conceptual abstractions would result in a loss of meaning for the informants. Informants can be asked to read their transcripts before reading a summary of the analysis provide by the researcher. Any changes, disagreements or additional information are then recycled into the ongoing analytical process. Credibility can also be established using existing literature that addresses the same general areas.

Transferability is not considered the responsibility of the investigator because the knowledge elicited is most influenced by each individual's life context and the situation (Lincoln & Guba, 1985). Indeed, the varied social constructions of knowledge are what the investigator is searching for. In its stead, the investigator's obligation is to accurately describe the contexts and techniques of the study so that subsequent follow-up studies can match them as closely as possible (Hirschman, 1986; Lincoln & Guba, 1985).

The dependability requirement ensures that, under the same circumstances, the same interpretation would occur. Independent investigators should analyze transcripts and tapes to confirm the plausibility of prior interpretations. This process is undertaken after the highest level of conceptual analysis (stage five). Further analysis by independent investigators is like a member check except that all levels of the analyses are reviewed. Should discrepancies arise, the differences are funneled back into the original analysis process.

Finally, it is not presumed that investigators can be neutral or personally detached from all facets of the investigation. Therefore, an auditor regularly reviews the interviews and analytical processes to confirm adherence to sound research practices. A detailed journal of all interviews, analyses and interpretations is kept to assist this process and the auditor acts as a "devil's advocate" to seek out and correct the personal biases of the investigator. With these trustworthiness strategies in place, the interviewing and analytic processes are less likely to submerge into "methodological anarchy." Interviewing actions and analyses are carefully reviewed to apply a consistency of rigor to the qualitative research process (Lincoln & Guba, 1985).

CONCLUSION

The understanding of tourism and the tourist experience, as interpreted by hosts and guests, has long been a focus for sociologists, anthropologists and psychologists. Despite a wide acceptance of qualitative methods in sociological and anthropological circles, the same acceptance has been limited in marketing and other disciplines that contribute to understanding tourism. Some people would suggest that a lack of qualitative research is due to the dominant culture of positivism and quantification while others place cause on the requirements of those who pay to know. Nevertheless, a slow but solid increase in qualitative research has been laid to question, not the wealth of evidence that quantitative researchers have gained, but the scope of their perspective. To assist in this continuing acceptance, researchers may prefer to start with qualitative methods that minimize the perception of bias and maximize the intent of objectivity. It is with this intent that quasi-structured interviewing and grounded theory analysis were been presented. Finding people's socially constructed knowledge may assist tourism researchers to better understand why people do what they do.

The commonsensical and taken-for-granted nature of socially constructed knowledge makes its identification difficult even though it has importance when subconsciously structuring peoples' life worlds. Although respondents cannot readily identify this knowledge they are more than able to tell stories or exemplars of their world. Through these stories, researchers can search for patterns or themes that underpin the defined topic. While no interpretive approach can be confidently objective [or indeed wants to be], the methods outlined are an attempt to bring a rigor and systematization to the qualitative research act that may enhance objectivity. What can be confidently expressed is that quasi-structured interview and grounded theory analysis are another way of knowing–beyond structured surveys and quantification.

Qualitative research might be described as investigation that takes place in the settings where subjects of interest exist, in an effort to bring meaning and understanding to different phenomena, as seen by the people who experience them. An addendum would also state that the data does not lend itself to quantification because the inquirer is seeking to describe parts of a complicated world through the situational and perspectival differences of people. Qualitative researchers know that the "truth" cannot be completely found but are trying to represent the knowledge as faithfully as possible. The argument of better or worse, and sound or unsound research is important but pales when compared to additional understanding of why people do what they do.

REFERENCES

Belk, Russell, Sherry, John & Wallendorf, Melanie (1988). A naturalistic inquiry into buyer and seller behavior at a swap meet. *Journal of Consumer Research*, 14: 449-470.

Berger, Peter & Luckman, Thomas (1966). *The Social Construction of Reality: A Treatise in the Sociology of Knowledge.* Garden City, NY: Doubleday.

Boorstin, Daniel (1964). *The Image: A Guide to Pseudo-Events in America.* New York: Harper.

Cauhape, E. (1983). *Fresh Starts: Men and Women after Divorce.* New York: Basic Books.

Cohen, Erik (1988). Traditions in the qualitative sociology of tourism. *Annals of Tourism Research,* 15: 29-46.

Cohen, Erik (1973) Nomads of affluence: Notes on the phenomenon of drifter tourism. *International Journal of Comparative Sociology,* 14: 89-103.

Crabtree, Benjamin & Miller, William (1992). *Doing Qualitative Research.* Newbury Park, CA: Sage.

Denzin, Norman (1989). *Interpretive Interactionism.* Newbury Park, CA: Sage.

Denzin, Norman & Lincoln, Yvonna (Eds.) (1994). *Handbook of Qualitative Research.* Thousand Oaks, CA: Sage.

Douglas, John (1985). *Creative Interviewing.* Beverly Hills CA: Sage.

Fontana, Andrea (1977). *The Last Frontier: The Social Meaning of Growing Old.* Beverly Hills, CA: Sage.

Fontana, Andrea & Frey, James (1994). Interviewing: The art of science. In N. Denzin & Y. Lincoln (Eds.). *Handbook of Qualitative Research* (pp. 361-376). Thousand Oaks, CA: Sage.

Garfinkel, H. (1967). *Studies in Ethnomethodology.* Englewood Cliffs, NJ: Prentice Hall.

Glaser, Barney (1972). *Experts versus Laymen: A Study of the Patsy and the Subcontractor.* New Brunswick, NJ: Transaction.

Glaser, Barney & Strauss, Anselm (1964). *Awareness of Dying.* Chicago: Aldine.

Glaser, Barney & Strauss, Anselm (1967). *The Discovery of Grounded Theory: Strategies for Qualitative Research.* Chicago, IL: Aldine.

Glaser, Barney & Strauss, Anselm (1968). *Time for Dying.* Chicago: Aldine.

Goldmann, Lucien (1980). *The Sociology of Literature.* St. Louis, MO: Telos Press.

Havitz, Mark (1994). *A personal and collective critique of methodological and ethical concerns in consumer behavior research* Unpublished keynote presentation at 1994, N.R.P.A. Symposium on Leisure Research, Minneapolis, MN.

Hekman, S. (1986). *Hermeneutics and the Sociology of Knowledge.* Notre Dame IN: University of Notre Dame Press.

Henderson, Karla (1991). *Dimensions of Choice: A Qualitative Approach to Recreation, Park and Leisure Research.* State College PA: Venture.

Hirschman, Elizabeth (1986). Humanistic inquiry in marketing research: Philosophy, method and criteria. *Journal of Marketing Research,* 21:237-249.

Hirschman, Elizabeth & Holbrook, Morris (1992). *Postmodern Consumer Research: The Study of Consumption as Text.* Newbury Park, CA: Sage.

Holbrook, Morris (1987). From the log of a consumer researcher: Reflections on the odyssey. *Advances in Consumer Research,* 14: 365-369.

Kassarjian, Harold (1987). How we spent our summer vacation. *Advances in Consumer Research,* 14: 367-377.

Kvale, Steinar (1983). The qualitative research interview: A phenomenological and hermeneutical mode of understanding. *Journal of Phenomenological Psychology,* 14: 171-196.

Lempert, L. (1992). *The crucible: Violence, help seeking, and abused women's transformation of self.* Unpublished doctoral dissertation, University of California-San Francisco.

Lincoln, Yvonna & Guba, Egon (1985). *Naturalistic Inquiry.* Beverly Hills: Sage.

Lofland, John (1971). *Analyzing Social Settings: A Guide to Qualitative Observation and Analysis.* Belmont, CA: Wadsworth.

Lofland, John & Lofland, Lyn (1984). *Analyzing Social Settings: A Guide to Qualitative Observation and Analysis.* Belmont, CA: Wadsworth.

MacCannell, Dean (1973). Staged authenticity: Arrangements of social space in tourist settings. *American Journal of Sociology,* 79(3): 589-603.

MacCannell, Dean (1976). *The Tourist: A New Theory of the Leisure Class.* New York: Schocken Books.

McCracken, Grant (1988). *The Long Interview.* Newbury Park CA: Sage.

Mannheim, Karl (1952). *Essays on the Sociology of Knowledge.* London: Routledge & Kegan Paul.

Marx, Karl (1970). *Capital: A Critique of Political Economy* (Vol. 1). London: Lawrence & Wishart.

Miles, Matthew & Huberman, Michael (1993). *Qualitative Data Analysis: A Sourcebook of New Methods.* Beverly Hills, CA: Sage.

Patton, Michael (1980). *Qualitative Evaluation Methods.* Beverly Hills, CA: Sage.

Riley, Roger (in press). Prestige Worthy Leisure Travel Behavior. *Annals of Tourism Research,* 22(3).

Schutz, Alfred (1964). *Collected Papers* (Vol. 2). The Hague, Netherlands: Martinus Nijhoff.

Seung, T. (1982). *Structuralism and Hermeneutics.* New York: Columbia University Press.

Spradley, J. P. (1979). *The Ethnographic Interview.* New York: Holt, Rinehart &Winston.

Strauss, Anselm (1987). *Qualitative Analysis for Social Scientists.* New York: Cambridge University Press.

Strauss, Anselm & Corbin, Juliet (1994) Grounded theory methodology: An overview. In N. Denzin & Y. Lincoln (Eds.). *Handbook of Qualitative Research* (pp. 273-285). Thousand Oaks, CA: Sage.

Strauss, Anselm & Corbin, Juliet (1990). *Basics of Qualitative Research.* Newbury Park, CA: Sage.

Taylor, C. (1985). *Philosophy and the Human Sciences.* Cambridge: Cambridge University Press.

Thompson, Craig, Locander, William & Pollio, Howard (1989). Putting consumer experience back into consumer research: The philosophy and method of existential phenomenology. *Journal of Consumer Research,* 16: 133-46.

Turner, Victor. (1973). The center out there: Pilgrim's goal. *History of Religions,* 12: 191- 230.

Turner, Victor. (1974). *The Ritual Process.* Harmondsworth: Penguin.

Wax, Rosalie (1971). *Doing Fieldwork: Warnings and Advice.* Chicago: The University of Chicago Press.

Wolff, J. (1975). *Hermeneutic Philosophy and the Sociology of Art: An Approach to Some of the Epistemological Problems of the Sociology of Knowledge and the Sociology of Art and Literature.* Boston MA: Routledge and Kegan Paul.

Tourists' Images of a Destination–
An Alternative Analysis

Graham M. S. Dann

SUMMARY. Tourism research has traditionally tackled the question of destination choice by asking visitors to rank attributes identified by the analyst and to indicate the degree to which they measure up to prior expectations. The current presentation offers an alternative qualitative methodology to the gauging of satisfaction, motivation and experience by focusing on tourists and examining the linguistic content of their mental images. The case study is that of Barbados and winter visitors to that Caribbean island. In supplying details of their own projected images and responses to pictorial stimuli in both pre and on-trip situations, they provide a framework for analysis at three levels. While cognitive appraisal of the destination is explored by means of mental comparison, the affective dimension reveals a vocabulary of motive. Finally, there is a cognitive component of imagery in which tourists project themselves into an imagined scenario as if they had already experienced it. These various layers of

Graham M. S. Dann is Professor, Department of Sociology, The University of the West Indies, Bridgetown, Barbados.

This paper was prepared for the conference on "Decision Making Processes and Preference Changes of Tourists: Intertemporal and Inter-Country Perspectives," held at Leopold-Franzens-Universität, Innsbruck, Austria, in November, 1993. In 1994 it was published under the title, "A Socio-Linguistic Analysis of the Cognitive, Affective and Conative Content of Images as an Alternative Means to Gauging Tourist Satisfaction, Motivation and Experience," pp. 125-139 in *Spoilt for Choice, Decision Making Processes–Intertemporal and Intercountry Perspectives,* R. V. Gasser and K. Weiermair (eds.). Innsbruck: Kulturverlag, Thaur. It is reproduced here with permission.

[Haworth co-indexing entry note]: "Tourists' Images of a Destination–An Alternative Analysis." Dann, Graham M. S. Co-published simultaneously in *Journal of Travel & Tourism Marketing* (The Haworth Press, Inc.) Vol. 5, No. 1/2, 1996, pp. 41-55; and *Recent Advances in Tourism Marketing Research* (ed: Daniel R. Fesenmaier, Joseph T. O'Leary, and Muzaffer Uysal) The Haworth Press, Inc., 1996, pp. 41-55.

subjective meaning may be collectively understood as analogous to the discourse of advertising.

INTRODUCTION

The term "images" is said to be "an abstract concept incorporating the influences of past promotion, reputation and peer evaluation of alternatives. Image connotes the expectation of the user" (Gensch, 1978 in Gartner and Hunt, 1987:15). According to Stringer (1984:149), in a socio-psychological sense, "image refers to a reflection or representation of sensory or conceptual information; . . . (it) is built on past experience and governs one's action (cf. Boulding, 1961) . . . It is not static or objective. There is an essential value component." An image is social to the extent that it is often shared by similar people who also form part of that image (Stringer, 1984 citing Moscovici, 1981).

Traditionally, tourism research has examined destination imagery by linking it to the question of destination choice. Visitors are supplied with standardized qualities of destinations and attention focuses on the various ways in which these attributes are rated or ranked. The characteristics appear as fixed format, close-ended questionnaire items; scores are assigned to replies, and subsequent application of statistical techniques affords comparisons, not only among rival destinations, but also within differential profile categories of respondent. A similar treatment is extended to the measurement of tourist satisfaction and the degree to which prior expectations are said to live up to or fail to meet the requirements of the visitor. Motivation (often understood as "basic need") is linked to such expectations, and the holiday experience is evaluated in terms of their fulfillment or otherwise.

Yet there are grounds for believing that these neo-positivist approaches may not be capturing the full dynamics or richness inherent in the process of destination choice. In the first place, it cannot be assumed that destination attributes on their own and in themselves are motivationally adequate to explain why individuals or groups gravitate towards one place and not to another. In fact, tourism advertising and promotion tend to operate from the opposite point of view, i.e., that psychological/structural dispositions in the consumer are the real motives of travel, and that these deep inner forces are only activated by the selective images of the destination (cf. Mayo and Jarvis, 1981; Uzzell, 1984).

Second, since the check list of items in a visitor motivation/satisfaction survey is usually generated by the researcher rather than the researched, there is a corresponding likelihood that subjective definitions of participants may be overlooked and replaced by so-called "objective" measures. Yet, while the latter can yield statistical reliability, they may do so at the expense of validity, given that the way situations are defined is ultimately associated with the perceived reality of effect (Thomas, 1951).

Third, and as a corollary of the above, it is often (incorrectly) supposed that questionnaire items which seek to gauge destination attractiveness each have one and only one meaning. Consequently, responses to such stimuli are reckoned to lie along a single dimension which can be graded as equally appearing intervals on a lone continuum. However, the more probable truth of the matter is that, since the stimuli are themselves images, they range from metaphoric to metanymic, from denotative to connotative, and are hence capable of multiple interpretation (cf. Cohen, 1993). Thus several continua may be operating on different layers. Some may be divergent; others may be convergent or intersecting. At the same time, the various units of measurement are likely to be different. Rarely will they be capable of comparison beyond the level of simple ordinality.

Fourth, it is also frequently assumed that such images are only of the verbal or mental variety and that the questionnaire is therefore the most appropriate instrument for dealing with these stimuli. Yet, the designers of brochures and allied promotional material, in surely rejecting such a claim, would quickly point to the important role of photography in relaying messages to target audiences. The semioticians would agree, and further engage in lengthy debate about the linguistic autonomy of pictures in a publicity setting (e.g., Eco, 1979; Barthes, 1982).

For these and other reasons some tourism researchers emphasize the need to reintroduce the subject, to bring the tourist back into their investigations. Gottlieb (1982:166), for instance, while lamenting the fact that "few authors attempt to explore the vacationers' own perspectives on the nature of the vacation," bases her innovative inversionist approach on the premise that "what the vacationer experiences is real, valid and fulfilling, no mater how 'superficial' it may seem to the social scientist" (Gottlieb, 1982: 167). Thus, instead of proposing yet another *a priori* typology of tourists, she prefers to go straight to the source, to construct a model inductively from conversations and interviews with the actual people who have undergone the vacation experience. Pearce (1982: 123-143) employs a similar methodology in seeking to examine the social role of the tourist, tourist motivation, contacts between tourists and hosts, and between tourists and the environment. In spite of the wealth of data generated, and the difficulties in coding such a vast array of open-ended material, Pearce believes that, when compared with satisfaction studies, the major merit of his approach is that it permits the airing of the participants' views in ways other than simply responding to preconceived survey categories. He further justified his "emic" perspective in relation to a travel career model of tourist motivation (Pearce, 1993).

More recently, Gartner (1993) has explored the processual nature of destination selection. In the early stages alternatives are discounted on such grounds as time constraints and insufficient discretionary income. Later, and as the number of viable options decreases, there is a growing emphasis on evaluation of attributes based on such criteria as activity performance and knowledge of performance characteristics. However, when potential tourists approach their final choice, it is motivation which comes into play. This crucial factor comprises not only "pull" motives which are linked to the destination's attractions, but also the extent to which they correspond to "push motives" of the prospective traveller (Dann, 1981). Furthermore, argues Gartner (1993), it is in the process of destination choice that the cognitive, affective and conative components of image become operational. These three dimensions are respectively associated with intellectual appraisal, motivational evaluation and projected behavioural activity on the part of the tourist.

The current presentation attempts to build on the foregoing insights by empirically examining Gartner's (1993) components of image in a sociolinguistic framework. By concentrating on tourists, what they are saying and how they are articulating their perceptions at the intellectual, motivational and experiential levels, it is hoped that a fuller understanding of the subjectivity at work in the process of destination selection will be attained.

THE PRESENT INVESTIGATION

The present research focuses on some 535 tourists visiting the Caribbean island of Barbados during the winter season of 1989. Details of the sample and other facets of the interview based study have been reported elsewhere (Dann, 1992; 1994b; forthcoming). Of interest here are the 200 or so pages of transcripts generated from open-ended replies to two items.

Early on in the interview, after respondents had been questioned as to their sources of information about Barbados, they were asked what sort of image they had of the destination:

a. prior to their ever having visited it, and
b. now that they were here (whether or not this was their first visit).

This before/after format permitted a comparison of the two sets of open-ended replies to no other stimulus than the simple question itself. Subsequently interviewees were shown four photographs which had featured in promotional material put out by the local authorities (Barbados Board of Tourism, n.d.; Official Guide, 1988-9), and which had been selected by the researcher on the theoretical basis of increasing strangerhood (Cohen, 1979) to the tourist. The pictures showed:

1. a young (visiting) couple on a beach at sunset;
2. a local woman serving in a hotel;
3. local children coming out of a country church; and,
4. a Rastafarian.

Using a similar format to the first question, interviewees were asked what these pictures meant to them:

a. before they had ever visited the island, and
b. now that they were here.

Again, a pre-trip/on-trip comparison could be made. So too could one contract the responses to these pictorial stimuli with those previously articulated (i.e., mental images) which had not benefited from visual aids.

Theoretical justification for the underlying socio-linguistic approach, along with the accompanying methodology and a number of findings as they related to the incidence and frequency of key words in respondents' descriptions, have been presented in another paper (Dann, forthcoming). There also has the rationale been supplied for the use of memory questions (cf. Boulding, 1961; Berger, 1972; Dann, 1993; Urbain, 1989) with respect to "induced" and "organic" imagery (i.e., that respectively based on publicity or visitation experience (cf. Gartner (1993: 197- 205)). On this occasion, however, attention is directed away from the quantitative patterning of responses and more towards their qualitative meaning.

THE COGNITIVE COMPONENT OF IMAGES

Gartner (1993:193), based on Scott (1965) and Boulding (1961), defines the cognitive image component as the evaluation of the known attributes of the product according to fact. Apart from the epistemological problem of whether facts exist, one can at least say that two operations are at work—the receipt of information and the formation of attitudes towards that information later expressed in one or more judgements.

In this study it was found that the cognitive appraisal of the destination was often expressed socio-linguistically via the strategy of mental comparison. The latter in turn was based on induced or organic sources. Table 1 provides some examples taken from accounts which articulate mental images and verbal reactions to the four pictures. Although in each case they involve five different respondents, in every before and after situation it is the same interviewee who speaks.

In every pre-trip situation the comparison is effected by means of recall and reference to a real or vicarious experience. In some cases there is a sense of "déjà vu"–"reminds me of"–an evocation of memory. There is also the use of the word "like" where the subject tries to make sense of one image by referring to a more familiar other.

The experience of being in Barbados variously modifies the pre-trip image. Whereas responses to picture 2 reveal a definite move in the positive direction, and those to picture 3 highlight a feeling of disillusionment, the remainder are more neutral in character. Since these expressions are

TABLE 1. Cognitive Images

Pre-Trip	**On Trip**
Without Pictorial Stimuli	*Without Pictorial Stimuli*
It's a tropical island like Martinique or St. Lucia.	It's a tropical island but not really like Martinique or St. Lucia. In the countryside there are some similarities but Barbados is very flat. The people drive on the wrong side of the road.
With Pictorial Stimuli	*With Pictorial Stimuli*
Picture 1 – Reminds me of Hawaii–A romantic getaway.	Picture 1 – I haven't seen a sunset yet. It's always been cloudy. There are palm trees.
Picture 2 – Southern culture–Plantation type thing.	Picture 2 – Lovely service and courteous people.
Picture 3 – Missionaries have been here. Looks less like Barbados than it does the South Pacific.	Picture 3 – Actually it is very heavily Anglican. Religion means a lot to you here.
Picture 4 – Reminds me of Bob Marley.	Picture 4 – They have their own religion and way of life.

more than mere descriptions, they can also be interpreted in terms of satisfaction or otherwise with the vacation experience, and the extent to which the latter exceeds, is on par with, or fails to live up to prior expectations. In other words, the analysis of linguistic expressions becomes an alternative method of gauging levels of satisfaction to the traditional questionnaire check list of destination attributes. In the case of mental images, the focus is more open-ended and it is the respondent who determines the area of significance. Once pictures are introduced, the discourse becomes more stimulus oriented.

THE AFFECTIVE COMPONENT OF IMAGES

The affective component of images relates to the vocabulary of motive, a crucial topic which tourism researchers have wrestled with for many years (cf. Dann, 1981; Pearce, 1982, 1993). According to Gartner (1993: 196), "Motives determine what we wish to obtain from the object being considered." For this reason he believes that the affective appraisal of alternative destinations can occur well before the final decision stage.

However, by treating motivation socio-linguistically, categories are no longer pre-determined a-priori by the researcher. Rather they emerge in an a-posteriori fashion from the discourse of the participants. Table 2 supplies some examples of this component. It employs the same format as the previous section.

In the first case (unaided by pictorial stimulus, and hence the most open-ended of the responses), there is a mixture of "push" and "pull" factors. In this particular example, the former comprise the need to relax and unwind (cf. Cohen's (1979) "recreational" mode) in a place that is more "low key" (i.e., less frenetic and alienating) than home. There is no quest for an elective centre in the "other" since "coming to" the place implies a return to one's own society. The "pull" of warm weather is indirectly contrasted with the (unmentioned) cold of the northern winter. However, the on-trip experience focuses attention more on the destination people (described as "friendly") and the environment is perceived as "clean" and "safe." Now the comparison with home is quite explicit and the experience is evaluated in favourable terms.

In response to the first picture, the interviewee articulates the pre-trip desire for companionship. The introduction of "paradise" (cf. Cohen, 1982) suggests an Eden-like situation where love and caring are framed with an intimate "ménage a deux." Yet reality fails to measure up to expectation. The respondent does not find the "secret" beach so necessary for the satisfaction of the previously identified motive.

TABLE 2. Affective Images

Pre-Trip	On Trip
Without Pictorial Stimuli	*Without Pictorial Stimuli*
A very relaxing place to come. A low key place to unwind with warm weather.	Very friendly people; clean and safe. More secure than other places. More safe than home.
With Pictorial Stimuli	*With Pictorial Stimuli*
Picture 1 – A lover's paradise. You can leave your worries behind.	Picture 1 – It is not a lover's paradise. I have not seen any secret beaches like this one here.
Picture 2 – Friendly, accommodating person. The smile makes you feel welcome.	Picture 2 – Typical of the Barbadian people I've met so far.
Picture 3 – Things are very old fashioned. People dress in beautiful colorful clothing.	Picture 3 – Old fashioned church. Typical of the West Indies. Very religious.
Picture 4 – Looks a bit saucy (teasing), flirtatious, feeling good about himself.	Picture 4 – Rastas generally look cheerful and carefree, but not flirtatious.

In the second picture, motivation is expressed in terms of belonging-ness. The interviewee sees in the maid a symbol of friendliness–the universally recognized smile which signifies welcome. A more neutral evaluation occurs in the on-trip situation since is is unclear from the account alone just how many Barbadian persons the respondent has met, and whether or not they are represented by more than simply those associated with the tourism industry. (For this information one has to turn to another section of the interview.) Hence, the cautionary "people I've met so far." Nevertheless the account suggests that friendliness is a generalizable quality, given that there is a subjective progression from "person" (pre-trip) to "people" (on-trip), while the picture itself shows just one local woman.

Reaction to the third picture reveals the well documented "nostalgia factor" (cf. Dann, 1994a; Graburn (forthcoming)) which increasingly seems to feature as a motive for travel in post-modern societies. At first sight "things are very old fashioned" seems rather patronising. However, the apparently disdainful remark is followed by a more positive evaluation in terms of "beautiful colourful clothing." Now, the drabness of the pre-trip home setting becomes alleviated by evoking a symbol of the exotic past which is located in the "other." In the on-trip situation, a religious interpretation is offered, thereby completing the cycle of nostalgia via the theme of tourism as a sacred quest for inner identity (cf. Graburn, 1989).

In the last case, the interviewee begins to identify with the subject to the extent that "saucy" and "flirtatious" are the pre-trip responses of the beholder. Such attributes are enhanced particularly in tourist-beachboy situations where the former is caucasian/female and the latter is black/male, and they may be interpreted as constituting an important part of the motivational ensemble associated with tourism in the Caribbean (cf. Karch and Dann, 1981). Yet, as with so many of these asymmetrical encounters, reality is often quite different from fantasy. Thus, in the on-trip situation "flirtation" becomes redefined as cheerfulness, and the potential intimacy of the interpersonal encounter is diffused by referring to Rastafarians in general.

THE CONATIVE COMPONENT OF IMAGES

Gartner (1993:196) speaks of the conative image component as the analogue of behaviour. It is the action component which builds on the cognitive and affective stages. Alternatively stated, during the destination decision process potential tourists can project themselves into an imag(e)-ined future situation as if they had already experienced it. By speaking to themselves in the future perfect tense, they are inserting themselves into the same socio-linguistic framework as the language of advertising (cf. Dann, 1993). However, in addressing their thoughts to others (e.g., an interview situation), the tense changes to the present continuous.

In perusing the transcripts of this study, it was discovered that the most frequent verbal strategy for articulating images in behavioural terms was that of personal identification with the portrayed scenario. In the absence of pictorial stimuli, such identification amounted to the mental construction of a scene and a subsequent self-immersion through introspection (Table 3).

In example one, the pre-trip vision moves from scenery, touristic pursuits and local people to the respondent and his wife, from the impersonal and passive to the personal and active. There is a parallel progression from friendliness to intimacy. The subsequent reflection of the on-trip conative image focuses on the relaxed pace of life and even suggests that the alternative lifestyle is preferable to the centre of the home society. One therefore senses that the tourist has moved away from the "recreational"

TABLE 3. Conative Images

Pre-Trip	**On Trip**
Without Pictorial Stimuli	*Without Pictorial Stimuli*
Scenery is absolutely beautiful—palm trees, beaches. That's what I vision in my head: water skiing, friendly people, being on the beach—the beach with my wife—that's what I envision.	It's everything I imaged, everything and better. It's total relaxation, a different world away from the hustle and bustle. Isolated from the world as far as the United States is concerned. I find generally it's a better life over here. I like the laid back attitude of the people toward life.
With Pictorial Stimuli	*With Pictorial Stimuli*
Picture 1 — My wife and I on the beach enjoying our 25th anniversary.	Picture 1 — Paradise. My wife and I on the beach enjoying our 25th anniversary. As beautiful as the picture.
Picture 2 — Gee, someone is going to give me breakfast in bed.	Picture 2 — Their friendly smile is genuine.
Picture 3 — It's like coming home. I feel at home with white, black, green or blue.	Picture 3 — I feel at home.
Picture 4 — The Rastaman is encouraging people to come and enjoy the beauty of Barbados.	Picture 4 — Barbados has a lot to offer visitors and they can really let themselves go.

and "diversionary" modes associated with mass tourism in search of an elective centre in the "other" (cf. Cohen, 1979). Significantly, and this time by way of omission, in the on-trip description there is no mention of the respondent's wife. She has been replaced by the destination people.

In the case of the first picture, once more there is identification with the scene through marital imagery. Interestingly too (as with most other similar examples in the transcripts) it is a male version of romance that is offered. On this occasion the 25th anniversary becomes the interpretative key to the portrayed romantic setting. Here the interviewee substitutes the two persons in the picture with himself and his spouse, even though the individuals featured are far younger than themselves. Tourism is thus perceived as providing a rejuvenating experience, one which permits the subject to step out of time and into the "reality" promised by the photograph. That such a possibility is described in real terms and that this "reality" is referred to as "paradise" (where by definition there is no time) lends further support to such an interpretation.

In the second picture, one encounters a typical instance of "the tourist as child" (Dann, 1989). Here the amply proportioned, benevolent black woman is cast in the role of nanny, if not mother. The plantation experience, the great house, the raising of white children by slave women are all selectively conjured up and personalised. As with nostalgia, inglorious features of the past are conveniently forgotten or overlooked. Interestingly, in the on-trip setting the smile is said to be "genuine," thereby introducing another frequently associated characteristic of conative imagery–that of perceived authenticity. As a matter of fact, re-read in this light, the images held by tourists of destinations as authentic can provide an alternative socio-linguistic input to one of the major debates in the academic treatment of tourism.

In the third picture, where children are shown on their way out of church, the interviewee personalises the scene by employing the expression "coming home," surely the establishment of an elective centre. For the respondent, the associated religious quest of pilgrimage (cf. Graburn, 1989 and Cohen's (1979) "existential" tourist) is addressed in terms of skin color (à la "United Colours of Benetton" advertisements). It is as if the essence of religion–the "coming home" outside one's own centre of existence–is to be found in a common humanity which knows no racial boundaries.

In the last example, a Rastaman beckons the viewer and thus becomes identifiable with the respondent. The conative imagery thereby moves from a passive situation of simple enjoyment to one promising active interpersonal involvement. Seen in this light, tourism becomes a form of release in which visitors can abandon the constraints of the home society. They can be as uninhibited as the unconventionality symbolized in the spirit of Rastafari.

CONCLUSION

According to Mayo and Jarvis (1981), destination choice is predicated on internalised mental pictures. These images in turn are based on selective perceptions, the various ways persons make sense of the world. When destinations are advertised, and pictorial/verbal messages are targeted at individuals, interpretation of such stimuli is grounded in personality, experiences, interests, needs, motives and mood. Consequently, Mayo and

Jarvis (1981: 42) maintain, "no two people see a destination in exactly the same way. Our perceptions are selective and they vary not only from person to person but from one country to another as well." Although the last point is more debatable, to the extent that it apparently denies the possibility of patterned experience, and hence of generalizability of comparison, the remainder of the thesis is quite germane to the present study.

Here too, it has been argued that destination choice is processual in nature and that is grounded in imagery. Moreover, the images of a destination can be understood in terms of their cognitive, affective and conative components, evaluative dimensions which respectively relate to the levels of intellect, motivation and experience. It has further been contended that their socio-linguistic expression, i.e., the verbal articulation of image, can be content analysed so as to yield more valid insights into tourist satisfaction and motivation than responses to questionnaire items which seek to measure the same crucial variables.

However, matters are far more complex than at first they might appear, and the various qualifications which follow should be taken into account by those interested in taking this line of inquiry any further.

In the first place, it should be noted that Gartner's (1993) image components are heuristic devices employed to simplify understanding by breaking down the decision process into discrete layers. Yet subjective reality itself is often much more intricate than the analytical constructs used to describe it. Indeed, destination evaluation is frequently an amalgam of components, one which switches back and forth, intersects, and projects forward in time while dealing with the past, rather than progressing in a smooth linear fashion or even in a rational manner. Consequently, although satisfaction may be gauged from a comparison of cognitive images in pre- and on-trip situations, so too can it be gleaned from the motivational and experiential components. By the same token, the vocabulary of motive may intrude into the discourse of mental comparison or projected behavioural activity.

Second, the transcripts from the study reveal that the interpretation of messages can take place at the literal or symbolic level. The picture of the Rastafarian, for example, was interpreted by some respondents in the former sense as simply a man with long hair. Yet far more frequent were connotative descriptions which read into the pictorial stimulus such selective and wide-ranging meanings as "a wild man," "savage," "looks like a beach bum or wino," "a radical," "black consciousness," "happy," "religious," "liberal minded and freedom oriented." Faced with such an array of interpretations, analysis of their socio-linguistic form and content should therefore also seek to discover the underpinning language of sign, signifier and signified. Barthes (1984), who deals with the semiotics of imagery in a unique and exciting way, has an interesting and related essay on the iconography of Abbé Pierre. What renders Barthes' account so relevant to the present example is that the bearded religious figure, like the Rasta, is said, through the signs of his image, to represent freedom and unconventionality.

Third, unlike most tourism research of this genre, which concentrates solely on the analysis of the pictorial/verbal content of brochures, travelogues, and other promotional material, in order to discern the message of the sender, this study additionally focuses on the message of the receiver. Thus, by examining the various ways in which potential visitors respond to destination images, it can help advertisers understand the extent to which they have correctly targeted their audiences in terms of the latters' socio-psychological requirements. However, the present investigation goes one stage further by placing the tourist in the role of sender when it explores imagery without the benefit of pictorial stimuli. The ensuing discourse which seeks to articulate mental images, since it does not depend on the skill or accuracy of an external promoter, but is rather generated internally and independently from within the subject, is therefore more likely to reveal the motivational forces behind the destination choice than socio-linguistic responses which are artificially created.

Finally, the introduction of two temporal periods in the same interview, i.e., pre-trip and on-trip, while possibly raising a few methodological eyebrows, can be theoretically justified when one considers the time transcendent nature both of advertising and the human personality. Whereas the former language speaks to the future by making its devotees dissatisfied with the present (Dann, 1993), receivers of such messages are additionally capable of introducing the past. Whenever they reflect, they bring into play experience through memory, and it is this turning back on themselves, this rendering of the Self as an object of consciousness, which necessarily precedes speech—in this instance the articulation of image. It is therefore not necessary, as some suggest, to go back in time and interview tourists before they depart, and then move forward in time to ascertain their on-trip and post-trip views. Nor is it sufficient, as many satisfaction studies unfortunately illustrate, simply to provide a check list of current destination resources and seek to evaluate them in terms of present attitude.

The foregoing qualifications, while demonstrating the complexity of investigations into the linkages between destination image and destination choice, nevertheless highlight some of the salient contributions made by the present study to several important issues in contemporary tourism research. It is to be hoped that others will continue along a similar path, or at least show through equally innovative approaches that there are alternative means to exploring the rich processes which connect the tourist with tourism in space and in time.

REFERENCES

Barbados Board of Tourism. n.d. Barbados. Hastings, Barbados: Cot Printery.

Barthes, R. (1982). Image, Music, Text. London: Fontana.

Barthes, R. (1984). Mythologies. London: Paladin.

Berger, J. (1972). Ways of Seeing. Harmondsworth: Penguin.

Boulding, K. (1961). The Image. Knowledge in Life and Society. Ann Arbor: University of Michigan Press.

Cohen, E. (1979). A Phenomenology of Tourist Experiences. Sociology 13:179-201.

Cohen, E. (1982). The Pacific Islands from Utopian Myth to Consumer Product. The Disenchantment of Paradise. Cahiers du Tourisme, série B no. 27.

Cohen, E. (1993). The Study of Touristic Images of Native People. Mitigating the Stereotype of the Stereotype. pp. 36-69 in D. Pearce and R. Butler (eds.) Tourism Research. Critiques and Challenges. London: Routledge.

Dann, G. (1981). Tourist Motivation: An Appraisal. Annals of Tourism Research 8:187-219.

Dann, G. (1989). The Tourist as Child: Some Reflections. Cahiers du Tourisme série C no. 135.

Dann, G. (1992). Predisposition Towards Alternative Forms of Tourism Among Tourists Visiting Barbados: Some Preliminary Observations. pp. 158-179 in V. Smith and W. Eadington (eds.) Tourism Alternatives. Potentials and Problems in the Development of Tourism. Philadelphia: University of Pennsylvania Press.

Dann, G. (1993). Advertising in Tourism and Travel. pp. 893-901 in M. Khan, M. Olsen and T. Var (eds.) Encyclopedia of Hospitality and Tourism. New York: Van Nostrand Reinhold.

Dann, G. (1994a). Tourism: The Nostalgia Industry of the Future. pp. 55-67 in W. Theobold (ed.) Global Tourism: The Next Decade. London: Butterworth-Heinemann.

Dann, G. (1994b). De Higher de Monkey Climb, de More 'e Show 'e Tail. Tourists' Knowledge of Barbadian Culture. Journal of International Consumer Marketing 6 (314): 181-204.

Dann, G. (forthcoming). A Socio-Linguistic Approach Towards Changing Tourism Imagery. In R. Butler and D. Pearce (eds.) Changes in Tourism: Peoples, Places and Processes. London: Routledge.

Eco, U. (1979). A Theory of Semiotics. Bloomington: Indiana University Press.

Gartner, W. (1993). Image Formation Process. Journal of Travel & Tourism Marketing 2 (2/3):191-215.

Gartner, W. and J. Hunt. (1987). An Analysis of State Image Change over a Twelve-Year Period (1971-1983). Journal of Travel Research 26 (2):15-19.

Gensch, D. (1978). Image-Measurement Segmentation. Journal of Marketing Research 15:384-394.

Gottlieb, A. (1982). Americans' Vacations. Annals of Tourism Research 9:165-187.

Graburn, N. (1989). Tourism: The Sacred Journey. pp. 21-36 in V. Smith (ed.) Hosts and Guests. The Anthrolopology of Tourism. 2nd ed. Philadelphia: University of Pennsylvania Press.

Graburn, N. (forthcoming). The Past in the Present in Japan: Nostalgia and Neo-Traditionalism in Contemporary Japanese Domestic Tourism. In R. Butler and D. Pearce (eds.) Changes in Tourism: People, Places and Processes. London: Routledge.

Karch, C. and G. Dann. (1981). Close Encounters of the Third World. Human Relations 34(4):249-268.

Mayo, E. and L. Jarvis. (1981). The Psychology of Leisure Travel. Boston: CBI.

Moscovici, S. (1981). On Social Representation. In J. Forgas (ed.) Social Cognition: Perspectives on Everyday Understanding. London: Academic Press.

Official Guide. (1988-9). Barbados. vol. 9. Bridgetown: Tourism Promotions.

Pearce, P. (1982). The Social Psychology of Tourist Behaviour. Oxford: Pergamon.

Pearce, P. (1993). Fundamentals of Tourist Motivation. pp. 113-134 in D. Pearce and R. Butler (eds.) Tourism Research. Critiques and Challenges. London: Routledge.

Scott, W. (1965). Psychological and Social Correlates of International Images. In H. Kelman (ed.) International Behavior: A Social-Psychological Analysis. New York: Holt, Rinehart and Winston.

Stringer, P. (1984). Studies in the Socio-Environmental Psychology of Tourism. Annals of Tourism Research 11:147-166.

Thomas, W. (1951). Social Behavior and Personality. E. Volkart (ed.). New York: Social Science Research.

Urbain, J. (1989). The Tourist Adventure and His Images. Annals of Tourism Research 16:106-118.

Modeling Vacation Destination Decisions: A Behavioral Approach

Ercan Sirakaya
Robert W. McLellan
Muzaffer Uysal

SUMMARY. The purpose of this study is to develop a multiple criteria decision-making instrument to model vacation destination-choice decisions of individuals based on the factors deemed to be important for vacation destination choice decisions. The study emphasizes the importance of individual differences in making vacation destination choice decisions. Although this research effort is explanatory in nature, the results reveal that application of behavioral decision theory is possible in modeling individuals' vacation destination decisions. *[Article copies available from The Haworth Document Delivery Service: 1-800-342-9678. E-mail address: getinfo@haworth.com]*

INTRODUCTION

The decision to purchase or refrain from purchasing a tourism product differs from the everyday buying of consumer goods in two fundamental

---

Ercan Sirakaya is a PhD candidate, and Dr. Robert W. McLellan is Professor, Department of Parks, Recreation and Tourism Management, Clemson University, 263 Lehotsky Hall, Clemson, SC 29634-1005. Dr. Muzaffer Uysal is Professor, Department of Hospitality and Tourism Management, Virginia Polytechnic Institute and State University, Blacksburg, VA 24061-0429.

[Haworth co-indexing entry note]: "Modeling Vacation Destination Decisions: A Behavioral Approach." Sirakaya, Ercan, Robert W. McLellan, and Muzaffer Uysal. Co-published simultaneously in *Journal of Travel & Tourism Marketing* (The Haworth Press, Inc.) Vol. 5, No. 1/2, 1996, pp. 57-75; and *Recent Advances in Tourism Marketing Research* (ed: Daniel R. Fesenmaier, Joseph T. O'Leary, and Muzaffer Uysal) The Haworth Press, Inc., 1996, pp. 57-75. Single or multiple copies of this article are available from The Haworth Document Delivery Service [1-800-342-9678, 9:00 a.m. - 5:00 p.m. (EST). E-mail address: getinfo@haworth.com].

aspects. First, the actual purchase and consumption of a tourism product occur at locations different from the purchaser's residence. Second, an individual or family may allocate a significant portion of their budget specifically for the acquisition of tourism products. Since the consumption of a tourism product will occur in the future at another site, the potential results of such a purchase are relatively uncertain; therefore, these purchases involve a high level of risk for the potential tourist. Tourists are involved in decisions such as whether to allocate part of their budget for tourism purposes, where to go, and which destination(s) to choose. Destinations, on the other hand, are competing not only with other destinations in terms of attracting these potential tourists, but also with other products, such as a new home, electronics, or an education. The outcome of such decisions are of interest to many public and private constituencies.

The process of decision-making has created a substantial body of scholarly literature in various fields such as economics, psychology, and management science (Louviere 1988; Fishbein 1976; Ericsson and Simon 1984). The theories and techniques developed within these disciplines have found useful applications in tourism settings (Goodrich 1978; Woodside and Lysonski 1989; Haider and Ewing 1990; Um and Crompton 1990; Vining and Fishwick 1991). Decision-making studies can be divided into two distinct groups: (1) structural models, and (2) process models. Basically, structural models examine the relationship between an input (stimulus) and an output (response) (Abelson and Levi, 1985). Tourism and recreation scholars have used these techniques extensively in describing vacation destination choices (Haider and Ewing 1990; Goodrich 1978) and park visitations (Louviere and Timmermans 1990). For example, two frequently used techniques are the Fishbein model (1976) and the multidimensional scaling. Fishbein (1976) suggests that the comparison among the characteristics of a given product such as a vacation destination and the expected set of attributes at that site influences the decision-making process. A destination that is most compatible with the potential tourists' expectations will be chosen by the traveler. Multidimensional scaling (MS) also explains the destination choice through a set of attributes of a potential site; moreover, it requires the tourists's assessment of the level to which a list of destinations offers desired characteristics. These two techniques are often criticized on the grounds of their concentration on the final phase of the decision-making process (Hammond, McClelland, and Mumpower 1980). Process models, on the other hand, examine the complete decision-making process of individuals by concentrating on the cognitive processes (transformation process between the input and output) which take place prior to arriving at a final decision (Abelson and Levi 1985). In other words, these models provide information on the actual decision-making behavior of individuals during the decision-making process, rather than on individuals' self-report of their behavior after they have arrived at a final decision. Therefore, the measured variable in a process model is the actual decision-making process and the factors that influence it (Stahl 1989). These process models—specifically, behavioral decision-making methodologies—can also be applied to tourism. Thus, the purpose of this study is to explore the utility of behavioral decision-making theory to decisions regarding vacation destination choices.

Any specific tourism product possesses multiple attributes that define the product and distinguish it from the alternatives. For example, a Caribbean destination may be a unique and differentiable tourism product from a European destination (such as Switzerland) based on its many differentiable attributes such as climate, an unpolluted natural environment, and distance from a traveler's point of origin. Potential travelers compare these attributes when deciding which destination to choose. However, according to Slovic, Fischhoff, and Lichtenstein (1977), most decision-makers cannot process multiple variables simultaneously; therefore, they use only a few criteria when making a decision. Moreover, a linear model with additive terms versus a model with multiplicative terms has been shown to explain nearly all of the error variance in descriptive models of decision-making.

Considering these arguments, researchers can infer that decision-makers may use only a few select criteria while making their decisions and therefore may utilize an additive approach in the decision-making process. Similarly, since tourism products have many attributes on which the decision-makers have to base their decisions, some factors may not be processed, and some may be ignored altogether. Therefore, from a marketing point of view, it is imperative and useful to identify the select few factors which play a crucial role in the final purchase decision, since consumer awareness can be created only if these chosen factors are included in the advertising message. Similarly, including unimportant factors in the message may cause the decision-maker to ignore the entire message (Mill and Morrison 1985). In fact, it is possible to determine which factors are most important to decision-makers by solely observing them process information on multiple variables in several decisions (Brunswik 1956).

Psychologists have developed many models to illustrate decision-making processes of individuals. Many of these models contain considerable measurement error, and have low reliability (Entwisle 1972; Fineman 1977). On the other hand, self-reported questionnaires may be biased toward social desirability. A decision-modeling methodology may be the appropriate modus operandi to examine the actual destination choice decisions of travelers, since respondents' immediate reactions to various scenarios may overcome the weaknesses inherent in self-reported question-naires and fantasy-based approaches (Stahl and Harrell 1982).

The aim of this study is to develop a model based on behavioral deci-sion-making theory to help explain vacation destination choice decisions. Specifically, a multiple criteria decision-making instrument will be devel-oped and tested for its reliability and validity based on the factors which decision-makers deem to be important in their selection of a vacation destination.

FACTORS INFLUENCING VACATION DESTINATION CHOICES

Tourism scholars have long acknowledged the importance of knowing why people travel, which destinations travelers choose, and the factors that play an important role in the selection of a vacation destination. They have devoted much literature to the notion of "pull factors" and "push factors" (Mak and Moncur 1980; Kucukkurt 1981; Haahti 1984; Phelps 1986; Shih 1986; Davis and Sternquist 1987; Chun 1989; Embacher and Buttle 1989; and Borocz 1990). Push factors (psychological motives) enable potential tourists to develop attitudes toward traveling in general. They involve dif-ferent cognitive processes such as the need for escape, socializing, belong-ing, self-esteem, and self-actualization. Pull factors, on the other hand, refer to man-made attractions (e.g., infrastructure and superstructure), natural attractions (e.g., scenic attractions, historical sights, beaches, climate), and socio-cultural attractions (e.g., accessibility, family and friends, tourist con-veniences, historical interest, suitability) (Sirakaya 1992).

The categories of attractiveness used by these researchers differ from one site to another, extending from natural and man-made attractions to those relating to socio-cultural resources. Yet, all the items are common in that they tend to draw visitors to an area. To test the applicability of behavioral decision-making theory to the destination choice decisions three attributes were selected (see Table 1):

- attractiveness,
- total cost of the trip (trip cost, on-site cost), and
- available time.

Table 1 below shows the many attributes that have been identified by research as exerting the most influence in travel destination choices.[1] The attributes given to the subjects as the only determinants of vacation deci-sions may not represent all the actual factors that play an important role in choosing a vacation destination; however, factors introduced by the

TABLE 1. Factors Affecting Travel Destination Choices

Physical Attractions		**Social-Psychological Attractions**	
Man-Made Tourist Attractions	*Natural Tourist Attractions*	*Social Cultural Attractions*	*Psychological Attractions*
−infrastructure −superstructure (facilities for sports and outdoor activities, casinos, hotels and resorts, shopping facilities) −publicity efforts	−scenic attractions (state parks, beautiful scenery, wilderness, landscape type, opportunities, trailing, hiking) −historical sights −beaches −climate (sun, snow) −hot springs	−attitudes of the host community (warm, hospitable) −cultural activities (theaters, museums) −nightlife and entertainment	−historical interest −(ancestry link) −family & friends −novelty of the destination −tourist conveniences −accessibility −suitability −good food −good accommodation −hotel room density −quietness of the place −common language

Exogenous Factors	**Total Travel Cost**		**Available Time**
	Transport Cost	*Holiday Cost*	
−political and social environments −political block affiliation −epidemics −natural disaster −terrorism	−cost of trip −time spent traveling −actual geographical distance	−exchange rate −reasonable prices (relative level of consumer prices) −good value for money (index of consumer prices)	−amount of travel time −amount of vacation time

authors corresponded highly to the factors named by the students with the exception of socio-psychological factors such as travelling with a partner. These attributes can be tested in order to assess the underlying principles which affect the decision-making processes of latent travelers.

MODEL DEVELOPMENT

There are three basic tenets utilized in the development of this model to explain travelers' decision process: (1) The assessment of the factors affecting a person's choice of a destination, (2) Brunswik's (1956) suggestions that most decision-makers employ few criteria when making their decisions, and (3) the premise that decision-makers process information additively. Utilizing the factors displayed in Table 1, a decision-making instrument was devised based on an instrument developed by Stahl and Harrell (1979, 1982) to measure managerial motivations which might influence an individual's job selection. This approach is reported to be free from social desirability bias, since the decision scores are based on the decision-making behavior of individuals rather than on individuals' self-reports of their behavior. Another strength of this technique is that it enables the researcher to assess the consistent decision-makers both by using a rigorous experimental design (a triple replicate of a 2 × 2 × 2 full factorial design) and by testing for potential random responses of each individual.

The mathematical model associated with the above decision-modeling approach is described in the following equation:

$$Y_j = B_1 (X_{1j}) + B_2 (X_{2j}) + B_3 (X_{3j}) + \varepsilon_{ij}$$

$$j = 1, 2, \ldots n \tag{1}$$

$$i = 1, 2, \ldots k$$

where

Y_j = value of destination choice decision;

B_1 = standardized regression coefficient or importance attributed to the X_1 criterion (attractiveness);

X_1 = the cue value, or information criterion of attractiveness of the destination;

B_2 = standardized regression coefficient (importance attributed to the X_2 criterion, or total travel cost);

X_2 = the cue value of total travel cost;

B_3 = standardized regression coefficient (importance attributed to the X_3 criterion, or available time);

X_3 = the cue value of available time;

ε_{ij} = error term;

j = the number of decisions; and

i = the number of variables or decision cues.

The standardized regression coefficients (B_i) are obtained from statistically regressing the Y_j on the X_{ij}. By keeping orthogonality of the design (factorial design which permits the estimation of all relevant effects with zero correlation), the standardized regression coefficients (beta weights) can be transformed to relative weights (RW_i), a conversion which enables the researcher to make an easy comparison between different respondents. Hoffman (1960) and Ward (1962) suggest the following equation for the manipulation of relative weights:

$$RW_i = B_i^2/R^2 \tag{2}$$

where

RW_i = the relative weight for the ith criterion;

B_i = the beta weight for the ith criterion; and

R^2 = the square of the decision-makers multiple correlation coefficient.

Darlington (1968) refers to the regression weights as "objective weights," since they are objectively calculated from the person's decisions. A third equation is associated with the use of subjective weights:

$$Y_j = SW_1 (X_{ij}) + SW_2 (X_{2j}) + \ldots\ldots + SW_i (X_{ij}) + \varepsilon_{ij} \tag{3}$$

where

SW_i = the subjective weight associated with the cue i.

The importance of the various criteria to decision-makers are used to determine the subjective weights. In other words, the respondents are asked to distribute 100 points among the cues in accordance with each cue's perceived importance. The transformation to relative weights provides several advantages. Stahl (1989) points out that the relative weights' sum is equal to 1.0 for each decision-maker. Therefore, by multiplying the relative weights by 100, they total to 100. Hence, this transformation enables direct comparison among decision-makers and comparison with subjectively stated measures of criterion importance (subjective weight). According to Slovic and Lichtenstein (1971), such a comparison enables a measure of cognitive insight into decision-making behavior.

INSTRUMENT DEVELOPMENT

The construction of the instrument used to examine the choice of a vacation destination centered around the review of tourism and travel literature. The characteristics of attractiveness, travel cost, and available time were utilized in the context of the kind of destination to which a person would be expected to visit. By keeping this in mind and by modifying Stahl and Harrell's Job Choice Exercise, a Vacation-Destination-Choice exercise was constructed; each subject was asked to indicate the possibility of travel to each of a number of hypothetical destinations. One example scenario is shown in Figure 1.

The exercise's instructions directed each subject to presume that s/he was taking a trip and that a number of travel destinations was available. These trips differed only in the degree to which the three key factors (attractiveness, cost, and time) were involved. The chance of these factors being present were either very high, or very low. These three factors served as the information cues that were provided to each subject as the possible basis for their decisions. Based on Stahl and Harrell's suggestion,

FIGURE 1. Example of Scenario for Destination Choice

DESTINATION X

For this trip, the following characteristics are present:

.. the attractiveness of the destination is .... VERY HIGH
.. the total travel cost is .... VERY HIGH
.. the time available to you is .... VERY HIGH

DECISION A: With these three factors in mind, indicate the likelihood that you will choose this destination

−5	−4	−3	−2	−1	0	+1	+2	+3	+4	+5
VERY									VERY	
UNLIKELY									LIKELY	

NOW:
given further information about hypothetical TRIP X, you must make a second decision about your likelihood of taking a trip.

FURTHER INFORMATION ABOUT DESTINATION X: If you decide to travel to this destination, the likelihood that you will be in a healthy, safe and secure environment is MEDIUM.

DECISION B: With all of the above information in mind, indicate the likelihood that you would choose this site as your vacation destination.

−5	−4	−3	−2	−1	0	+1	+2	+3	+4	+5
VERY									VERY	
UNLIKELY									LIKELY	

between each scenario a diversionary question was inserted, which asked for a second decision as to the likelihood of traveling to a previously chosen destination after being given additional information regarding the presence of a healthy, safe and secure environment. This item was given separately in order to facilitate a thought break as each individual makes his/her decision.

The basic design was a full-factorial with each of the three cues at two levels, for a total of eight basic destinations (2^3). Since the questionnaire also contained an item on safety presented at three levels (low, medium, high), the eight different scenarios were each replicated three times: once at the high level for each primary factor, once at the low level for each primary factor, and once at the medium level for each primary factor. A triple replicate of a 2^3 (= 8) decisions yielded a total of 24 values of destination decisions (3×2^3). Using Stahl's (1982) suggestion, six preparatory scenarios were added at the beginning of the decision-making exercise as warm-up decisions, resulting in a total of 30 destination decisions. These additional six scenarios were not used in the computation of the three decision criterion scores; they merely allowed the individual to become familiar with the methodology before responding to the 24 scored values of destination choices regarding attractiveness, cost, and time. Therefore, the complete vacation destination choice exercise consisted of 30 destinations, 24 of which are scored.

DATA COLLECTION

The data for this study were gathered through administration of the instrument to a group of college students at a land-grant university in the southeastern part of the United States. After being pretested on 37 students, the Vacation-Destination-Choice Exercise was administered during regular class hours to 279 students from various classes in the Spring of 1991. An attempt was made to obtain a truly representative sample of college students at the selected institution; however, the prime reason for obtaining the data was not to explain the preferred destination attributes by students per se but to develop a decision model.

INSTRUMENT ANALYSIS

A program was written to recode cue values of very high and very low respectively to +1 and −1 to preserve orthogonality. The reformatted data was then analyzed by a methodology similar to that of Stahl and Harrell (1982, 1989) who used a multiple regression model based upon each subject's response to each of the 24 scenarios. The dependent variable was each subject's response while the regressors were the cue values.

Reliability and Internal Consistency

The data analysis first involved both a reliability test of the questions and testing the internal consistency of decision-makers. First, the reliability of questions was checked through the examination of three pair-wise correlations for the eight possible Destinations combinations. Correlation among repeated questions was examined to determine consistency. Coefficients ranged from a low of .49 to a high of .73. Summary results are shown in Table 2.

Second, the internal consistency of decision-makers was examined through R-squares resulting from individual regressions on the three main effects in order to identify random decision-makers. Any individual with an R^2 below 0.31 (alpha = 0.05) was dismissed from further consideration. This was established through the calculation of the F-test as proposed by Intrilligator (1978, p.128) in the following equation:

$$\frac{R^2/ \ (k - 1)}{(1 - R^2) \ / \ (n - k)} = F \ (k - 1, \ nk) \tag{4}$$

TABLE 2. Summarized Mean of Three Pairwise Correlation Coefficients for the Eight Possible Destinations

Hypothetical Destinations	Level of the Cues*	Mean Correlation Coefficient
7, 18, 26	High/Low/Low	.60
8, 17, 23	Low/Low/High	.63
9, 16, 29	Low/High/High	.49
10, 21, 28	High/Low/High	.62
11, 20, 27	High/High/High	.73
12, 19, 24	Low/High/Low	.69
13, 15, 25	Low/Low/Low	.66
14, 22, 30	High/High/Low	.63

*Order of cues: attractiveness/cost/available time

By setting the significance level at .05, a significant F-value for 4-1 degrees of freedom in the numerator and 24-4 degrees of freedom in the denominator yields .314. Individuals with R^2 below this value can be considered as responding to the instrument in a random manner (Intrilligator 1978). The desired R^2 can be solved through the use of known degrees of freedom and the significant F-value. Only four individuals were identified as random decision-makers. The distribution of the R^2 from all 279 respondents are represented in Table 3. A mean R^2 of .80 and an R^2 range from .33 to .97 indicated that the remaining decision-makers (275) were internally consistent in the application of their destination decisions.

Group Regression Model

The next step in analyzing the data was to compute group regression with the remaining 275 decision-makers, 6600 decisions; note that the actual number of observations in data set was 6696. The explanatory power of interactive terms did not contribute to a significant increment in explainable variance (.008); therefore, the remainder of the analysis is based upon the main effects only. The group regression results for this study are presented in Table 4 and Table 5. Results showed that, although respondents have different decision-making styles, the R^2 is quite high. However, compared to the average individual R^2 of .80 from 275 separate regressions, the group R^2 of .58 is considered low. Therefore, a dramatic increase is observed in error variation by fitting a common group model. This implies that vacation destination decision-making styles are individual-specific.

TABLE 3. Distribution of R^2 Values Based on Intriligator's F-Test

R^2 Range	Frequency
.90 - 1.00	50
.80 - .89	117
.70 - .79	59
.60 - .69	25
.50 - .59	10
.315 - .49	8
Below .314*	4
TOTAL	275

Note: mean R^2 = .80
* below .314 value is considered as responding to the instrument in a random manner; thus those individuals that have an R^2 value of .314 or less should be dropped from further analysis

TABLE 4. Group Regression Results (n = 6600)

Decision Cues	Standardized Estimate	t-score
Attractiveness (X_1)	2.07 *	82.34
Total Cost (X_2)	– .81 *	– 32.20
Available Time (X_3)	.95 *	38.00

* Significant at P ≤ .05.
Note: n = 6600 because of deletion of decision-makers who were not consistent in their decisions

TABLE 5. Multiple R-Squares of Group Regression

Model	R^2
Common Group Model	.58
Model After Elimination of Error due to Repetition	.75
Model After Elimination of Error due to Individual Differences	.97

Elimination of Errors in the Model

A common group model contains three types of error: those due to individual differences, those due to the repetition of questions, and those due to statistical error. As the next step, a group regression model considering the error that is attributable to repetition of questions was computed. Errors due to repetition of questions were eliminated to increase explainable variance of the decision-making model. This manipulation was done by averaging differences among responses to repeated questions into the model containing only the main effects, increasing the multiple R^2 from .58 to .75.

After examination of the change that resulted from including the repetition-to-repetition error into the model, another group regression was calculated across all decision-makers by including the error caused by individual differences in making destination-choice decisions. Error due to individual differences was eliminated by averaging responses of 275 respondents to questions pertaining to levels of cues, increasing the R^2 to .97.

Computation of Relative Weights

The transformation of standardized regression coefficients (beta weights) to relative weights allows researchers to compare the relative importance of decision-making cues among decision-makers and to facilitate the comparison of research based results with subjectively stated measures of cue importance. Table 6 displays distributions of relative weights.

Test of Insight

The subjective weights were obtained by asking the students to distribute 100 points across the decision-making criteria. Table 7 contains means only on the three cues for the relative and subjective weights which resulted from comparisons made by decision-makers of subjective and relative weights through a three paired sample t-test. The safety item was not incorporated into the analysis as mentioned before, since it was utilized to facilitate a thought-break between scenarios. Therefore, the students were asked to make only one decision regarding the first three key factors. Table 7 indicates a bias pattern emerging from significant differences between the relative weights and the subjective weights. This pattern is consistent with previous findings of Slovic and Lichtenstein (1971).

TABLE 6. Distribution of Relative Weight Values

Cues	Mean	Standard Deviation	Minimum	Maximum
Attractiveness	62.59	25.30	.6000	100
Total Cost	18.46	13.56	.00	95.9
Available Time	19.21	12.38	.00	76.1

TABLE 7. Comparison of Average Relative and Subjective Weights

Decision Cues	Mean Relative Weights	Mean Subjective Weights	t-values
Attractiveness	67.15	41.74	8.37*
Total cost	13.14	33.20	−7.30*
Time available	19.46	24.80	−2. 17*

* Significant at P ≤ .05.

Subjects tend to underemphasize the importance they claim to give to a highly important factor, such as attractiveness, and over-emphasize the importance they claim to give to a low-importance factor. According to Slovic and Lichtenstein (1971), if subjectively stated weights and objectively calculated weights of decision-makers (beta weights) are close to one another, researchers can conclude that decision-makers are more insightful into their own decision-making styles. Therefore, according to these results, the students in this study did not appear to demonstrate good insight into their decision-making styles.

LIMITATIONS

There are three potential problems which may impose limitations on the results of this research. First, decision modeling exercises based on hypothetical situations are simulations of reality; decisions may differ from "simulated" conditions to "real" conditions. Therefore, this approach might not capture the actual essence of the decision-making process of individuals (Christoph 1985). However, as long as the decision-makers bring their past experiences into the decision-making exercise (Jemison and Sitkin 1986), what is measured in the exercise may be very close to the real decision-making process.

A second limitation of this study involves the validity of the attributes presented to the students. Since the main purpose was solely to model vacation decision-making process of individuals, no attempt was made to validate the construct of the attributes to a more universal model. The authors acknowledge that the items given to the students as the sole determinants of vacation decisions may in reality not represent all the actual factors which play an important role for a choice of a vacation destination; in fact, when the authors asked students to name which factors were important to them while selecting a destination ninety-seven percent of the students listed attractiveness as a decisive factor in selecting a vacation site, followed by seventy-nine percent who considered the cost of taking the trip. Twenty-three percent of students listed "person with whom I travel" as an important factor followed by "novelty of the destination" (16%) and 11 percent listed a safe, secure and healthy environment. Available time, however was listed by only five percent of the students. Factors introduced by the authors corresponded highly to the factors listed by the students with the exception of socio-psychological factors such as travel partner and novelty of the destination (which can be considered as part of attractiveness). The condensed list of the factors affecting travel destination choice decisions and the percentage distribution of the factors presented by students are presented in Table 8.

A third limitation of this study is the external validity of the results. The results may not be generalized beyond this sample of college students.

DISCUSSION

The construction of the instrument to examine the choice of a vacation destination involved the review of the relevant literature. Three factors were used to represent the characteristics of a destination: (1) attractiveness, (2) total travel cost, and (3) available time. By modifying Stahl and Harrell's Job Choice Exercise, a Vacation-Destination-Choice exercise was constructed that asked each subject to indicate the possibility of travel to each of a number of hypothetical destinations. Between each scenario a diversionary question was inserted, which asked for a second decision as to the likelihood of traveling to a previously chosen destination after being given additional information regarding the presence of a healthy, safe and secure environment. This item was given separately in order to facilitate a thought break as each individual makes his/her decision. The basic design was a full-factorial with each of the three cues at two levels, for a total of eight basic destinations (2^3). The eight different scenarios were each replicated three times, since the questionnaire has also incorporated an item on safety presented at three levels (low, medium, high). A triple replicate of a 2^3 (= 8) decisions yielded a total of 24 values of destination decisions (3×2^3).

Instrument analysis involved testing the reliability of the questions and computation of individual regression equations in order to examine the internal consistency of the decision-makers and dismissal of inconsistent

TABLE 8. List of Factors Stated by Students as Affecting Travel Destination Choice Decisions

Attributes	Percentage Distribution
Attractiveness (physical)	97%
Cost of the trip	79%
Travel partner	23%
Novelty (activity)	16%
Safe, secure and healthy environment	11%
Available time	5%

decision-makers. Any individual with R^2 that fell below 0.314 (at $\alpha = 0.05$) was dropped from further study. The mean individual R^2s was .80 indicating internal consistency of the decision-makers. Group regressions, however, resulted with an R^2 of .58 which is significantly lower than individual R^2s. Therefore, a dramatic increase was observed in error variation by fitting a common group model. This implies that vacation destination choice decision-making styles are individual specific.

A common group model contains three types of error; those due to individual differences, those due to the repetition of questions, and those due to statistical error. Errors due to question repetition have been eliminated, increasing the multiple R^2 by 17 percent to 75 percent. Error due to individual differences was eliminated, increasing the R^2 to 97 percent. Then, standardized regression coefficients were transformed to relative weights to enable the researchers to perform a test of insight, an easy comparison with subjectively stated weights.

Unlike the interviews and Likert type scale questionnaires commonly referred to in tourism and travel literature, the instrument developed in this study provides information on the actual decision-making behavior exhibited by potential travelers, rather than on their self-reported behavior. Thus, it is less affected by social desirability bias, wherein an individual gives an answer to the researcher partly as a function of what the individual considers to be an "acceptable" or "appropriate" answer. Moreover, this instrument gives the researcher the opportunity to analyze the individual decision-maker, since the model can evaluate the equation for each traveler.

Although this research effort is explanatory in nature, its results reveal that the application of behavioral-decision-theory is possible in modeling individuals' vacation-destination decisions. Moreover, this study showed that its instrument is reliable for examining destination-choice decisions. Future research should be oriented toward establishment of the validity of this instrument. The question of whether the developed instrument is measuring the actual destination-choice decisions or something else remains unsolved; however, research can be undertaken for identifying more specific factors that are important for travelers in the selection of a specific destination. This would aid the researcher in segmenting the market. From a planning and marketing point of view, these attributes may enable host communities and destination marketers to develop and promote their tourism product more effectively by stressing the importance of each factor according to its relative weight. When designing vacation tours, an increased awareness and possible preference of a certain destination can only be created if more important factors can be included in a promotional message. Similarly, attention must be paid by marketers to eliminate any non-essential factors from their messages, since the inclusion of these factors may lead the decision-makers to ignore the entire message (Mill and Morrison 1985). Moreover, identification of important factors can be used by host communities to actually create positive images of their communities or perhaps correct negative images, if there are any. By employing a different version of this instrument with the resources that a specific community considers to be important for tourists' selection of their community as a vacation destination, host destinations may determine the importance attributed to each factor by potential markets, leading them to concentrate on the effective development of those resources. For example, attractiveness is commonly defined by such attributes as beautiful scenery, an unpolluted natural environment, good food, a friendly attitude in the host community, and so on. Designing a new instrument that refers to these items would reveal the true weights attached to each item. This would in turn help bring about more efficient orientation of promotion campaigns through stressing attributes according to their relative importance. Hence, decision-makers would be involved indirectly in designing and developing the promotion materials and the resources of the host community. In addition, further research should be oriented toward examining the interaction of "pull factors" and "push factors" in the context of decision-making by using a broader representative sample.

Unlike other studies in travel and tourism, this study accentuates the different decision-making policies of potential travelers. Each traveler should be treated differently from the other, since people behave individually according to their varying needs and wants. Unfortunately, orientation and adaptation of the tourism product to individual needs is certainly not feasible; however, recognizing individual differences and their true needs on tour operation may well serve the dual purpose of creating a better service to potential travelers and enabling tour agencies to employ individual-specific marketing strategies.

This research has shown that decision modeling of vacation destination-choices is possible. Further studies may lead to a more comprehensive and refined model to help answer other elusive questions concerning destination decisions.

NOTE

1. The atttributes given to the subjects as the only determinants of vacation decisions may not represent all the actual factors that play an important role in choosing a vacation destination; however, factors introduced by the authors correspond highly to the factors named by the students with the exception of socio-psychological factors such as traveling with a partner.

BIBLIOGRAPHY

Abelson, R. P. and Levi, A. (1985). *Decision-Making and Decision Theory.* In: Lindzey, G. and E. Aronson, (eds.), *The Handbook of Social Psychology* (3rd ed.), Vol.1, New York: Random House.

Borocz, J. (1990). Hungary as a Destination 1960-1984. *Annals of Tourism Research,*17(1): 19-35

Brunswik, E. (1956). *Perception and the Representative Design of Psychological Experiments* 2nd Ed., Berkeley: University of California Press.

Christoph, Richard T. (1985). Divestiture Decision Modeling Utilizing the Capital Asset Pricing Model. *Clemson University Dissertation,* Clemson, S.C.: Clemson University Press.

Chun, Kye-Sung. (1989). Understanding Recreational Traveler's Motivation, Attitude and Satisfaction. *The Tourist Review,* 44(1): 3-7.

Darlington, R. B. (1968). Multiple Regression in Psychological Research and Practice. *Psychological Bulletin,* 69(3), 161-182.

Davis, Bonnie D. and Sternquist, Brenda. (1987). Appealing to the Elusive Tourist: An Attribute Cluster Strategy. *Journal of Travel Research,* 25(4): 25-32.

Embacher, J. and Buttle, F. (1989). A Repertory Grid Analysis of Austria's Image as Summer Vacation Destination. *Journal of Tourism Research,* 27(3) 3-8.

Entwisle, D. R. (1972). To Dispel Fantasies about Fantasy-Based Measures of Achievement Motivation. *Psychological Bulletin,* 77(6): 337-391.

Ericsson, K.A. and Simon, H.A. (1984). *Protocol Analysis: Verbal Reports as Data.* Cambridge, MA: The MIT Press.

Fineman, S. (1977). The Achievement Motive Construct and Its Measures: Where Are We Now? *British Journal of Psychology,* 68(1): 1-22.

Fishbein, M. (1976). Attitude and the Prediction of Behavior. *Readings in Attitude Theory and Measurement.* New York: John Wiley and Sons (pp. 477-492).

Goodrich, J. N. (1978). The Relationship Between Preferences for and Perceptions of Vacation Destinations: Application of a Choice Model. *Journal of Travel Research,* 17(3): 8-13.

Haahti, Antti J. (1984). Finland's Competitive Position as a Destination. *Annals of Tourism Research,* 13(1): 11-35.

Haider, W. and Ewing, G. O. (1990). A Model of Tourist Choices of Hypothetical Caribbean Destinations. *Leisure Sciences,* 12: 33-47.

Hammond, K. R., McClelland, G. H., and Mumpower, J. (1980). *Human Judgement and Decision-Making: Theories, Methods, and Procedures.* New York: Preager.

Hoffman, P. J. (1960). The Paramorphic Representation of Clinical Judgment. *Psychological Bulletin,* 57(2): 116-132.

Intrilligator, M. D. (1978). *Econometrics Models, Techniques, and Applications.* Englewood Cliffs, N.J: Prentice Hall Inc.

Jemison, David B. and Sitkin, Sinn B. (1986). Corporate Acquisitions: A Process Perspective. *Academy of Management Journal,* 2(1): 145-163.

Kucukkurt, Mehmet. (1981). Factors Affecting Travel Destination Choice: An

Expectancy Theory Framework for Studying Travel Behavior. *Dissertation.* Troy, New York: Rensselear Polytechnic Institute.

Louviere, J. J. and Timmermans, H. (1990). Using Hierarchical Information Integration to Model Consumer Response to Possible Planning Actions: A Recreation Destination Choice Illustration. *Environment and Planning*, 22(A): 291-308.

Louviere, J. Jordan. (1988). *Analyzing Decision-Making: Metric Conjoint Analysis.* Newbury Park, Ca.: Sage Publications.

Mak, J. and Moncur, J. E. T. (1980). The Choice of Journey Destinations and Lengths of Stay: A Micro Analysis. *Review of Regional Studies*, 10(3): pp. 38-40.

Mill, R. C. and Morrison, A. M. (1985). *The Tourism System.* Englewood Cliffs, New Jersey; Prentice-Hall, Inc.

Phelps, Angela. (1986). Holiday Destination Image–The Problem of Assessment: An example developed in Menorca. *Tourism Management*, 7(3): 168-180.

Shih, David. (1986). VALS as a Tool of Tourism Market Research: The Pennsylvania Experience. *Journal of Travel Research*, 24(4): 2-12.

Slovich P. and Lichtenstein, S. (1971). Comparison of Bayesian and Regression Approaches to the Study of Information Processing in Judgment. *Organizational Behavior and Human Performance*, 6: 649-744.

Slovich P., Fischhoff, B., and Lichtenstein, S. (1977). Behavioral Decision Theory. *Annual Review of Psychology*, 28: 1-39.

Sirakaya, E. (1992). Modeling Vacation Destination Choice Decisions: Development of an Instrument. *Clemson University Masters Thesis.* South Carolina, U.S.A: Clemson University.

Stahl, M. J. (1989). *Strategic Executive Decisions: An Analysis of the Difference Between Theory and Practice.* New York: Quorum Books.

Stahl, M. J. and Harrell, A. M. (1979). Behavioral Decision Theory: Need for Achievement and Academic Performance. *Proceedings, Western AIDS Meeting.* Reno: Western AIDS (pp. 162-164).

_____ (1982). Evolution and Validation of a Behavioral Decision Theory Measurement Approach to Achievement, Power, and Affiliation. *Journal of Applied Psychology*, 67(6): 744-751.

Um, Seoho and Crompton, John L. (1990). Attitude Determinants in Tourism Destination Choice. *Annals of Tourism Research*, 17(3): 432-448.

Vining, J. and Fishwick, L. (1991). An Exploratory Study of Outdoor Recreation Site Choices. *Journal of Leisure Research*, 23(2): 114-132.

Ward, J. (1962). Comments on the Paramorphic Representation of Clinical Judgment. *Psychological Bulletin*, 59(1): 74-76.

Woodside, A. G. and Lysonski, S. (1989). A General Model of Traveler Destination Choice. *Journal of Travel Research*, 27(4): pp.8-14.

Consumer-Defined Dimensions
for the Escorted Tour Industry Segment:
Expectations, Satisfactions,
and Importance

Charles R. Duke
Margaret A. Persia

SUMMARY. Using issues defined by tour participants, underlying dimensions of escorted tours were developed for pre- and post-tour evaluations and importances. Expectation dimensions emphasized itinerary issues whereas pre-tour importances concentrated on value, comfort, and safety. The items that make up these factors should be considered in pre-tour promotions. Personal enjoyment issues were combined in the primary post-tour satisfaction dimension whereas itinerary issues combined to create the primary post-tour importance factor. Tour designs should ensure that personal enjoyment issues are satisfied but should attempt to continually improve itineraries to better satisfy tour participants. *[Article copies available from The Haworth Document Delivery Service: 1-800-342-9678. E-mail address: getinfo@haworth.com]*

A satisfied customer normally provides a company with repeat business and also creates goodwill that is expressed by positive word-of-mouth

Charles R. Duke is Assistant Professor, Department of Marketing, Clemson University, Box 341325, Clemson, SC 29634-1325. Margaret A. Persia is Instructor, Department of Hospitality Management, East Stroudsburg University, East Stroudsburg, PA 18301-2999.

[Haworth co-indexing entry note]: "Consumer-Defined Dimensions for the Escorted Tour Industry Segment: Expectations, Satisfactions, and Importance." Duke, Charles R., and Margaret A. Persia. Co-published simultaneously in *Journal of Travel & Tourism Marketing* (The Haworth Press, Inc.) Vol 5, No. 1/2, 1996, pp. 77-99; and *Recent Advances in Tourism Marketing Research* (ed: Daniel R. Fesenmaier, Joseph T. O'Leary, and Muzaffer Uysal) The Haworth Press, Inc., 1996, pp. 77-99. Single or multiple copies of this article are available from The Haworth Document Delivery Service [1-800-342-9678, 9:00 a.m. - 5:00 p.m. (EST). E-mail address: getinfo@haworth.com].

recommendations. The tourism industry, along with other service businesses, has explored ways to understand and measure this satisfaction. One approach is to obtain ratings from tourists on issues critical to their trips and then to see if these issues coalesce along similar factors or dimensions, normally by using factor analysis. Researchers and practitioners have developed dimensions to characterize tourist attitudes (cf. Um and Crompton, 1991), expectations (cf. Chon, 1990), satisfactions (cf. Ross and Iso-Ahola, 1991), and importance (cf. Persia and Gitelson, 1993). Understanding important factors helps tour designers to improve response to consumer needs by altering tour features. However, most prior studies have been of limited usefulness to tour designers by using factors established for some other purpose, measuring limited constructs, using too broad a sample of vacations or leisure activities, or limiting the use of analytical methods. The intent of this study was to provide insight into tourists' expression and definition of their expectations, satisfactions, and importances (that is, multiple constructs) across an entire industry segment (escorted tours) using multiple firms and destinations. This approach should provide the escorted tour industry segment with a more complete picture of generalizable tourist evaluations that can guide tour design. Additionally, this study evaluated differences in tour design strategy that can arise from altering factor analysis techniques and assumptions.

ISSUES IN TOUR DIMENSION RESEARCH

An examination of tourism research reveals specific issues and choices made by the researchers in completing their work. These alternative approaches present limitations on the generalizability or applicability of the results. A comparison across some of these issues for some tourism studies that seem relevant in developing tourist dimensions is given in Table 1. This comparison emphasizes that many studies concentrate on *a priori* dimensions, using a single construct, and using a single factor analytic rotation method without specific rationale given. Because their purposes differed, these prior studies varied in the number and composition of dimensions. However none of these studies examines a specific segment of the industry, and comparisons of evaluation timing (pre- and post-tour) is uncommon. The following discussion details the rationale for choosing the approaches taken in the study reported here.

A Priori versus Consumer Defined Dimensions

Research into underlying dimensions of attitude, behavior, etc., begins with work that defines relevant issues of importance. These issues may be developed from assumed dimensions with multiple scales used to measure a theorized construct (cf. Lounsbury and Hoopes, 1985; Um and Crompton, 1991). Conversely, issues may be developed from qualitative responses of the individuals in the population of interest. The critical issues noted in exploratory research can be converted into items to provide measurement scales for descriptive analysis (cf. Dorfman, 1979; Pearce, 1980). This type of extensive exercise is necessary when the population or the issues are diverse or the application is specific. If the issues and dimensions are theoretically universal, then basic research provides guidance on the dimensions and items that should be included in future work (Lounsbury and Hoopes, 1985).

Comparing new research on established dimensions can possibly build on prior theoretical and practical research. Theory construction should build and evolve on prior work rather than simply ignore progress made (cf. Anderson, 1983). However when applying the same dimensions across differing groups and situations, the interpretation of research results must recognize the limitations imposed by *a priori* assumptions. Generalization of *a priori* dimensions to specific applications must be carefully considered based on the appropriateness of dimensions and factors. This study did not rely on prior dimensions but rather permitted consumers to define their own critical issues and then developed specific underlying dimensions from their ratings in this industry segment. Exploratory research assisted in early stages of developing multiple statements or scale items, eliciting input from the targeted tourist group, and evaluating underlying dimensions which result from specific data. In this way, tour designers can use the expressed needs and desires of the consumer to evaluate their tour services. Comparisons can be made against prior research dimensions to evaluate differences.

Pre-Tour versus Post-Tour Evaluations

The choices of when to collect evaluations are varied. Disconfirmation theory suggests that expectations prior to an event or purchase are the appropriate benchmark against which the consumer makes a judgment (cf. Oliver, 1980). Others suggest that, since expectations change during the product use experience, expectations of what should occur on the *next* tour might be measured from the experiences of tourists immediately after their *current* tour (cf. Cote, Foxman, and Cutler, 1989). Whether compared against an expectations benchmark or not, satisfaction measures are assumed to be the primary determinant of repeat business and positive word of mouth (Chon, 1990; Yau and Chan, 1990). The choice of mea-

TABLE 1. Comparison of Tourism Evaluation Dimension Studies on Major Assumptions

Study	Purpose	A Priori versus Consumer Defined	Pre versus Post Tour	Factor Rotation	Construct Measured	Major Factors
Chon 1990	Disconfirmation of expectations	A Priori – single destination	Pre & Post	Oblique	Expectation and Satisfaction	Shopping People Safety/security Scenery/attractions History/culture Travel resources General attitude
Yau & Chan 1990	Destination choice – limited to Asian destinations and comparisons	A Priori – researcher defined – multiple destination ratings – single destination used for collection	Mid-tour	Orthogonal	Satisfaction Importance	Shopping/transportation Entertainment/attractions Services Price Food Weather
Urn & Crompton 1991	Travel attitudes	A Priori – researcher defined	Post	Oblique	Satisfaction	Social agreement Active needs Travelability Passive needs Intellectual needs
Lounsbury & Hoopes 1985	Vacation satisfaction – all vacation types	A Priori – researcher defined – life satisfaction scales	Post	Orthogonal	Satisfaction	Relaxation & leisure Natural environment Escape Marriage & family Food & lodging

Study	Purpose	A Priori versus Consumer Defined	Pre versus Post Tour	Factor Rotation	Construct Measured	Major Factors
Beard & Ragheb 1980	Leisure satisfaction – all leisure activities	A Priori – factor to confirm	Post	Oblique	"Importance" through Likert	Psychological Educational Social Relaxation Physiological Aesthetic
Pearce 1980	Leisure satisfaction – all leisure activities	Combined – some prior literature factors – some consumer defined factors	Post	Cluster analysis	"Importance" through Likert	Achievement Relaxation Intimacy Time filling Power Sociability Intellectual Transcendence Constructiveness
Persia & Gitelson 1993	Agency choice	Combined – some prior literature factors – consumer defined factors	Post	Oblique	Importance	Information search Interactive agent quality Physical aspects Buyer value Technical skill Specialized services

surement timing depends on which method provides a better indication of critical issues needed for the study.

Expectation measures have been collected prior to tour experiences (cf. Chon, 1990) or from recall of expectations (cf. Dorfman, 1979). Pre-tour expectations seem more appropriate to reflect the tourist's purchase parameters (cf. Cote, Foxman, and Cutler, 1989). Respondent capability to correctly recall prior expectations casts content and external validity doubt on measures not collected prior to tours (cf. Lounsbury and Hoopes, 1985). Other expectation results have been developed as *post hoc* inferences from satisfaction ratings (cf. Manning and Ciali, 1980; Stewart and Carpenter, 1989) which may be acceptable in suggesting new lines of research but has little credible value to suggest managerial action (Lounsbury and Hoopes, 1985).

Travel or destination satisfactions are normally measured after the tourist has completed the tour experience (cf. Lounsbury and Hoopes, 1985). Satisfactions are crucial to services such as tours (cf. Parasuraman, Zeithaml, and Berry, 1988) but may not fully reflect the consumer decision-making process (cf. Chon, 1990; Cote, Foxman, and Cutler, 1989). Yau and Chan (1990) collected satisfactions and destination ratings while tourists were still at the destination. This hybrid measure is difficult to compare with others since it does not fit normal construct definitions from expectancy or dissonance theories. To minimize construct validity problems, a preferred approach is to use actual measures of either pre- or post-tour expectation to compare with post-tour satisfaction information (cf. Lounsbury and Hoopes, 1985). This current study used pre-tour expectations and post-tour satisfactions so that the dimensions for two different tour participant attitude structures could be developed and compared. Importance of both pre- and post-tour measures were also used.

Factor Analysis Rotations: Orthogonal versus Oblique

Factor analysis is often augmented by rotation techniques that are intended to increase the loading factors on the dimensions. The reference axes are moved to improve interpretation by reducing ambiguity in unrotated factor solutions. Rotations should help to simplify factor structure by redistributing variance from higher variance factors to lower variance ones. Orthogonal rotation extracts the primary factor as the linear combination with the highest explanation of variance. Other factors (or dimensions) are then developed perpendicular to the first. Orthogonal rotation is commonly accomplished in attitudinal research to maximize the independence of dimensions (Kerlinger, 1986). This analysis method is appropriate when the correlations among the dimensions is small and are necessary when the dimensions are to be used for regression or some other linear prediction model. However, some researchers consider that orthogonal structures may be unrealistic in scientific investigation because factors are seldom independent (Um and Crompton, 1991). Oblique rotations can help to increase loading factors and more clearly define underlying dimensions even though the factors may be intercorrelated (Kerlinger, 1986).

Both techniques have been used in tourism research. Tour designers need to understand the impact of deciding on factors that can be used for prediction as well as theory construction (orthogonal rotation) versus those useful only for examining theoretically related issues (oblique rotation). Either may be appropriate depending on the purpose of the analysis. Orthogonal, independent factors are prevalent in tourism literature (cf. Lounsbury and Hoopes, 1985; Yau and Chan, 1990) and are appropriate when independent factors are needed such as for predictive models (Kerlinger, 1986; Hair et al., 1993). However, oblique analysis has been used without orthogonal factors reported (cf. Chon, 1990) and is suggested for analysis of theoretical development where prediction may not be as critical (Kerlinger, 1986; Hair et al., 1993). Both orthogonal and oblique rotation structures have been used in analyses where initial orthogonal structures are considered to be too highly correlated (cf. Beard and Ragheb, 1980; Pearce, 1980; Um and Crompton, 1991). Analysis in this study considered both types of factor analysis rotation to illustrate the variation in results and the impact this might have on tour design.

Additional Issues

A universal set of tourist dimensions has been the goal of some studies (Um and Crompton, 1991; Lounsbury and Hoopes, 1985; Beard and Ragheb, 1980; Pearce, 1980) along the same lines as the SERVQUAL effort (Parasuraman, Zeithaml, and Berry, 1988). This universal dimensions approach presumes that common dimensions can be consistently generated across tour locations, services, and offerings with a standardized set of questions and dimensions. However, the usefulness of this universal approach appears to lack application to the broad field of tourism because of the large number of differences within the industry (cf. Babakus and Boller, 1992). As with most other industries, prior research in tour dimensions provides a variety of frameworks with dissimilar measures, features, or benefits (cf. Chon, 1990; Dorfman, 1979; Lounsbury and Hoopes, 1985; Ross and Iso-Ahola, 1991; Um and Crompton, 1991; Yau and Chan, 1990). This dissimilarity may appear to be inconsistent to the tour designer since the purposes of each study varied from evaluating a single destination (Chon, 1989) to the very broad issues of all leisure activities (Pearce, 1980; Beard and Ragheb 1980). But research based on perceptions of tourists across an industry segment may be more appropriate for tourism given the varied travel experiences available. The large number of different vacation and leisure *styles and objectives* suggest that consistent dimensions across different vacations (or products) should be neither expected nor plausible (Babakus and Inhofe, 1991). This study considers underlying dimensions, or factors, in tourism across a large number of tour providers, destinations, etc., by concentrating on one tour style (escorted tours). Using a tourism industry segment appears to be the highest level of generalization permissible to maintain similar tour characteristics. By using multiple firms and destinations, the study reported here avoided limiting the study's application to a single location.

Satisfaction has been measured as a single item (Manning and Ciali, 1980), as a short multiple item scale relating only to the satisfaction construct (Stewart and Carpenter, 1989; Yau and Chan, 1990), and as a longer multiple item scale relating to a broader range of satisfaction dimensions (Dorfman, 1979; Lounsbury and Hoopes, 1985; Prizan, Neumann, and Reichel, 1978; Ross and Iso-Ahola, 1991). Single measures have been considered inadequate as managerial information due to an inability to interpret response (Shelby, 1981; Yi, 1990). Shorter multiple item scales provide an adequate basic impression of overall satisfaction with some insight into various dimensions (Ditton, Graefe, and Fedler, 1981). Longer multiple item scales are considered to be good in providing detailed analytical information (Lounsbury and Hoopes, 1985). But some researchers are skeptical of the correlation of these scales to overall satisfaction measures (Dorfman, 1979). Expectation measures are most often longer multiple item scales (cf. Dorfman, 1979). Importance has been used to demonstrate the versatility of multi-item scales (Persia and Gitelson, 1993). This current study developed a longer multiple item scale list that reflected tourist concerns over a variety of issues.

TOUR DIMENSIONS STUDY:
PRE- AND POST-TOUR EVALUATIONS

Study Objectives

This study compared tourist evaluations of escorted tours. Information was obtained from a national sample of U.S. travelers who booked escorted tours through a large number of tour agencies and operators. The objectives were to use tourist-defined critical issues for the escorted tour industry segment (1) to evaluate underlying dimensions for expectation, satisfactions, and importances and (2) to illustrate differing tour design strategies that can be drawn from using alternative factor analysis rotation methods.

Design

Pre-tour and post-tour evaluation issues were developed in an exploratory study. Pre-tour expectation evaluations were then obtained on multiple items from a national sample of escorted tour purchasers. After completing their travels, respondents provided post-tour satisfaction ratings on the same issues. Factor analysis was used to develop dimensions.

Sampling

Travel agencies and tour operators from throughout the United States were asked to assist in data collection (Duke and Persia 1993). Agencies were selected randomly from a list of those approved by the Airline Reporting Corporation, the widest sample frame available. Tour operators were selected randomly from a list of members of the National Tour Association (NTA). Firms were asked to distribute surveys to escorted tour clients booked on upcoming tours. To maintain confidentiality, responses were not associated with the distributing firm. Responses were obtained from 149 tour participants for the pre-tour expectations data collection. This represents an appropriate sample size for Longwoods' (1990) estimate of America's touring market (2,975,200) at a confidence interval of 99 percent and a tolerance of 10 percent given the widest standard deviation resulting from responses to items on the questionnaire (cf. Tull and Hawkins, 1991; Lehmann, 1989). Post-tour data was requested from each of the pre-tour participants. A 60% response rate from the pre-tour participants produced 89 satisfaction observations.

Respondent characteristics were similar to those given from Longwoods (1990) domestic escorted tours (Duke and Persia 1993). Additionally, these demographics were similar to a previous European escorted tour study (Quiroga, 1990). The majority of respondents were female, and most participants were between the ages of 61 and 75. Education level was relatively high. Respondents reported that they were experienced group travelers with a large majority having participated in previous escorted tours. European tours outnumbered all other foreign destinations which included a highly diverse set of destinations. Approximately one-third of the respondents indicated that they had visited their tour destination before. Tours occurred in every month of the year except January. Respondents resided in 29 different states.

Instrument

The evaluation statements used were derived from an exploratory study of escorted tour participants. Specific statements generated from this exploratory study reflected consumer concerns in their own terminology which increases content and external validity from the consumers' perspective (cf. Peter and Ray, 1984). Issues of concern noted in this exploratory study included many of those found in prior studies such as itinerary, personal satisfaction, social interaction, services provided, and scenery. Responses to open-ended questions regarding expectations, important issues, critical events on the tour, feature of the tours, etc., were coded. High frequency responses were used to develop evaluation statements, and pretests with members of the target group reduced overlapping or superfluous questions. Additional content validity for the evaluation statements was obtained by soliciting suggestions from industry research professionals (cf. Beard and Ragheb, 1980). The research departments from the National Tour Foundation and the American Society of Travel Agents reviewed the statements and suggested refinement, consolidation, or elimination based on their experiences with field data collection. The final statements (Table 2) were again pretested and considered appropriate by consumers who were a part of the target group but not a part of final data collection. Subjects responded to the statements by completing Likert scales rating pre-tour expectations and post-tour satisfactions (+2 = strongly agree, − 2 = strongly disagree) as well as itemized scales rating pre- and post-tour importance (+2 = very important, +1 = important, 0 = neutral, − 1 = unimportant).

RESULTS AND DISCUSSION

Pre-Tour Expectation and Importance

Pre-tour expectation ratings were analyzed with conventional orthogonal rotation factor analysis yielding dimensions shown in Table 3. Factors were selected using eigenvalue criteria (1.0 or higher) combined with skree tests. The primary factor emphasized *itinerary issues* such as impor-

TABLE 2. Tour Dimension Study Evaluation Statements Developed from Exploratory Study

—I expect the scenery will be a source of enjoyment on this tour.

—I expect to be treated as a special person.

—I expect the tour escort in particular to make this tour enjoyable.

—I expect to be comfortable on this tour.

—I expect to make friends with other passengers on this tour.

—I expect the atmosphere among the group to be friendly.

—I don't expect to be alone often.

—I expect to learn new things about myself on this tour.

—I expect to get my money's worth on this tour.

—I expect to relax on this tour.

—I expect this tour will be the best way I personally could visit this destination.

—I expect I won't have to make major decisions on this tour.

—I expect to do what I couldn't do alone on this tour.

—I expect we will see as much as possible.

—I expect this tour to be adventurous.

—I expect never to be bored on this tour.

—I expect that stops at interesting places will be long enough to see what is important.

—I expect to be shown the most important attractions during this tour.

—I expect this tour to be educational.

—I expect to be safe from harm or injury on this tour.

tant attractions, scenery, length of stops, and escorts. The second factor emphasized *social and safety* features with a more relaxed, comfortable, and friendly atmosphere. Other factors indicated *education and adventure*, *planned group activities*, and the unique nature of tours as the *best way to visit* an attraction. Expectation importance factors were somewhat different from expectation rating factors. The primary factor projected the *value, comfort,* and *safety* of tours as the best way to visit important attractions. The second factor emphasized *social relaxation* in a friendly, exciting group atmosphere. Other factors emphasized *education and adventure, stops and scenery,* and choosing tours as the *best way to visit.* One approach to using attitude importance scores is to create linear combinations (expectation rating times importance rating). Multiplicative combinations of expectation and importance scores for this data indicated

TABLE 3. Factor Comparison of Pre-Tour Evaluations (Expectations; n = 149)

	Expectations	Score	Importance	Score	Multiplicative Model	Score
Factor 1	(v = 34.3%; α = .78; E = 6.85)		(v = 33.4%; α = .90; E = 6.68)		(v = 39.1%; α = .79; E = 7.82)	
	stop long enough	.793	Money's worth	.852	Money's worth	.844
	Important attractions	.753	Important attractions	.851	Safe from harm	.829
	Enjoyable scenery	.683	Comfortable	.818	Comfortable	.815
	Enjoyable escort	.537	Best way to visit	.807	Important attractions	.794
	See all possible	.489	Safe from harm	.793	New friends	.700
			New friends	.590	Best way to visit	.679
			See all possible	.560	See all possible	.488
Factor 2	(v = 8.3%; α = .81; E = 1.66)		(v = 9.7%; α = .73; E = 2.09)		(v = 10.4%; α = .73; E = 2.08)	
	Relaxed	.730	Relaxed	.673	Not often alone	.768
	Safe from harm	.708	Not often alone	.643	Never bored	.711
	Friendly atmosphere	.640	Friendly atmosphere	.613	Released	.657
	Comfortable	.560	Never bored	.552	Friendly atmosphere	.580
	New friends	.555	Enjoyable escort	.483	Treated special	.535
	Money's worth	.537	Treated special	.441	Enjoyable escort	.487

Factor 3	(v = 7.4%; α = .69; E = 1.49)		(v = 8.5%; α = .66; E = 1.38)		(v = 6.7%; α = .68; E = 1.33)
	Learn about self	.830	Educational	.781	Educational	.771
	Adventurous	.704	Adventurous	.771	Adventurous	.729
	Educational	.575	Learn about self	.698	Learn about self	.700
	Treated special	.388				
Factor 4	(v = 6.1%; α = .71; E = 1.21)		(v = 6.6%; α = .56; E = 1.30)		(v = 6.3%; α = .65; E = 1.26)
	No decisions	.779	Stop long enough	.818	Stops long enough	.818
	Not alone often	.691	Enjoyable scenery	.610	Enjoyable scenery	.684
	Never bored	.343				
Factor 5	(v = 5.0%; α = .73; E = 1.00)		(v = 5.5% α = .55; E = 1.00)		(v = 5.2%; α = .52; E = 1.03)
	Do what can't alone	.814	Do what can't alone	.800	Do what can't alone	.795
	Best way to visit	.807	No decisions	.634	No decisions	.508
	Total Variance Explained, %	61.0	Total Variance Explained, %	63.8	Total variance Explained, %	67.6

Note: v = variance explained; α = coefficient alpha; E = eigenvalue (orthogonal rotations); ss = sum of squares loading (oblique rotations).

factors similar to importance ratings. Because the individual items were generated directly from consumers, Cronbach's alpha for some of the factors were anticipated to be low such as the latter factors in importance and the multiplicative model. However, these levels of correlation were compatible with scales generated from exploratory research (cf. Kerlinger, 1986).

The high variance explained by primary, concrete tour issues in this study is larger than the variance explained by these issues in prior expectation studies (cf. Chon, 1990; Yau and Chan, 1991). Because the dimensions in this analysis were developed from consumer generated issues rather than *a priori* theory, the traveler's primary concerns of basic tour design were highlighted here. Other dimensions were associated with features of prior studies such as safety, social interactions, and entertainment. Although important, these other dimensions seemed to be considered by tour purchasers only after the concrete tour features were evaluated.

These results also showed that expectation and importance scores were related but were not surrogates for each other. The differences in the factors indicated that concrete tour features account for more expectation variances, but personal issues combine with some of these tour issues to account for higher importance variation. Both constructs (expectation and importance) are valuable and should be considered in tour design. But this analysis suggests that they are not always good proxies for each other. Importance scores dominated the multiplicative model which is suggested in compensatory decision models. Caution should be used in combining these constructs if expectation scores are more highly valued in a particular research effort.

Satisfaction and Importance

Factor analysis on post-tour satisfaction measures resulted in four factors (Table 4). The *personal enjoyment* primary factor is more complicated than the pre-tour evaluations. Items which were most significant included social issues, such as not being alone or bored, along with concrete issues such as long stops, seeing as much as possible, and enjoyable escorts. The second factor emphasized more classic *itinerary* tour aspects such as the best way to visit important attractions as well as a relaxed, yet adventurous, trip. The third factor indicated *safety, scenery, and comfort* whereas the last factor emphasized *education and social*. Satisfaction importance differed by producing the largest number of factors of all the evaluations (Table 4). The primary factor emphasized more concrete *itinerary* features. The second factor indicated *social and personal* issues. Other factors suggested *structured visits, relaxed comfort, enjoyable escorts*, and *adventurous education*. A multiplicative model of satisfaction and importance scores resulted in even more complex factors. Some *itinerary* features accounted for the highest variance in the primary factor. *Personal and social* created the second factor. The third factor indicated *exciting stops*, and the fourth factor emphasized *education and adventure*. Cronbach's alpha for satisfaction dimensions were acceptable, but correlations among the lower factors in the importance analysis indicate that this sample provided a very diverse set of responses for importances. This diversity is reflected in the last factor of the multiplicative model.

The personal enjoyment primary satisfaction factor might be similar to prior satisfaction results indicating social, psychological, or leisure issues (Beard and Ragheb, 1980; Lounsbury and Hoopes, 1985; Um and Crompton, 1991). Itinerary issues appeared to explain less satisfaction variance although they explain more of the satisfaction importance variance.

These evaluations of post-tour ratings indicated that satisfaction and importance were separate constructs similar to the conclusions from the expectations ratings. In contrast to pre-tour evaluations, the multiplicative model did not follow the same factor structure as either satisfactions or importance. This indicated that pre-tour evaluations may be more homogeneous whereas individual experiences differ enough to create more diverse post-tour impressions.

Pre-Tour versus Post-Tour Comparison

The underlying dimensions of both expectations (Table 3) and satisfactions (Table 4) have a common education factor, but other factors are not easily comparable. This reinforces the construct differences between satisfactions and expectations. Major variances explained by concrete itinerary expectations were replaced by variations explained by personal enjoyment satisfactions. Fewer factors evolved from satisfactions, but interpretation is more difficult.

The question of when evaluations should be measured (pre-tour versus post-tour) depends on the purpose. That is, the researcher must clearly determine if management decisions involve pre-experience expectations for evaluations prior to more learning (such as designing promotional literature) or post-experience evaluations which include learning from the tour (such as assuring satisfactory tour features). Specific and varied information can be obtained for these different approaches. However, managers and researchers should exercise caution when inferring post-experience expectation from satisfaction ratings (cf. Stewart and Carpenter, 1989) or mid-tour satisfactions (cf. Yau and Chan, 1990). This study

TABLE 4. Factor Comparison of Post-Tour Evaluations (Satisfactions; N=89)

	Satisfaction	Score	Importance	Score	Multiplicative Model	Score
Factor 1	(v = 48.9%; α = .89; E = 9.78)		(v = 25.7%; α = .67; E = 5.14)		(v = 41.9%; α = .75; E = 8.39)	
	Not alone often	.732	Important attractions	.642	Best way to visit	.781
	Never bored	.713	Do what can't alone	.626	Important attractions	.735
	See all possible	.690	See all possible	.625	Enjoyable escort	.660
	Stops long enough	.679	Stops long enough	.565	Do what can't alone	.619
	Enjoyable escort	.655	Enjoyable scenery	.484	Enjoyable scenery	.618
	No decisions	.621			No decisions	.557
	Treated special	.610				
	Do what can't alone	.541				
Factor 2	(v = 7.9%; α = .86; E = 9.78)		(v = 9.8%; α = .72; E = 1.95)		(v = 7.3%; α = .80; E = 1.47)	
	Important attractions	.793	Friendly atmosphere	.728	New friends	.724
	Best way to visit	.793	New friends	.700	Not often alone	.662
	Relaxed	.629	Treated special	.571	Treated special	.653
	Adventurous	.607	Not often alone	.523	Relaxed	.603
	Money's worth	.467	Safe from harm	.426	Comfortable	.593
					Friendly atmosphere	0.58
					Learn about self	.575
					Safe from harm	.507
Factor 3	(v = 6.9%; α = .76; E = 1.39)		(v = 7.5%; α = .51; E = 1.51)		(v = 6.7%; α = .78; E = 1.34)	
	Safe from harm	.816	No decisions	.749	Never bored	.714
	Enjoyable scenery	.709	Best way to visit	.710	Stops long enough	.599
	Comfortable	.647			Money's worth	.598
					See all possible	.569

Factor 4 (v = 5.2%; α = .75; E = 1.04)	(v = 7.2%; α = .65; E = 1.44)	(v = 6.3%; α = .50; E = 1.25)
Learn about self .717	Relaxed .779	Educational .798
New friends .699	Comfortable .649	Adventurous .506
Educational .697	Money's worth .504	
Friendly atmosphere .599		
Factor 5	(v = 6.1%; α = .41; E = 1.23)	
	Enjoyable escort .783	
	Never bored .564	
Factor 6	(v = 5.8%; α = .56; E = 1.15)	
	Educational .882	
	Adventurous .552	
	Learn about self .531	
Total Variance Explained, % 69.0	Total Variance Explained, % 62.1	Total Variance Explained, % 62.2

Note: v = variance explained; α = coefficient alpha; E = eigenvalue (orthogonal rotations); ss = sum of squares loading (oblique rotations).

illustrates the dramatic differences in the pre-tour (expectation) and post-tour (satisfaction) factor structures which might skew the results of expectation research. For example, inferring expectations from the first satisfaction factor in this study would mask the primary pre-tour factor explicitly emphasizing concrete tour feature or even the specific expectation factor 4 combination. Inferred expectations from satisfaction measures must be considered risky and questionable.

Factor Rotation Comparisons

Primary analysis of data was performed under conventional orthogonal rotation of factors to maximize variance explained. Oblique rotations were performed to compare independent factors with solutions that do not emphasize independence. Table 5 shows an oblique solution for expectations derived from a principal components extraction method. This factor structure is very similar to the orthogonal solution (Table 3) except that the order of the factors has changed. For example, the educational factor accounts for more variation in the oblique rotation than in the orthogonal.

Other extraction methods are available to analysts such as the alpha extraction which emphasizes closer relationships among scale items instead of maximizing variance explained. An expectations oblique factor solution with alpha extraction produced similar factors but altered the order of extraction for the primary and third factors (Table 5).

An attempted oblique (principal components) rotation for satisfaction ratings did not converge. However, a satisfaction oblique rotation with alpha extraction (Table 5) developed similar factors to the orthogonal (principal components) rotation (Table 4) although the order of extraction was different. Cronbach's alpha for all oblique rotations that converged were acceptable.

In this study, rotation procedures and factor extraction methods did not show dramatically different dimension structures. However, the order of extraction (and thus their importance in the factor structure) varied among the different styles of factor solution techniques. Researchers should be aware of these potential differences in factor order, but the underlying dimensions in this investigation appear to be stable under varied solution techniques.

CONCLUSIONS

Prior travel research has provided tour designers with indications of the tourist preferences from more theoretical perspectives. This study developed dimensions with issues defined by tour-goers rather than *a priori* theoretical dimensions. Compared with prior studies (Table 1), these results indicated that concrete tour issues account for more variance, but personal issues hold signicicant importance. Task-oriented issues become more critical concepts where consumer defined constructs are used such as in Pearce (1980) as well as Persia and Gitelson (1993). Factor rotation techniques varied in prior studies (Table 1) but this evaluation suggests that the basic issues of evaluation are robust across rotation procedures although the relative importance and variance explained changes.

Pre-tour expectations indicated that concrete itinerary issues should be emphasized by tour planners in promotions and advertising. Social and safety features along with other features can be used to augment pre-tour information. Issues in the primary expectations importance factor should also be emphasized to attract new tour-goers. Multiplicative factors gave little new information for pre-tour analysis.

Satisfaction factors emphasized personal enjoyment issues whereas satisfaction importance concentrated on itinerary issues. Tour designers should ensure that personal enjoyment issues are specifically addressed during the tour experience. The continuing importance of itinerary indicates the necessity for careful planning, but with a realization that the tour experience may increase the tourist's appetite for even more time and access devoted to important attractions.

Factor analysis can be a valuable tool in developing tour design issues. This particular study generalized across a relatively coherent segment, but other specific applications may require special considerations to issues not addressed here. Uncertainty over rotation and extraction methods should not deter tour professionals from using factor techniques. In this case, the factors themselves were relatively robust, but the order of importance for each factor changed with differing rotation and extraction procedures. A basic process of orthogonal procedures is likely to provide most of the critical information necessary, especially when implicitly predicting from factors by using the analysis to change tour designs. Tour planners should realize that this analysis used the entire population without using such market segmenting variables as gender, experience with tours, geographical location, tour destination, etc., which may have some impact on tour dimensions. This analysis suggests, however, that the basic dimensions will likely remain consistent even though the relative importance of the dimensions may vary.

TABLE 5. Factor Comparison of Oblique Rotations

	Expectations Principal Components	Score	Expectations Alpha Extraction	Score	Satisfactions Alpha Extraction	Score
Factor 1	(v = 34.3%; α = .81; E = 6.85)		(v = 31.7%; α = .78; ss = 6.34)		(v = 47.0%; α = .90; ss = 9.41)	
	Stops long enough	.825	Safety	.592	Not often alone	.743
	Important attractions	.734	Relaxed	.547	Never bored	.738
	Enjoyable scenery	.708	Friendly atmosphere	.499	See all possible	.700
	Money's worth	.556	Comfortable	.397	Stops long enough	.686
	Enjoyable escort	.492	New friends	.395	No decisions	.580
	See all possible	.417			Treated special	.562
					Do what can't alone	.475
					Comfortable	.321
Factor 2	(v = 8.3%; α = .67; E = 1.66)		(v = 5.9%; α = .69; ss = 1.18)		(v = 5.6%; α = .80; ss = 1.11)	
	Learn about self	.851	Learn about self	.846	New friends	−.692
	Adventurous	.676	Adventurous	.555	Learn about self	−.610
	Educational	.537	Educational	.407	Educational	−.596
			Treated special	.280	Friendly atmosphere	−.547
					Adventurous	−.476
Factor 3	(v = 7.4%; α = .78; E = 1.49)		(v = 5.0%; α = .81; ss = 1.01)		(v = 5.2%; α = .65; ss = 1.05)	
	Relaxed	.728	Stops long enough	.757	Safety	.711
	Safety	.656	Important attractions	.704	Enjoyable scenery	.481
	New friends	.519	Enjoyable scenery	.586		
	Friendly atmosphere	.587	Money's worth	.491		
	Comfortable	.4296	Enjoyable escort	.399		
			See all possible	.346		

Factor 4	(v = 6.1%; α = .73; E = 1.21)		(v = 3.9%; α = .73; ss=.77)		(v = 3.7%; α = .87; ss = .74)	
	Do what can't alone	.861	Do what can't alone	.789	Important attractions	.813
	Best way to visit	.852	Best way to visit	.734	Best way to visit	.813
					Relaxed	.580
					Do what can't alone	.552
Factor 5	(v = 5.0%; α = .74; E = 1.00)		(v = 2.5%; α = .71; ss = .51)			
	No major decisions	.811	No decisions	−.689		
	Not often alone	.702	Not often alone	−.581		
	Treated special	.309	Never bored	−.219		
	Never bored	.278				
	Total Variance Explained, %	61.0	Total Variance Explained, %	49.1	Total Variance Explained, %	61.5

Note: v = variance explained; α = coefficient alpha; E = eigenvalue (orthogonal rotations); ss = sum of squares loading (oblique rotations).

REFERENCES

Anderson, Paul F. (1983), "Marketing, Scientific Progress, and Scientific Method," *Journal of Marketing*, 47 (4), 18-31.

Babakus, Emil and Boller, Gerald W. (1992), "An Empirical Assessment of the SERVQUAL Scale," *Journal of Business Research*, 24 (3, May), 253-268.

Babakus, Emil and Inhofe, Mary (1991), "The Role of Expectations and Attribute Importance in the Measurement of Service Quality," in *Enhancing Knowledge Development in Marketing*, Mary C. Gilly et al., eds., Chicago: American Marketing Association, 142-144.

Beard, Jacob G. and Ragheb, Mounir G. (1980), "Measuring Leisure Satisfaction," *Journal of Leisure Research*, 12 (1), 20-33.

Chon, Khe Sung (1990), "Traveler Destination Image Modification Process and its Marketing Implications," in *Developments in Marketing Science: Proceedings of the Thirteenth Annual Conference of the Academy of Marketing Science*, Vol. 13, R.L. King (ed.), New Orleans: Academy of Marketing Science, 480-482.

Cote, Joseph A., Foxman, Ellen R., and Cutler, Bob D. (1989), "Seeking an Appropriate Standard of Comparison for Post-Purchase Evaluations," in *Advances in Consumer Research*, 16, T.K. Srull, ed., Provo, UT: Association for Consumer Research, 502-506.

Ditton, R. B., Graefe, Alan R., and Fedler, A. J. (1981), "Recreational Satisfaction at Buffalo National River: Some Measurement Concerns," in *Some Recent Products of River Recreation Research*, GTR NC-63, St. Paul, MN: USDA Forest Service, North Central Forest Experiment Station 61.

Dorfman, Peter W. (1979), "Measurement and Meaning of Recreation Satisfaction, A Case Study in Camping," *Environment and Behavior*, 11 (4), 483-510.

Duke, C.R. and Persia, M.A. (1993). "Foreign and Domestic Escorted Tour Expectations of American Travelers," *Journal of International Consumer Marketing*, 6 (3), 61-77.

Hair, Joseph F., Anderson, Rolph E., Tatham, Ronald L., and Black, William E. (1993), *Multivariate Data Analysis*, New York: Macmillian.

Kerlinger, Frederick N. (1986), *Foundations of Behavioral Research,* New York: Holt, Rinehart, and Winston.

Lehmann, Donald R. (1989), *Market Research and Analysis*, 3rd Edition, Boston: Irwin.

Longwoods Travel (1990), *National Tour Foundation Group Travel Report*, Longwoods International, USA.

Lounsbury, J.W. and Hoopes, L.L. (1985), "An Investigation of Factors Associated with Vacation Satisfaction," *Journal of Leisure Research*, 17 (1), 1-13.

Manning, Robert E. and Ciali, Charles P. (1980), "Recreation Density and User Satisfaction: A Further Exploration of the Satisfaction Model," *Journal of Leisure Research*, 12 (4), 329-345.

Oliver, Robert L. (1980), "A Cognitive Model of Antecedents and Consequences of Satisfaction Decisions," *Journal of Marketing Research*, 17 (November), 460-469.

Parasuraman, A., Zeithaml, Valerie A., and Berry, Leonard L. (1988), " SERVQUAL: A Multiple-Item Scale for Measuring Consumer Perceptions of Service Quality," *Journal of Retailing*, 64 (Spring), 12-43.

Pearce, Philip L. (1980), "A Favorability-Satisfaction Model of Tourists' Evaluations," *Journal of Travel Research*, 19 (Summer), 13-17.

Persia, Margaret A. and Gitelson, Richard J. (1993), "The Differences Among Travel Agency Users in the Importance Ratings of Agency Service Features," *Journal of Travel& Tourism Marketing*, 2 (3), 77-98.

Peter, J.P. and M.I. Ray (1984), *Measurement Readings for Marketing Research*, Chicago: American Marketing Association.

Prizan, Abraham, Neuman, Yoram, and Reichel, Arie (1978), "Dimensions of Tourist Satisfaction with a Destination Area," *Annals of Tourism Research*, 5 (3), 314-322.

Quiroga, Isabel (1990), "Characteristics of Package Tours in Europe," *Annals of Tourism Research*, 17 (2), 185-207.

Ross, E.L.Dunn and Iso-Ahola, Seppo E. (1991), "Sightseeing Tourists' Motivation and Satisfaction," *Annals of Tourism Research*, 18 (2), 226-237.

Shelby, Bo (1981), "Encounter Norms in Backcountry Settings," *Journal of Leisure Research*, 13 (2), 129-138.

Stewart, William P. and Carpenter, Edwin H. (1989), "Solitude at Grand Canyon: An Application of Expectancy Theory," *Journal of Leisure Research*, 21(1), 4-17.

Tull, Donald S. and Hawkins, Del I. (1991), "*Marketing Research: Measurement and Method*, 5th Edition, New York: Macmillan.

Um, Seoho and Crompton, John L. (1991), "Development of Pleasure Travel Attitude Dimensions." *Annals of Tourism Research*, 18 (4), 500-504.

Yau, Oliver H. M. and Chan, C.F. (1990), "Hong Kong as a Travel Destination in Southeast Asia: A Multidimensional Approach," *Tourism Management*, 11 (June), 123-132.

Yi, Youjae (1990), "A Critical Review of Consumer Satisfaction," in *Review of Marketing 1990*, V.A. Zeithaml, ed., Chicago: American Marketing Association, 68-123.

Major Determinants
of International Tourism Demand
for South Korea:
Inclusion of Marketing Variable

Choong-Ki Lee

SUMMARY. This study identifies the major determinants of international inbound tourist expenditures in South Korea using regression models. Income, relative prices, exchange rates, promotional expenditures, and dummy variables are incorporated into the models. The empirical results show that the coefficient of income was statistically significant and was highly elastic. The coefficients of relative prices and exchange rates were generally significant and elastic. The coefficient of promotional expenditures was found to be significant, but appeared to be inelastic. The findings of this study provide useful marketing information on how to promote international tourism demand for Korea. *[Article copies available from The Haworth Document Delivery Service: 1-800-342-9678. E-mail address: getinfo@haworth.com]*

Choong-Ki Lee is affiliated with the Department of Tourism, Dongguk University, Sukjangdong, Kyungju City, Kyunbuk, South Korea 780-714. His research interests are in the areas of forecasting tourism demand and the economic impact of tourism.

The author thanks Professor Turgut Var and Dr. Thomas W. Blaine for their constructive comments and suggestions. Special thanks are extended to Dr. Kyung-Sang Kwon for his assistance in data collection.

[Haworth co-indexing entry note]: "Major Determinants of International Tourism Demand for South Korea: Inclusion of Marketing Variable." Lee, Choong-Ki. Co-published simultaneously in *Journal of Travel & Tourism Marketing* (The Haworth Press, Inc.) Vol. 5, No. 1/2, 1996, pp. 101-118; and *Recent Advances in Tourism Marketing Research* (ed: Daniel R. Fesenmaier, Joseph T. O'Leary, and Muzaffer Uysal) The Haworth Press, Inc., 1996, pp. 101-118. Single or multiple copies of this article are available from The Haworth Document Delivery Service [1-800-342-9678, 9:00 a.m. - 5:00 p.m. (EST). E-mail address: getinfo@haworth.com].

INTRODUCTION

Tourism has emerged as the largest industry in the world, producing US$3.5 trillion in gross output and creating 127 million jobs (World Travel & Tourism Council 1992). Tourism receipts as an invisible export contribute to the balance of payments through foreign exchange earnings in many countries. Furthermore, tourism generates additional business turnover, household income, employment, value-added, and government revenue. Edgell (1990) maintains that the growing significance of tourism has been attracting increasing attention from public and private sectors with an interest in economic development throughout the world. Many countries have recognized tourism as a considerable benefit toward the economy and environment, and have concentrated their resources on tourism planning and development.

Forecasting tourism demand will play an important role as an essential element of tourism planning and resource allocation. Accurate estimates of tourism demand not only ensure the successful implementation of a tourism policy, but also provide the tourism planners and practitioners with considerable benefits in terms of the quality of their decisions and investment efforts. Determinants of tourism demand and elasticities provide useful marketing information on how to increase international tourism to Korea. Therefore, forecasting tourism demand based on appropriate analytical methods is an absolute necessity for the decision-making process by public and private sectors. In this respect, the objective of this paper is to (1) identify major determinants of international inbound tourist expenditures in South Korea through a set of regression models; and (2) investigate the effect of marketing variables on international tourism demand for Korea by incorporating promotional expenditures.

TOURISM IN SOUTH KOREA

As can be seen in Table 1, in 1965, the total number of foreign tourist arrivals in South Korea was 33,464 with almost US$21 million of tourism receipts at current prices. In 1973, foreign tourist arrivals totaled 679,221, a dramatic increase of 83.3% over the previous year and the tourism receipts reached $269 million, accounting for a 224.5% rise over the previous year. However, in the following year, tourism in South Korea experienced its first decline due to the world economic recession caused by the first oil price shock. In 1978, the 1 millionth foreign tourist mark was achieved with tourism receipts of $408 million, mainly attributed to a large influx of Japanese tourists.

TABLE 1. International Tourist Arrivals and Tourism Receipts in South Korea, 1965-1989

Year	Foreign Tourist Arrivals	Annual Growth Rate(%) (Tourists)	Normal Tourism Receipts (US$ 1,000)	Annual Growth Rate(%) (Receipts)	Real Tourism Receipts[1] (US$ 1,000)	Real Annual Growth Rate(%)
1965	33,464	34.1	20,798	32.4	239,057	28.6
1970	173,335	418.0	46,772	124.9	297,911	24.6
1971	232,795	34.3	52,383	12.0	292,642	−1.8
1972	370,656	59.2	83,011	58.5	417,141	42.5
1973	679,221	83.3	269,434	224.5	1,307,932	213.5
1974	517,590	−23.8	158,571	−41.1	619,418	−79.7
1975	632,846	22.3	140,627	−11.3	438,090	−29.3
1976	834,239	31.8	275,011	95.6	743,273	69.7
1977	949,666	13.8	370,030	34.6	909,165	22.3
1978	1,079,396	13.7	408,106	10.3	875,764	−3.7
1979	1,126,100	4.3	326,006	−20.1	591,662	−32.4
1980	976,415	−13.3	369,265	13.3	520,825	−12.0
1981	1,093,214	12.0	447,640	21.2	520,512	−0.1
1982	1,145,044	4.7	502,318	12.2	544,223	4.6
1983	1,194,551	4.3	596,245	18.7	624,995	14.8
1984	1,297,318	8.6	673,355	12.9	689,913	0.1
1985	1,426,045	9.9	784,312	16.5	784,312	13.7
1986	1,659,972	16.4	1,547,502	7.3	1,505,352	91.9
1987	1,874,502	12.9	2,299,156	48.6	2,171,063	44.2
1988	2,340,462	24.9	3,265,232	42.0	2,876,856	32.5
1989	2,728,054	16.6	3,556,279	8.9	2,966,038	3.1

[1]Real tourism receipts were calculated by dividing the normal tourism receipts by CPI (1985 = 100).
Sources: IMF (1986-1991); MOT and KNTC (1987-1989).

Tourism in South Korea experienced a second decrease from 1979 to 1980, as a result of the world economic recession caused by the second oil price shock and internal political instability. After the slump, tourist arrivals began to grow at an annual rate of 10% during the period of 1981-1985. Tourism continued to increase thanks to Korea's economic growth and the hosting of the 1986 Asian and 1988 Olympic Games which greatly enhanced the awareness and attractiveness of Korea's tourism. In 1986, the year of the Asian Games, 1.7 million tourists visited South Korea and expenditures on these trips were $1.5 billion. These tourism receipts were a dramatic increase (91.9%) over the previous year, in real terms. During the Seoul Olympics, 160 nations participated, resulting in 241,000 foreign inbound tourists and an expenditure of $259 million (Ministry of Transportation, hereafter "MOT" 1990). In that year, Korea's tourism surpassed 2.3 million foreign tourists and totaled almost $3.3 billion in tourism receipts. This represented a 24.9% and 42.0% increase over the previous year, respectively. International inbound tourism for South Korea continued to increase by an annual average rate of 16.6% for tourist arrivals and 8.9% for tourism receipts after the Seoul Olympics.

As shown in Table 2, Japanese tourists appear to dominate the Korean inbound tourism market, representing 47.7% of total tourist arrivals in 1984-89. Tourist arrivals from the USA ranked as the second largest inbound market, accounting for 15.2% of total tourist arrivals for the same

TABLE 2. International Tourist Arrivals to South Korea by Major Markets, 1984-1989

Thousands of Visitors

Nationality	1984	1985	1986	1987	1988	1989	Market Share (%)
Japan	576	638	791	894	1,124	1,380	47.7
U.S.A.	213	239	285	326	347	317	15.2
Taiwan	94	100	95	110	124	157	6.0
Hong Kong	47	47	55	54	62	67	2.9
U.K.	19	21	24	25	33	34	1.4
FR. Germany	17	19	21	23	31	31	1.3
Canada	13	17	20	22	25	25	1.1
Sub Total	979	1,081	1,291	1,454	1,746	2,011	75.6
Others	318	345	369	421	594	717	24.4
Total	1,297	1,426	1,660	1,875	2,340	2,728	100.0

*Percentage of average market share from 1984 to 1989.
Source: MOT and KNTC (1989).

period. The USA market dominated inbound tourism by the late 1960s, but the Japanese market surpassed the USA market since the early 1970s. The dominance of the Japanese tourists in the Korean inbound market is largely attributable to Japan's proximity, appreciation of the yen against the US dollar, the excess foreign exchange holdings, the project to send ten million Japanese tourists abroad, cultural similarity, and accessibility.

Although the Taiwanese share of the Korean inbound market has fallen to 6% for the last decade, it is the third largest tourist-generating country for Korea. Hong Kong ranks fourth in the inbound market with 3% of total tourist arrivals. All the tourists from Canada, UK, and FR. Germany represent only about 4% of the Korean inbound market in 1984-1989, but they are still important in terms of market diversification. The European market to Korea consists of 6.3% of the Korean inbound market in 1984-1989 in which the UK accounts for 20% of the European market, followed by FR. Germany with 18% of the market. In 1989, the Asian market consisted of 67.7% of the total; the Americas, 13.2%; Europe, 6.3%; and the ethnic market of Korean residents overseas, 11.8%, respectively (MOT and KNTC 1990). Strong promotional efforts have been made by the Korea National Tourism Corporation (KNTC) in order to attract the European market which is regarded as one of the highest potential markets.

DETERMINANTS OF INTERNATIONAL TOURISM DEMAND

Economic theory suggests that the income of tourists and the prices of substitutes are the major factors of determining demand for international travel (Crouch 1994). Demand theory also implies that demand for international tourism may be influenced by promotional expenditures and other special factors such as international mega-events, political disturbances, and economic recessions.

Income

A review of the past research by Crouch (1994) reveals that the income variable has been incorporated into demand models as the single most important determinant of international tourism demand. Demand theory implies that the higher the per capita income, the more people are likely to travel, *ceteris paribus*. Like in many goods and services, the demand theory hypothesizes that the demand for international tourism is a positive function of income. This hypothesis has been supported and estimated income elasticities have been found generally high, exceeding unity, in most cases (Gray 1966; Laber 1969; Artus 1972; Barry and O'Hagan 1972; Di Matteo and Di Matteo 1993; Kwack 1972; Jud and Joseph 1974; Loeb 1982; Sheldon 1993; Smeral, Witt, and Witt 1992; Stronge and Redman 1982; Witt and Witt 1990; Uysal and Crompton 1984). The high income elasticity indicates that international tourism is regarded as a luxury product (Martin and Witt 1989). In this study, the income variable is incorporated into demand models in the form of real per capita income.

Prices

International tourists would be responsive to changes in prices in the destination country and the effect of such relative prices would be significant as a determinant of demand for international tourism (Loeb 1982). Barry and O'Hagan (1972) suggest three aspects of price: (1) the costs of living at the destination; (2) transportation costs; and (3) exchange rates. Demand theory hypothesizes that the demand for travel is an inverse function of relative prices. That is, the greater (lower) cost of living in the destination country relative to the origin country, the lower (greater) tourism demand, other factors being held constant. This hypothesis has been supported by previous research and, in most cases, the relative prices variable has been statistically significant (Kwack 1972; Loeb 1982; Quayson and Var 1982; Smeral, Witt, and Witt 1992; Uysal and Crompton 1984). Since price is a highly complex variable and data on tourism prices are rarely available, the consumer price index (CPI) has been most frequently used as a proxy for tourism prices (Crouch 1992). In this sense, this study includes the variable of relative prices using CPI between origin and destination country.

The variable of transportation costs may determine the level of demand for international travel. That is, an increase (decrease) in transportation costs is likely to decrease (increase) the demand for international tourism. Researchers frequently encounter difficulties in measuring appropriate transportation costs because they vary depending on the mode (airline, surface, etc.), season, and whether or not the tourist is travelling first class. Furthermore, the presence of multicollinearity sometimes occurs between income and air fare (Fujii and Mak 1980; Quayson and Var 1982). These reasons frequently force researchers to exclude the variable (Loeb 1982; Uysal and Crompton 1984; Witt and Martin 1987) or yield insignificant results (Gray 1966; Jud and Joseph 1974; Quayson and Var 1982; Stronge and Redman 1982). In this respect, this study excludes this variable in estimating demand for international tourism.

Exchange rates may also have a significant effect on demand for international travel. Most tourists are seldom completely aware of prices in advance and thus, the level of price recognized by them will highly rely on the rate of exchange (Gray 1966). Thus, it is expected that the depreciation of a destination's currency *vis-à-vis* the origin country's currency would lead to an increase in international tourism demand for the destination. Inclusion of this variable produced significant results in some studies (Gerakis 1965; Artus 1972; Uysal and Crompton 1984), whereas it yielded unsatisfactory results in other studies (Gray 1966; Loeb 1982; Quayson and Var 1982). Var et al. (1990) had mixed results that eleven of twenty cases were found to be significant. It is therefore unclear whether exchange rate is a contributing explanatory variable for international tourism demand. Nevertheless, the exchange rate variable is included in this study on the grounds that foreign tourists may be sensitive to exchange rates. The theory of purchasing power parity asserts that, ignoring transportation costs and trade barriers, long run exchange rates should perfectly reflect the costs of living between countries (Gordon 1981). However, it is well known that short run deviations between exchange rates and costs of living are often substantial (Peebles 1988). As a consequence, this study uses real exchange rates adjusted by relative CPIs as a separate independent variable in each equation.

Marketing

Promotional expenditure will play an important role in increasing international tourism demand. However, few researchers incorporated marketing variables into demand models largely because of the lack or unavailability of relevant data (Crouch 1994). Nonetheless, some studies attempted to examine the effect of marketing expenditures on international tourism demand, but the results were mixed. Barry and O'Hagan (1972) included marketing expenditure with income, price, and credit restriction variables but excluded marketing variable due to the presence of muticollinearity. However, they argued that the exclusion of important explanatory variables such as marketing expenditure might cause over-estimation of the income elasticity. Uysal and Crompton (1984) incorporated promotional expenditure with income, price, exchange rate, and dummy variables. The results show that six of eleven cases for tourist numbers and one of eleven cases for tourist expenditure were statistically significant and that none of them were elastic. They concluded that the impact of promotional expenditure on international tourism to Turkey was minimal. Reviewing past literature of international tourism demand, Crouch (1994) found that marketing expenditure was highly significant in influencing the level of international tourism demand in some studies. In this study, real promotion expenditure is incorporated as a demand determinant in order to investigate the impact of marketing expenditure on international tourism demand.

Other Special Factors

Demand for international tourism may be affected by special factors. Many studies included dummy variables into demand models in order to explain the effect of special events on demand (Crouch 1994). Three dummy variables are included in this study in order to represent the effects of: (1) the first oil crisis in 1974; (2) the second oil crisis and internal political disturbances in 1980; and (3) the Seoul Olympic Games in 1988.

MODEL SPECIFICATION AND ESTIMATION PROCEDURES

The regression model as one of the quantitative techniques is based on the assumption that a dependent variable has a cause-and-effect relationship with one or more explanatory variables (Var and Lee 1993). Thus, the objective of this model is to establish the form of a relationship between a dependent and several independent variables and then, predict the values of the dependent variable. This model involves several steps: (1) identify determinants of each equation; (2) determine the functional form of that equation (e.g., linear or logarithm); (3) estimate the parameters of that equation; (4) test the statistical significance of the results using t or F tests; and (5) check the validity of underlying regression assumptions (Makridakis and Wheelwright 1978).

Based on a review of related literature, this study identifies income, relative prices, exchange rates, promotional expenditure, and dummy variables as the important determinants of international tourism demand for Korea. Then, this study determines a functional form of the demand equation. Almost all previous studies have taken a double logarithmic formation (Artus 1972; Barry and O'Hagan 1972; Chadee Mieczkowski 1987; Di Matteo and Di Matteo 1993; Fujii and Mak 1980; Gray 1966; Jud and Joseph 1974; Laber 1969; Loeb 1982; Quayson and Var 1982; Stronge and Redman 1982; Uysal and Crompton 1984; Var, Mohammad, and Icoz 1990; Witt and Martin 1987). The double-log specification has two underlying advantages: (1) the estimated coefficients can be interpreted as the demand elasticities; and (2) the double-log form has relatively low residual variance, compared to other functional forms with the same data sets (Jud and Joseph 1974). The preliminary estimation indicates that double logarithmic forms fit the data better than do linear forms in terms of expected signs and statistical significance. Thus, the following model to estimate international tourism demand for Korea is specified in the double-logarithmic form with the exception of dummy variables:

$$\ln EXP_{i,Korea} = \beta_0 + \beta_1 \ln RYPC_i + \beta_2 \ln RPRC + \beta_3 \ln REXC + \beta_4 \ln RPE + \gamma_1 DM_1 + \gamma_2 DM_2 + \gamma_3 DM_3 + \varepsilon \tag{1}$$

where:

$EXP_{i,Korea}$ = real tourist expenditure (measured by dividing total real tourist expenditures by population in the origin country *i*),

$RYPC_i$ = real per capita income in the origin country *i* (measured by dividing GNP_i by both population$_i$ and CPI_i),

$RPRC$ = relative prices (measured as the ratio of CPI_{Korea} to CPI_i),

$REXC$ = real exchange rate (measured as the units of currency$_{Korea}$ per unit of currency$_i$ and then multiplying by the ratio of CPI_i to CPI_{Korea}),

RPE = real promotional expenditure (measured by dividing promotional expenditure by CPI_{Korea}),

DM_1 = dummy variable portraying the effect of the 1974 oil crisis; 1 if 1974, 0 otherwise,

DM_2 = dummy variable reflecting the effect of the 1980 oil crisis and internal political instability; 1 if 1980, 0 otherwise,

DM_3 = dummy variable representing the effect of the 1988 Seoul Olympic Games; 1 if 1988, 0 otherwise,

$\beta_0, \beta_1, \beta_2, \beta_3, \beta_4, \gamma_1, \gamma_2, \gamma_3$ = coefficients to be estimated,

ε = random error term,

i = subscript denoting the tourist-generating country (or the origin country).

The specified model posits that real tourist expenditure made by each of the tourist-generating countries is a function of per capita real income, relative prices, real exchange rate, real promotional expenditure, and dummy variables. Then, it is hypothesized that:

$$\beta_1 > 0, \beta_2 < 0, \beta_3 > 0, \beta_4 > 0, \gamma_1 < 0, \gamma_2 < 0, \text{ and } \gamma_3 > 0$$

Equation (1) is estimated using ordinary least squares (OLS) for the following seven major tourist-generating countries based on market share: Japan, USA, Taiwan, Hong Kong, FR. Germany, UK, and Canada. OLS estimation sometimes suffers from the presence of serial correlation and multicollinearity which violate assumptions underlying the classical linear regression model. Serial correlation is encountered in time series data when the disturbance terms in a certain time period are correlated with those in a future time period.

In the presence of serial correlation, the estimated coefficients are still unbiased and consistent but inefficient. Loss in efficiency implies that the normal t and F tests are no longer valid. The most commonly used test for serial correlation is the Durbin-Watson (DW) test. Since the range between d_i and d_u leaves many cases with inconclusive results, this study obtains a DW probability to detect serial correlation more precisely. When serial correlation is detected on the basis of DW probability at the level of 5%, the regression model is re-estimated using a Cochrane-Orcutt procedure which involves a series of iterations to yield a better estimate of ϱ, or a correlation coefficient associated with errors (see Pindyck and Rubinfeld 1981):

$$\varepsilon_t = \varrho\varepsilon_{t-1} + v_t$$

where:

ε_t = residual in time t,

ϱ = autocorrelation coefficient,

v_t = non-autocorrelated error term.

In addition, multicollinearity occurs when two or more independent variables are highly correlated to each other. When multicollinearity exists, the standard errors associated with the regression coefficients are so large that estimates of true parameters become unstable, thus producing low t-values. Furthermore, it is difficult for the analysts to separate contribution of explanatory variables to a dependent variable. Multicollinearity can be diagnosed by inspecting the pairwise correlation matrix. A high correlation coefficient between two explanatory variables (close to 1) indicates a possible presence of collinearity. Belsley, Kuh, and Welsch (1980) proposed another diagnostic procedure with double conditions: (1) condition index greater than or equal to 30 or 100; and (2) at the same time, at least two numbers in a variance proportion row greater than or equal to 0.5. When severe multicollinearity is present, the regression model is re-estimated using ridge regression which is designed to decrease overall mean square error by introducing a slight bias of k (diagonal matrix of non-negative constants) in the estimates at the expense of achieving efficiency (Hoerl and Kennnard 1970). The appropriate value of k can be determined by using ridge-trace procedure in which the value of k gradually increases between 0 and 1 until the estimated coefficients become stable. The results from the study by Fujii and Mak (1980) show that when severe multicollinearity exists, ridge regression performs better than does OLS in terms of forecast errors.

DATA SOURCES

The data used in this study cover 20 annual time series data for the period 1970-1989 (1971-1990 for USA). Data on foreign tourist expenditures were obtained from *Annual Statistical Report on Tourism* published by MOT and KNTC (1980-1990). Consumer price indices, gross national product and population for measure of income, and exchange rate were obtained from *International Financial Statistics* published by the International Monetary Fund (1986-1991), *Trends on Average Exchange Rates of Korean Won Against the Major Currencies* published by the Korea Exchange Bank (1970-1990), and *Statistics on Exchange Rates of Korean Won Against Foreign Currency* published by Bank of Korea (1994). Data for Hong Kong were obtained from *Foreign Economic Trends and Their Implications for the United States* published by U.S. Department of Commerce/Bureau of International Commerce (1970-1990). Additional data for Taiwan were obtained from *Industry of Free China* published by Council for Economic Planning and Development of Republic of China (1990). Data for promotional expenditure were obtained from KNTC (1994), but the data covered only the period 1980-1993 and several countries.

EMPIRICAL RESULTS

The empirical results estimated from Equation (1) when including promotional expenditure is shown in Table 3. The coefficients associated with non-dummy variables can be interpreted as demand elasticities because all variables of the equations except the dummy variables were estimated in the natural logarithmic form. Three models (for Japan, USA, and Hong Kong) were re-estimated using the Cochrane-Orcutt (CORN) procedure since DW probability indicated the presence of serial correlation at the 5% significant level. In addition, two models (for Taiwan and FR. Germany) were re-estimated using the ridge regression because multi-

TABLE 3. Regression Results of Determinants of International Tourist Expenditures in South Korea Including Marketing Variable[a]

Origin Count	Coefficients Constant	RYPC	RPRC	REXC	RPE	DM_1	DM_2	DM_3	R^2	DW	Estimation Technique[b]
Japan	-28.787 (-8.15)	11.656* (11.77)	-4.504* (-4.72)	0.116 (2.90)	0.073** (1.42)	-0.790* (-2.78)	-0.287 (-1.14)	N/S	0.919	1.654	CORN
USA	-41.153 (-5.71)	8.458* (7.67)	-1.817 (-3.16)	0.909 (1.34)	0.068* (2.20)	0.093 (0.53)	N/S	0.197	0.908 (1.17)	1.330	CORN
Taiwan	3.727 (2.296)	1.177* (4.05)	0.538 (1.22)	0.830* (1.38)	N/A	N/S	N/S	N/S	0.915	1.823	RIDG
Hong Kong	-12.065 (-4.33)	3.275* (8.37)	-1.363* (-2.36)	1.921* (3.25)	0.048* (2.33)	-0.597* (-2.46)	-0.762 (-3.13)	N/S	0.952	1.722	CORN
FR. Germany	11.817 (3.11)	6.772* (5.97)	-0.859 (-2.42)	0.612 (1.23)	0.023 (1.18)	N/S	-0.699* (-2.34)	N/S	0.897	1.708	RIDG
UK	27.92 (8.61)	6.593* (12.84)	-2.448* (-3.86)	-0.265 (-0.73)	N/A	N/S	N/S	N/S	0.930	1.799	OLS
Canada	-1.921 (-0.09)	13.946* (2.93)	0.063 (0.03)	5.335* (1.80)	N/A	N/S	N/S	N/S	0.679	1.646	OLS

[a]All models were estimated in double-logarithmic form except dummy variables.
[b]OLS, CORN, and RIDG indicate estimation of the equations by ordinary least squares method, the Cochrane-Orcutt procedure, and ridge regression, respectively.
*, **, *** indicate significance at the 95%, 90%, and 80% confidence intervals, respectively.
The figures in parentheses indicate t-statistics associated with the estimated coefficients.
N/A indicates not available for the data on promotional expenditure.
N/S means that inclusion of variable(s) is not significant and does not improve goodness of fit, as well.

collinearity was detected through diagnostic procedures as mentioned early. R^2 indicates that all cases account for 90% of the variation in the dependent variable except Canada (68%). This indicates a high level of goodness-of-fit for six of seven models.

However, the relatively poor fit to the data for one model might have been caused by the omission of some important explanatory variables from the model.

Income Variable

The estimated coefficients of income variable were found statistically significant for all cases at the 95% confidence intervals and the signs of the coefficients all were also positive as expected. The estimated income elasticities were generally high, ranging from a low of 1.18 to a high of 13.95. The highest elasticity was found for the Canadian market (13.95), indicating a 1% increase in their income, leading to about a 14% increase in their travel expenditures in Korea. The Japanese market had the second highest elasticity of 11.66, followed by the USA market (8.46). Overall, the results show that income is the most important variable as the major determinant of international tourism for Korea. Furthermore, the income elasticity implies that international tourism demand for Korea is highly sensitive to tourist income.

Relative Prices Variable

The estimated coefficients of relative prices were found statistically significant for five of seven cases at the 95% confidence interval and the signs of them were negative as expected. Contrary to expectation, two cases had the positive signs where none of them were significant, as well. The estimated price elasticities ranged from a low of 0.86 to a high of 4.50. The highest elasticity was found for the Japanese market, followed by the UK (-2.45), the USA (-1.82), and Hong Kong (-1.36), indicating sensitiveness to changes in relative prices. However, the elasticity was less than -1 for FR. Germany. In general, the variable of relative prices appears to be important as determinant of international tourism for Korea.

Exchange Rate Variable

The estimated coefficients of exchange rates had the expected positive signs for all countries except for the UK which was not significant. The coefficients for four countries were found statistically significant; two cases (Japan and Hong Kong) at the 95%, one case (Canada) at the 90%, and one case (Taiwan) at the 80% level of confidence interval. The elasticities of exchange rates ranged from a low of 0.12 to a high of 5.34. The highest elasticity was found for Canada, followed by Hong Kong (1.92), indicating high responsiveness on changes in exchange rates. However, the Japanese and the Taiwanese markets were inelastic with regard to exchange rates. In general, the exchange rate variable appears to be one of important explanatory variables in influencing international inbound tourism for Korea.

Marketing Variable

The variable of promotional expenditure was only included in four models (Japan, USA, Hong Kong, and FR. Germany) due to the lack of data. The estimated coefficients of this variable had the expected positive signs in all four cases and were found significant except FR. Germany. The elasticities of promotional expenditure were inelastic in all cases, ranging from 0.05 to 0.07. The elasticity implies that a 10% increase in promotional expenditure in Japan and the USA results in a 0.7% increase in international tourist expenditures in Korea, respectively. The results suggest that the variable of promotional expenditure is still significant but has low impact on international tourist expenditures in Korea.

Dummy Variable

Dummy variables were omitted in most cases because inclusion of these variables did not improve regression models resulting in insignificance in most cases. The dummy variable for the first oil crisis was found significant with the expected negative signs in Japan and Hong Kong. The dummy variable for the second oil crisis had the expected negative signs in three cases, but one case was significant. The dummy variable for the Seoul Olympic Games was included in the model of the USA, where the sign of the coefficient was positive but insignificant. An interesting note is that the dummy variable portraying the '88 Seoul Olympic Games was not significant for any country. It was typically high tourist season in Korea when the Olympic Games were held in Seoul. Foreign tourists who did not secure their airline seats and accommodations in advance might have changed their schedule and stayed in neighboring countries, especially in Japan. This might have psychologically caused the insignificant results. Loeb (1982) observed similar results in that the dummy variable for the Canadian Olympics was not significant in seven of nine cases.

CONCLUSIONS AND MARKETING IMPLICATIONS

This study identified the major determinants of international inbound tourist expenditures in South Korea by constructing regression models for seven tourist-generating countries. As in other previous studies, income was found to be the most important contributing determinant of international tourism demand for Korea. The income elasticity was also found to be high, indicating that Korea is regarded as a luxury destination by tourists from the selected countries. Particularly, new industrialization of Asian countries has brought wealth and economic growth, providing these people with greater disposable incomes and leisure time. The higher income elasticity implies that an increase in income of these people increases the demand for international tourism. Furthermore, an intra-regional travel pattern is generally dominant (intra-regional travel represents around 50% in the north eastern region). Therefore, the Korean government, including the tourism industry, should make effective promotional efforts to these countries on a continual basis in order to increase the international inbound tourism for Korea.

The variables of relative prices and exchange rates were found to be generally significant, indicating important determinants of international tourism demand for Korea. In the area of marketing tourism, the variable of tourism prices may be easier to control by the host country (e.g., tax incentives to hotels and domestic airlines) as compared to that of income. According to the research by Usui (1994), Japanese intentions of visiting Korea appear to be lower than those of visiting of Singapore and Hong Kong because they perceive Korea to be expensive as compared to Singapore and Hong Kong. Furthermore, Americans perceive Korea to be less expensive than Japan, but more expensive than Hong Kong (Fesenmaier 1994). The relative price elasticity also indicates that foreign tourists are sensitive to prices in their travelling and spending in Korea. This implies that an increase in tourism prices causes a decrease in the level of tourism demand. Thus, tourism policy-makers and industry managers should keep prices low to be competitive, while maintaining a high quality of service.

Even though its elasticity was relatively low, the variable of promotional expenditure was found to be significant. This implies that promotional activities by national tourism organizations along with airlines are important to increase the level of international tourism demand. A special marketing program should be developed to create awareness and a positive image toward Korea among target markets with effective media. In addition, as markets become more segmented, Fesenmaier (1994) suggests that a marketing program should be developed to build relationships with travel agents, hotels, airlines, and the potential Korean-American market.

REFERENCES

Artus, Jacques R. (1972). An Econometric Analysis of International Travel. *IMF Staff Papers*, 19(3): 579-613.

Bank of Korea (1994). *Statistics on Exchange Rates of Korean Won Against Foreign Currency.* Seoul, Korea: Government Printers.

Barry, Kevin, & O'Hagan, John (1972). An Econometric Study of British Tourist Expenditure in Ireland. *Economic and Social Review*, 3(2): 143-161.

Belsley, D. A., Kuh, E., & Welsch, R. E. (1980). *Regression Diagnostics, Identifying Influential Data and Sources of Collinearity.* New York, NY: Wiley.

Chadee, D., & Mieczkowski, Z. (1987). An Empirical Analysis of the Effects of the Exchange Rate on Canadian Tourism. *Journal of Travel Research*, 26(1): 13-17.

Council for Economic Planning and Development (1990). *Industry of Free China.* Republic of China, No. 74.

Crouch, Geoffrey I. (1992). Effect of Income and Price on International Tourism. *Annals of Tourism Research*, 19(4): 643-664.

Crouch, Geoffrey I (1994). The Study of International Tourism Demand: A Review of Findings. *Journal of Travel Research*, 33(1): 12-23.

Di Matteo, Livio, & Di Matteo, Rosanna (1993). The Determinants of Expenditures by Canadian Visitors to the United States. *Journal of Travel Research*, 31(4): 34-42.

Edgell, David L. (1990). *International Tourism Policy.* New York, NY: Van Nostrand Reinhold.

Fesenmaier, Daniel R. (1994). Strategies for Marketing Korea to Visitors in the United States. *International Symposium on the Image Strategy of Korea for Overseas Tourism Promotion.* Paper presented at the Korea Transport Institute, Seoul, Korea.

Fujii Edwin T., & Mak, James (1980). Forecasting Travel Demand When the Explanatory Variables are Highly Correlated. *Journal of Travel Research*, 18(4): 31-34.

Gerakis, Andreas S. (1965). Effects of Exchange-Rate Devaluations and Revaluations on Receipts from Tourism. *IMF Staff Papers*, 12(2): 365-384.

Gordon, Robert J. (1981). *Macroeconomics*, 2nd ed. Boston: Little, Brown.

Gray, H. Peter (1966). The Demand for International Travel by the United States and Canada. *International Economic Review*, 7(1): 83-92.

Hoerl Arthur E., & Kennard, Robert W. (1970). Ridge Regression: Applications to Nonorthogonal Problems. *Technometrics*, 12(1): 69-82.

International Monetary Fund (1986-1991). *International Financial Statistics Yearbook.* Washington, DC: International Monetary Fund.

Jud G. Donald, & Joseph, Hyman (1974). International Demand for Latin American Tourism. *Growth and Change*, 5(1): 25-31.

Korea Exchange Bank (1970-1990). *Trends on Average Exchange Rates of Korean Won Against the Major Currencies.* Seoul, Korea: Government Printers.

Korea National Tourism Corporation (1994). *Promotional Expenditure by Region, 1980-1993.* Seoul, Korea: Unpublished Government Printers.

Kwack, Sung Y. (1972). Effects of Income and Prices on Travel Spending Abroad, 1960 III - 1967 IV. *International Economic Review,* 13(2): 245-256.

Laber, Gene (1969). Determinants of International Travel Between Canada and the United States. *Geographical Analysis,* 1(4): 329-336.

Loeb, Peter D. (1982). International Travel to the United States: An Econometric Evaluation. *Annals of Tourism Research,* 9(1): 7-20.

Makridakis, Spyros, & Wheelwright, Steven C. (1978). *Forecasting: Methods and Applications.* New York, NY: Wiley/Hamilton.

Martin, Christine A., & Witt, Stephen F. (1989). Tourism Demand Elasticities. In S. F. Witt & L. Moutinho (Eds.), *Tourism Marketing and Management Handbook* (pp. 163-167). Hemel Hempstead: Prentice-Hall.

Ministry of Transportation (1990). *Tourism Statistics.* Seoul, Korea: Government Printers.

Ministry of Transportation and Korea National Tourism Corporation (1980-1990). *Annual Statistical Report on Tourism.* Seoul, Korea: Government printers.

Peebles, Gavin (1988). *Hong Kong's Economy: An Introductory Macroeconomic Analysis.* New York, NY: Oxford University Press.

Pindyck, Robert S., & Rubinfeld, Daniel L. (1981). *Econometric Models and Economic Forecasts,* 2nd ed. New York, NY: McGraw-Hill.

Quayson, Jojo, & Var, Turgut (1982). A Tourism Demand Function for the Okanagan, BC. *Tourism Management,* 3(2): 108-115.

Sheldon, Pauline J. (1993). Forecasting Tourism: Expenditures versus Arrivals. *Journal of Travel Research,* 32(1): 13-20.

Smeral, Egon, Witt, Stephen F., & Witt, Christine A. (1992). Econometric Forecasts: Tourism Trends to 2000. *Annals of Tourism Research,* 19(3): 450-466.

Stronge, William B., & Redman, Milton (1982). U.S. Tourism in Mexico: An Empirical Analysis. *Annals of Tourism Research,* 9(1): 21-35.

U.S. Department of Commerce/Bureau of International Commerce (1970-1990), *Foreign Economic Trends and Their Implications for the United States—Hong Kong.* Washington D.C.: Government Printers.

Usui, Shigeru (1994). Image Strategy of Korea to Japanese Traveling Overseas. *International Symposium on the Image Strategy of Korea for Overseas Tourism Promotion.* Paper presented at the Korea Transport Institute, Seoul, Korea.

Uysal, Muzaffer, & Crompton, John L. (1984). Determinants of Demand for International Tourist Flows to Turkey. *Tourism Management,* 5(4): 288-297.

Var, Turgut, & Lee, Choong-Ki (1993). Tourism Forecasting: State-of-the Art Techniques. In Mahmmod Khan, Michael Olsen, & Turgut Var (Eds.), *VNR's Encyclopedia of Hospitality and Tourism* (pp. 679-696). New York, NY: Van Nostrand Reinhold.

Var, Turgut, Mohammad, Golam, & Icoz, Orhan (1990). Factors Affecting International Tourism Demand for Turkey. *Annals of Tourism Research,* 17(4): 606-610.

Witt, Christine A., & Witt, Stephen F. (1990). Appraising an Econometric Fore-casting Model. *Journal of Travel Research*, 28(3): 30-34.

Witt, Stephen F., & Martin, Christine A. (1987). Econometric Models for Fore-casting International Tourism Demand. *Journal of Travel Research*, 25(3): 23-30.

World Travel & Tourism Council (1992). *Economic Powerhouse*. 2nd Annual Report. Brussels, Belgium.

A Neural Network Approach
to Discrete Choice Modeling

Jiann-Min Jeng
Daniel R. Fesenmaier

SUMMARY. Conventional disaggregate choice models consider choice to be an outcome of individual preferences. A variety of estimating procedures have been developed to calibrate these models and can be considered "mapping mechanisms" which link a dependent variable (e.g., choice of destination) with independent variables (e.g., individual characteristics such as age, gender, and income and destination-related attributes including attractiveness and cost). A new approach has been developed to achieve this "mapping" and is generally referred to as "artificial neural networks" (ANNs).

The goal of this study was to evaluate the usefulness of artificial neural networks for modeling individual choice behavior. The two specific objectives of this study were to compare the accuracy in prediction of a conventional conjoint model and an ANN model and to compare part-worth utilities or preference structure of the respective models. Comparison between a conventional disaggregate choice model (e.g., the conjoint model) and a back-propagation neural network (BPNN) model was based upon a study involving on-site interviews of visitors to five Illinois Highway Welcome Centers.

The findings of the study indicate that the back-propagation neural network approach is a useful approximator or pattern matcher for discrete choice models. The BPNN model performs equally well or

Jiann-Min Jeng is a PhD candidate and Daniel R. Fesenmaier is Associate Professor, Department of Leisure Studies, University of Illinois at Urbana-Champaign.

[Haworth co-indexing entry note]: "A Neural Network Approach to Discrete Choice Modeling." Jeng, Jiann-Min, and Daniel R. Fesenmaier. Co-published simultaneously in *Journal of Travel & Tourism Marketing* (The Haworth Press, Inc.) Vol. 5, No. 1/2, 1996, pp. 119-144; and *Recent Advances in Tourism Marketing Research* (ed: Daniel R. Fesenmaier, Joseph T. O'Leary, and Muzaffer Uysal) The Haworth Press, Inc., 1996, pp. 119-144. Single or multiple copies of this article are available from The Haworth Document Delivery Service [1-800-342-9678, 9:00 a.m. - 5:00 p.m. (EST). E-mail address: getinfo@haworth.com].

119

better than the more traditional conjoint model in terms of goodness-of-fit and prediction rate. However, the findings of BPNN analysis also exhibited contradictory results to conjoint analysis. Two out of six models calibrated provided totally different results. Implications of the findings for travel and tourism marketing are discussed. *[Article copies available from The Haworth Document Delivery Service: 1-800-342-9678. E-mail address: getinfo@haworth.com]*

INTRODUCTION

Discrete choice models have been used extensively in tourism research to develop a better understanding of the destination choice process (Haider and Ewing, 1990; Lue, Crompton and Stewart, 1994), to assess the impact of price on travel behavior (Morely, 1994a,b; Bojanic and Calantone, 1990), to measure the image of ski resorts in British Columbia (Carmichael, 1992) and to examine alternative designs of various tourism products and services (Roehl, Ditton, Holland and Perdue, 1992; Fesenmaier, 1994). Conventional disaggregate choice models consider choice to be an outcome of individual preferences. Choosing one alternative in a given choice set is based upon criteria which decision-makers *a priori* construct in order to maximize expected utility (Louviere, 1988a; Timmermans, 1984a). That is, individuals' preferences among choice alternatives are assumed to be a combination of attributes by some simple algebraic rules–i.e., adding/subtracting and multiplying/dividing (Anderson, 1981, 1982, 1990).

A variety of procedures have been developed to calibrate disaggregate choice models including logit and probit formulations, linear, nonlinear and weighted least squares and linear programming (Ben-Akiva and Lerman, 1985; Louviere, 1988a; Louviere and Woodworth, 1983). These approaches can be considered "mapping mechanisms" which link a dependent variable (e.g., choice of destination, travel mode and route, or brand) with independent variables (e.g., individual characteristics such as age, income, gender, price and cultural background and destination-related characteristics such as attractiveness and travel cost). A new approach has been developed to achieve this "mapping" and is generally referred to as "artificial neural networks" (ANNs) (Nelson & Illingworth, 1991; Jost, 1993; Schalkoff, 1992). ANNs are designed to simulate the human brain in terms of how an individual stores and recalls information and makes judgments. With the rapidly emerging computation technology, ANNs have been applied to diverse fields such as pattern recognition and classification, speech recognition, optimization, predicting stock market (Dutta & Skekhar, 1988; White, 1988), image recognition (Castelaz, 1988), financing risky identification (Collins, Ghosh, & Scofield, 1988), tourism market segmentation (Mazanec, 1992), and traveler route choice (Yang, Kitamura, Jovanis, Vaughn & Abdel-Aty, 1993).

The goal of this study was to evaluate the usefulness of the artificial neural network model for modeling individual choice behavior. There are two specific objectives of this study: (1) to compare the accuracy in prediction of a conventional discrete destination choice model and an ANN model; and, (2) to compare part-worth utilities or preference structure of a conventional discrete choice model and an ANN model.

THEORETICAL CONSIDERATIONS

Two main streams of disaggregate choice models can be categorized as revealed choice models and stated preference models (Louviere, 1988b; Louviere & Timmermans, 1990). Revealed choice models include discrete choice models (Louviere, 1976, 1988a, b; Louviere & Timmermans, 1990) and logit models (Richards & Ben-Akiva, 1975). Stated preference models include decompositional multiattribute preference models (Timmermans, 1984a, b, c), conjoint methods (Batsell & Louviere, 1990; Green, Carroll, & Goldberg, 1981; Green & Srinivasan, 1978; Louviere, 1988a, b) and part-worth models (Louviere, 1988a; Louviere & Timmermans, 1990).

These two approaches differ substantially in terms of the nature of data they use to model the choice process (Batsell & Louviere, 1991; Louviere, 1983; Louviere & Timmermans, 1990; Timmermans, 1984a, b). Revealed choice models are based upon choice probabilities which are derived from *observed* choices. However, stated preference models are based on individuals' expressed overall utility (preference) for *hypothetical* choice alternatives. Recently, however, Louviere (1988a) argued that the basic theories and methodologies which underlie these two approaches are similar and therefore should be considered part of a "family" of disaggregate choice models. The following discussion of conventional disaggregate choice models will focus on: (1) model specification; (2) methods of data collection; and (3) model estimation and parameter calibration of these two forms of disaggregate choice models.

Choice Model Specification

The revealed choice model relies on random utility theory and assumes choice behavior to be probabilistic (Batsell & Louviere, 1991; Louviere & Timmermans, 1990). Random utility theory is based upon the assumption that an individual is a "rational economic man" who utilizes imperfect (partial) information to maximize his/her expected utility. The difference or variation across individuals is defined as random error and is assumed to be distributed independently and identically across the population (Louviere, 1988a, b; Timmermans, 1984a; Timmermans & Golledge, 1990; Richards & Ben-Akiva, 1975). A second important underlying assumption of probabilistic choice models is "independence of irrelevant alternatives" (IIA) which assumes that choice alternatives are "mutually exclusive and exhaustive" (Batsell & Louviere, 1991; Louviere, 1988a, b; Louviere & Timmermans, 1990; Timmermans & Golledge, 1990; Richards & Ben-Akiva, 1975). That is, the probability of choosing an alternative from a choice set remains the same whether an alternative is added or removed from the choice set (Timmermans & Golledge, 1990). Timmermans and others have shown that the "strict utility function" of a logit model causes problems when choice alternatives are not comparable (Timmermans, 1984c).

The general form of the revealed choice model is:

$$P(i:A_t) = Prob[u_{it} \geq u_{jt}, \forall_t, i \neq j] \tag{1}$$

Where:

i, j =   as each alternative in choice set;

t =   individual choice-maker;

A_t =   the set of alternative choices available to individual t.

The utility function of u_{it} for each individual t and each alternative I can be denoted as:

$$u_{it} = u_t(x_i, s_t) + \varepsilon_{it} \tag{2}$$

Where:

x_i =   the physical and social characteristics of alternative i ;

s_j =   the socio-economic characteristics of individual;

ε_{it} =   random error term.

Assuming that the random error is independently and identically distributed with a double (extreme value) exponential distribution, it can be shown that the choice model takes the form of the multinomial logit model as follows (Timmermans, 1984c; Richards & Ben-Akiva, 1975):

$$P(i : A_t) = \frac{\exp^{U_i(X_i, S_t)}}{\displaystyle\sum_{j \epsilon A_t} \exp^{U_j(X_j, S_t)}} \tag{3}$$

Where:

t =   an individual choice maker;

A_t =   the set of relevant alternatives for individual t;

$P(i{:}A_t)$ =   the probability that individual t will choose alternative I out of the set of alternatives A_t;

U_{it} =   the utility of alternative I to individual t.

Stated preference models are based on individuals' expressed overall utility (preference) for *hypothetical* choice alternatives. The underlying assumption is that an individual perceives each choice alternative as a combination of attributes with different attribute levels (Batsell & Louviere, 1991; Fesenmaier, 1990; Lieber & Fesenmaier, 1984; Timmermans, 1984a). Timmermans and Golledge (1990) indicate that the stated preference model is based on the basic assumption that an individual processes a variety of information in order to make a judgement using a specified combination rule (Anderson, 1981, 1982, 1990; Green & Srinivasan, 1978). The combination rules are generally assumed to be one of three major forms: the additive rule, the multiplicative rule, and the mix (averaging) rule (Anderson, 1981, 1982, 1991).

A number of approaches have been developed to select attributes for inclusion in the model. In-depth interviews, process tracing (Olshavsky, 1979; Payne, 1976; Payne, Bettman, & Johnson, 1992), repertory grid analysis (Hallsworth, 1988), and direct questioning can be used for identifying the determinants of individual choice behavior (Green & Srinivasan, 1978; Timmermans, 1984a). Timmermans (1984b) suggested the individual-specified influential attributes yield a totally disaggregate approach where the choice dimension, measurement of utility functions, model specification and prediction of overt choice behavior all take place at the individual level. Green and Srinivasan (1978) pointed out that, in terms of number of attributes, attributes have to account for both the reliability and validity of estimation procedure. Inclusion of a large number of attributes which may influence one's decision may yield higher validity; however, redundant attributes may lead to unreliable estimation. Timmermans (1984a) suggested that the ratio of the number of choice alternatives (n) and the number of estimated parameters (T) should be as large as possible.

In stated preference models, two methods are typically used for presenting hypothetical choice alternatives: full-profile design and trade-off design (Green & Srinivasan, 1978; Timmermans, 1984a). In a full-profile design, every possible combination of all attribute levels (i.e., possible choice alternatives) are presented; hence, individual responses provide measurement of overall utility or preference of alternatives. With the trade-off design, on the other hand, individuals consider two factors at a time and provide the response of utility or preference with respect to all possible combinations of paired attribute levels. However, both designs usually result in a problem of information overload (Green & Srinivasan, 1978; Louviere & Timmermans, 1990; Timmermans, 1984b,c). For example, a full-profile design with 10 attributes and 3 levels creates 59,049 (3^{10}) different combinations; a trade-off design creates 810 stimuli (i.e., $10*(10-1)/2*(3*3)$). Thus, an individual usually becomes exhausted and therefore can not make consistent and errorless responses. Considering the ratio of hypothetical choice alternatives and the number of attributes, Timmermans (1984a, p. 196) suggested the "full-profile approach will give better results in cases where the number of attributes describing the choice alternatives is relatively small and/or the interattribute correlations are relatively large whereas the trade-off approach is likely to provide more accurate results where the number of attributes is large and/or the interattribute correlations are small." Due to oversized full-profile designs, researchers suggested using a fractional factorial design (Batsell & Louviere, 1991; Louviere, 1988; Louviere & Timmermans, 1990). The fractionalized choice sets consider a smaller number of hypothetical choice alternatives and therefore, reduces the exercise to a manageable size. A fractional factorial design, however, restricts the model which may be calibrated.

According to Green and Srinivasan (1978), another important consideration in design is the believability and validity of a stimulus set as reflected by the range and variation of attribute levels and interattribute correlation. For example, one design can reduce the believability and hence, provide less valid responses by increasing the range of attribute levels (i.e., whether or not the levels are realistic in terms of respondents' knowledge and/or experiences) and by decreasing the interattribute correlation to zero (i.e., whether or the pre-specified attribute levels are independent).

Research has shown that orthogonal designs improve the accuracy of the parameter estimation for a given level of validity for the preference judgement (Green & Srinivasan, 1978; and Timmermans, 1984a).

Model Estimation and Parameter Calibration

A variety of approaches have been developed to estimate discrete choice models including logit and probit formulations, linear, nonlinear and weighted least squares and linear programming. These approaches have used a number of analytical and statistical procedures whereby aspects describing the choice alternatives are "mapped" onto individuals' expressed preferences for one or more choice alternatives. Many of the different estimation procedures and mapping algorithms have been incorporated into various computer packages (Batsell & Louviere, 1991; Louviere, 1988a, b; Louviere & Timmermans, 1990; Richards & Ben-Akiva, 1975). Timmermans (1984a) categorized four types of methods used for calibrating additive models based on the method of data collection, profile design vs. trade-off design, and the scale of the choice alternative, ordinal vs. internal scale. As shown in Table 1, linear programming is used for the ordinal-type data including LINMAP, PREMAP, UNICON, and logistic regression. For interval-type data, however, multiple regression including

TABLE 1. Estimation Methods for Discrete Choice Model

Method of Data Collection	Dependent Variable	
	Ordinal Scale	Interval Scale
Profile Design	1. Badness-of-fit measure (UNICON, monotonic regression, PREMAP) (Timmermans, 1984a); 2. linear programming (LINMAP) (Green & Srinivasan, 1978); 3. Sum-of-absolute-error.	1. Ordinary linear/nonlinear least square (OLS); 2. Weight least square.
Trade-Off Design	1. Linear programming (LINMAP); 2. Johnson's non-metric trade-off procedure (Green & Srinivasan, 1978; and Timmermans, 1984a); 3. Logistic regression (LOGIT, or PROBIT-like model).	1. Ordinary linear/nonlinear least square (OLS); 2. Weight least square.

ordinary linear/nonlinear least squares (OLS) and weighted least squares (WLS) is used.

ARTIFICIAL NEURAL NETWORKS (ANNs) MODEL

The artificial neural network (ANNs) model was developed in the early 1960s by Mclloach-Hopfield (Jost, 1993; NeuralWare, 1993; Simpson, 1990) and consists of a set of nodes (i.e., neurons) for processing incoming information (i.e., stimulus, input data) and a set of connections (i.e., synaptic strengths, connection weights) for "memorizing" information (Simpson, 1990). Through replicative learning processes (i.e., by feeding example patterns and repeatedly adjusting the weights of connections) and associative memory (i.e., storage and recall of information by association with other information) the neural network model can almost errorlessly classify information as pre-specified patterns (Muller and Reinhardt, 1990; Simpson, 1990). In other words, a neural network model is a "device" which learns from examples and can provide desired results by giving new information.

A typical architecture of neural network models include one input layer, one or two hidden layer(s), and one output layer (Simpson, 1990; Neural-Ware, 1993). Each layer consists of numerous processing nodes (Figure 1). The "input layer" is considered a set of "sensors" which receive stimuli from the outside world and can be used to represent the independent variables of a discrete choice model. The "output layer" can be thought of as the dependent variable (e.g., destination choice). The "hidden layer," on the other hand, contains "neurons" which are considered the center of the neural network; this layer acts as a filter (or series of filters) which rescales or "remaps" the input data onto the output.

Simpson (1990) described 27 different neural networks which are basically derived from two learning methods—*supervised* and *unsupervised* learning and two architectures—*feedforward* and *feedback* recall (see Table 2). A supervised learning method is defined by outputs, the weight is adjusted corresponding to the difference between desired output and actual output (California Scientific Software, 1990; Nelson & Illingworth, 1991; Rumelhardt et al., 1990; Simpson, 1990). An unsupervised learning method "is a process that incorporates no external teacher and relies upon only local information and internal control" (Nelson & Illingworth, 1991; Simpson, 1990; Hiotis, 1993). In the unsupervised learning model, data is organized by computing the degree of similarity between "objects" which can be used to group or classify the respective objects (NeuralWare, 1993; Simpson, 1990). Feedforward recall is a one-directional information processing

FIGURE 1. General Neural Network Architecture

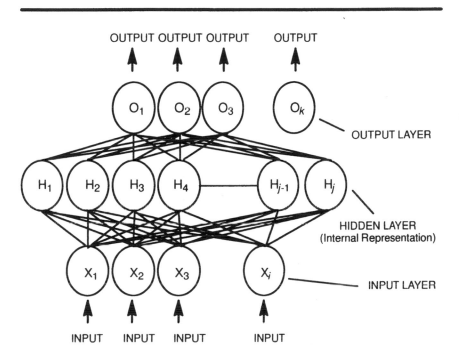

neural network in which each node is allowed only to receive information from the preceding neuron. Feedback recall is a bi-directional information processing method in which each node is not only receiving information from the proceeding layer but also allowing the feedback to later layers.

The back-propagation neural network (BPNN) model is an advanced multiple regression analysis neural network model that is capable of dealing with more complex and non-linear data relationships than standard regression analysis (Jost, 1993). An important distinction between conventional statistical regression methods and the BPNN model is that regression methods relate independent variables directly to the dependent variable. BPNN models, on the other hand, relate independent variables (the input layer) indirectly to dependent variables (output layer) by establishing a number of hidden nodes. The function of the hidden layer is believed to "represent the internal structure of input data" which, in turn, yields a better approximation in terms of mapping input data onto output patterns (Rumelhart et al.,1986). At a sufficient number of hidden nodes,

TABLE 2. Types of Neural Networks Models

	Learning Method	
	Supervised	Unsupervised
Feedforward	Perceptron Adaline/Madaline Backpropagation (BP) Boltzman Machine (BM) Cauchy Machine (CM) Adaptive Heuristic Critic (AHC) Associative Reward-Penalty (ARP) Avalanche Mathed Filter (AMF)	Learning Matrix (LM) Drive-Reinforcement (DR) Sparse Distributed Memory (SDM) Linear Associative Memory (LAM) Optimal Linear Associative Memory (OLAM) Fuzzy Associative Memory (FAM) Linear Vector Quantizer (LVQ) Counterpropagation (CPN)
Feedback	Brain-State-in-a-Box (BSB) Fuzzy Cognitive Map (FCM)	Additive Grossberg (AG) Shunting Grossberg (SG) Binary Adaptive Resonance Theory (ART 1) Analog Adaptive Resonance Theory (ART2) Discrete Autocorrelator (DA) Continuous Hopfield (CH) Discrete Bidirectional Associative Memory (BAM) Adaptive Bidirectional Associative Memory (ABAM) Temporal Associative Memory (TAM)

Adapted from Simpson (1990)

the BPNN model can minimize error and provide a better approximation (White, 1989; Rumelhart et al., 1986).

Estimation and Parameter Calibration

Parameter calibration of a BPNN model is conducted through a "replicative learning" process. The process is conducted by iteratively and simultaneously changing the weights of each connection to minimize the error between desired outputs and actual outputs (White, 1989; Simpson, 1990). The learning process is usually a time-consuming process which ultimately approximates the global (universal) minimum. Therefore, in terms of the development of neural networks, most model builders focus attention on developing algorithms which can minimize the error (i.e., approximating global minimum) and speed up the learning process (NeuralWare, 1993). The process is conducted by iteratively and simultaneously changing the weights of each connection to minimize the error (Euclidean distance) between desired outputs and actual outputs–Δw (White, 1989; Simpson, 1990). The global error–Δw is obtained by equation 4.

$$\Delta w_{k,t} = \frac{\sum_{k1}^{k} (o_k - \hat{o}_k)^2}{2} \tag{4}$$

Where:

$w_{k,t}$ = the k-th error between actual output and desired output at t-th iteration;

o_k = the k-th actual output;

$\hat{o}_k$ = the k-th desired output.

The processes of model estimation include four steps including selecting training examples, specifying model structure, deciding the acceptance level of model estimation, and examining the weighting of each input variable. First, a set of training "examples," which represents major characteristics of the samples, is selected. Typically, the rest of the data (observations) are used to cross-validate the model and to test the stability of the established model. The second step is to specify the numbers of hidden nodes and number of the hidden layers. The number of hidden nodes usually depends on the complexity of a given estimation task. Currently, no established guidelines exist for deciding the optimal number of nodes (and layers) needed either for higher approximation or efficient estimation process. However, the model estimation is usually a process of numerous trial-and-error; and thus, is time-consuming. Third, two criteria are usually employed for deciding the acceptance level of model estimation; these are the root mean square (Δw) and the classification rate (percentage of correctly assigned). These two statistics calculated in the training process indicate the internal validity of the model and the values obtained in the cross-validation process provide measures of external validity.

In summary, there are substantial differences between conventional choice models (both revealed choice model and stated preference model) and the BPNN model. Conventional choice models employ statistical methods which link dependent variables directly to independent variables whereas the BPNN model links dependent variables to independent variables indirectly by means of a "hidden" layer. In terms of operation of model estimation and error of estimation, BPNN requires a time-consuming learning process whereas the conventional choice can be estimated relatively easily using standard estimation procedures.

METHODOLOGY

Comparison of the two choice modeling approaches (i.e., conventional disaggregate choice model and the BPNN model) was based upon a study involving on-site personal interviews of visitors to five Illinois Highway Welcome Centers (Fesenmaier, 1994). The goal of the study was to assess visitors' preferences for alternative strategies for locating and configuring tourist information centers off the interstate. This was accomplished by first identifying those attributes of tourist information centers which determine their relative "attractiveness." Based upon the literature, the following six attributes were identified: (1) the ease of highway access (i.e., on the frontage road to the interstate vs. within 1/3 mile of the interstate); (2) the service setting (i.e., the number of services nearby including gas stations and restaurants); (3) whether or not the tourist information center stands alone or is physically part of another type of service; (4) the format with which travel information is made available (i.e., tourist brochures vs. interactive computer without paper printout); (5) the availability of travel counselors; and (6) whether or not the tourist information center is publicly or privately owned and operated (see Table 3). Sixty-four (64) different profiles or scenarios were generated (six attributes with two levels) and fractionalized by factorial design (Louviere, 1988a, b, c; Louviere & Timmermans, 1990; Timmermans, 1984a, b, c,). As shown in Table 4, eight alternatives were used based upon the *anchor-point* design which provides sufficient information with which to evaluate the relative importance of each attribute in tourist decision on using off-interstate tourist information centers (Louviere and Timmermans, 1990; Louviere, 1983). The dependent variable was the choice between two hypothetical alternatives—Information Center A and Information Center B.

Data were collected using a systematic process of visitor to five Illinois welcome centers. The five Centers where the surveys were completed are located on high traffic interstate highways at each border of the state: (1) Lake Forest Oasis (at I-94, 12 miles south of Wisconsin border); (2) Mississippi Rapids (at I-80, 1 mile east of Iowa border); (3) Highland

TABLE 3. Description of Attributes and Levels Used in Choice Experiment

Attribute	Level 1	Level 2
Highway access:	On the frontage road next to interstate	Within 1/3 mile of interstate
Service setting:	No gas station or restaurants nearby	Many gas stations and restaurants nearby
Type of facility:	Part of a gas station, restaurant, store	By itself
Type of information:	Computerized tourist information system without paper printout	Tourist brochures (including attractions, shopping, and hotels)
Availability of travel counselors:	Counselors available 8 a.m. to 5 p.m.	No counselors available
Type of ownership:	Privately owned and operated	Owned and operated by the state of Illinois

Silver Lake (at I-70, 27 miles east of St. Louis); (4) Rend Lake (at I-57); and (5) Cumberland Road (at I-70, 8 miles west of Effingham). While each tourism information center had its own unique characteristics the Lake Forest Oasis deserves special notice. The Lake Forest Oasis is highly commercialized (Wendy's and a number of other vendors provide services) and the tourist information center is located in an inconspicuous area entering the building. The relative inaccessibility of the tourist information center appears to limit the ability of travel counselors to service incoming traffic effectively. On two selected days (one weekday and one weekend day) during the first two weeks of August, 1992, approximately every 10th person visiting the tourist information center was approached between operating hours of 8:00 a.m. to 5:00 p.m. and invited to participate in the study. In total, 382 tourist information center visitors were approached and yielded 238 completed surveys (62.3%) yielding 1804 choice decisions (i.e., each respondent made eight decisions corresponding to the eight choice situations); one hundred of the choice responses (5%) were dropped due to incomplete/ inadequate data.

Model Calibration

Three programs were used for data analysis: (1) SPSS V. 6.0 for Windows (SPSS Inc, 1993); (2) SYSTAT Logit Regression with the module of

TABLE 4. Layout Design for Choice Experiments

Welcome Center Attributes

Choice Scenario	Choice Alternative	Highway Access	Service Setting	Type of Facility	Type of Information	Availability of Counselors	Type of Ownership
1	A	1/3 mile	No gas, etc.	Part of facility	Computer	Counselors	State
	B	Frontage	Many gas, etc.	Stand alone	Brochures	No counselor	Private
2	A	1/3 mile	Many gas, etc.	Stand alone	Brochures	Counselors	State
	B	Frontage	No gas, etc.	Part of facility	Computer	No counselor	Private
3	A	Frontage	Many gas, etc.	Part of facility	Computer	No counselor	Private
	B	1/3 mile	No gas, etc.	Stand alone	Brochures	Counselors	State
4	A	Frontage	No gas, etc.	Part of facility	Brochures	No counselor	State
	B	1/3 mile	Many gas, etc.	Stand alone	Computer	Counselors	Private
5	A	1/3 mile	Many gas, etc.	Part of facility	Brochures	Counselors	Private
	B	Frontage	No gas, etc.	Stand alone	Computer	No counselor	State
6	A	Frontage	No gas, etc.	Stand alone	Brochures	Counselors	Private
	B	1/3 mile	Many gas, etc.	Part of facility	Computer	No counselor	State
7	A	Frontage	Many gas, etc.	Stand alone	Computer	Counselors	State
	B	1/3 mile	No gas, etc.	Part of facility	Brochures	No counselor	Private
8	A	1/3 mile	No gas, etc.	Stand alone	Computer	No counselor	Private
	B	Frontage	Many gas, etc.	Part of facility	Brochures	Counselors	State

discrete choice analysis (SYSTAT, Inc., 1993); and, (3) NeuralWare V. 5.0 for IBM (NeuralWare, 1993). Two sets of analyses were conducted to compare the results of parameter estimation for both discrete choice model and BPNN model. The first set of analyses focused on calibration of the discrete choice model using logistic regression (Fesenmaier, 1994). The second set of analyses used a back-propagation neural network (BPNN) model to examine the factors affecting respondents' choices.

Calibration of the BPNN model was based on batch learning and the momentum was added to speed up the learning process. Individuals' choice between alternatives A or B (the dependent variable) was coded as "1" or "2." Parameter estimates were normalized in model calibration for both inputs and outputs in the neural network model (NeuralWare, 1993). Part-worth utility estimates were interpreted by measuring the relative contribution (i.e., percentage share) of each attribute to the total variance of the dependent variable. A goodness-of-fit value (R^2) was also calculated to evaluate performance of network model; these R^2 values were calculated by comparing the root mean squared error (RMS) between desired output and actual output divided by the variance of desired output and are similar to R^2 coefficients provided in multiple regression analysis (Glass & Hopkins, 1984).

Three stages of analyses were required in calibrating the BPNN model. A preliminary study was conducted to evaluate differences in performance between neural network model architectures. A follow-up study using the cross-validation training methods was conducted to identify the "best" model architecture. Last, a cross-validation training process was used to minimize the size of hidden layers. Criteria for selecting a specified model for follow-up analyses were on the basis of prediction rate, R^2 value, and size of hidden layers. Four three-layered neural network architectures were initially used for the preliminary evaluation which are 6-6-1 (i.e., with respect to the number of nodes for input-hidden-output layer), 6-12-1, 6-18-1, and 6-30-1.

For the cross-validation training procedure (NeuralWare, 1993; Wiggins et al., 1992), the original sample was spilt into a "training" and a "testing" data set. Approximately 75% of the sample was randomly selected as the training set and the rest (25%) of the sample was used as the testing set. The cross-validation training was set up by holding the best testing result for 100 retest cycles; every re-test was conducted after 1,000 training cycles (NeuralWare, 1993). If the best testing result did not change after 100 retries the network stopped learning. Model stability was measured by the number of training cycles the networks needed to reach the best result. Control strategies for the batch learning process required changes in the learning rate and momentum over the training cycle. Initially, a 0.4 momentum value and a 0.4 learning rate value was used; after 10,000 training cycles, values of 0.3 and 0.2 were used, respectively; after 30,000 cycles, values of 0.015 and 0.05 were used; after 120,000 cycles, 0.0017 and 0.00312 were used; and finally, after 150,000 cycles, 0.0 and 0.00001 were used. A sigmoid transfer function and generalized-delta-rule (cumulative delta rule) were used to improve the training speed.

If choice frequency is used, a typical approach for parameter estimation is through the maximum likelihood estimation. "A maximum likelihood estimator is the value of the parameters for which the observed sample is most likely to have occurred" (Ben-Akiva and Lerman, 1985, p. 20). Ben-Akiva and Lerman (1985) also indicated that the maximum likelihood estimator is consistent, asymptotically normal and efficient; however, the drawback of maximum likelihood estimation is somewhat biased or inefficient when the sample is not sufficiently large. The McFaddan's *rho*-square (ϱ^2) statistic also provides an index describing the goodness-of-fit of models calibrated using maximum likelihood estimation. The *rho*-square statistic has the same statistical meaning as the R^2 statistic in multiple regression analysis in that it measures the extent to which the dependent variable (i.e., the choice outcome) can be predicted by observed independent variables.

RESULTS AND INTERPRETATION

The choice experiment was based on six attributes which were *a priori* identified to be influential of individual choices among different configurations and/or designs of off-interstate information centers. Specifically, respondents were asked to make a series of decisions between alternative off-interstate tourist information centers which differ with respect to *highway access, service setting, type of facility, type of information provided, presence and availability of travel counselors*, and *type of ownership*. Eight choice situations were presented enabling the identification of each attri-bute and attribute level combination (Louviere, 1988a, b). Respondents were allowed to "drop out"; that is, they were allowed to choose whether they *would continue on highway without stopping* or *would have stopped anyway*, which was given the condition that the information center was the only rest area. Thirty-five percent (35%) of the respondents indicated they *would have stopped anyway*, and 13 percent of the respondents indicated they *would have continued on*. Hence, approximately 52 percent of the respondents appeared to consider the off-interstate tourist information center as an alternative option for travel information. Comparison between visitors across the five tourist information centers shows that Mississippi Rapids visitors were more willing to consider off-interstate tourist information centers (75%) than visitors to the other four respective information centers (see Table 5).

Results of the Conventional Choice Model Calibration

The results of the choice experiment were first obtained using a series of logit regression analyses. Results presented in Table 6 indicate that the

TABLE 5. Frequency of Choice Outcomes by Tourist Information Center

Tourist Information Center	Choice A	Choice B	Would Have Continued	Would Have Stopped	Number of Choices
Lake Forest Oasis	31%	23%	16%	30%	337
Mississippi Rapids	39%	35%	14%	12%	372
Rend Lake	25%	22%	8%	45%	361
Highland Silver Lake	20%	17%	19%	43%	355
Cumberland	26%	24%	13%	47%	379
Overall Sample:	**28%**	**24%**	**13%**	**35%**	
Total Number of Responses:	509	429	227	639	1804

models developed (for the overall model and for each individual tourist information center) are significant predictors of individual choice ($p < 0.05$). For the overall model, the results show that *service setting* (with many gas stations and restaurants nearby) was the most important attribute (with a coefficient of -0.566) influencing choice, while *highway access* (-0.382) was the second most important attribute. Nevertheless, *type of ownership* (-0.319) and *presence of travel counselor* (-0.280) were also significant to attract highway travelers. However, *type of facility* was the least important and non-significant attribute (-0.086, $p > 0.05$).

Comparison of the model calibration results for the five tourist information centers shows substantial variation of important aspects of off-interstate travel information centers. *Service setting* was statistically significant for visitors to Lake Forest Oasis (-1.104), Mississippi Rapids (-0.702), and Cumberland (-0.322); Mississippi Rapids visitors were more concerned about the *type of information* (-0.325), *presence of counselor* (-0.383), and *type of ownership* (-0.534) whereas *highway access* was more important to the Cumberland visitors (-0.366). Visitors to Rend Lake and Highland Silver Lake tended to emphasize more on highway accessibility (-0.546 and -0.742, respectively); Rend Lake visitors were concerned about the availability of a travel counselor (-0.388) whereas visitors to Highland Silver Lake were concerned about the ownership (-0.461).

Results of Back-Propagation Neural Networks Model Calibration

The BPNN model was specified as three-layered architecture with one input layer, one hidden layer and an output layer. As indicated earlier, a preliminary cross-validation study was conducted with four network

TABLE 6. Importance Weightings of Off-Site Tourist Information Center Attribute by Tourist Information Center Location

Information Center Attributes:	Overall Model	Tourist Information Center				
		Lake Forest Oasis	Mississippi Rapids	Rend Lake	Highland Silver Lake	Cumberland
Constant	0.172[1] (0.071)[2]*	0.327 (0.176)	0.155 (0.135)	0.074 (0.167)	0.141 (0.198)	0.258 (0.162)
Highway access: (1 = On frontage road 2 = within 1/3 mile of interstate)	−0.382 (0.073)*	−0.123 (0.178)	−0.282 (0.147)	−0.546 (0.169)*	−0.742 (0.201)*	−0.366 (0.162)*
Service setting: (1 = many gas/restaurants nearby 2 = no gas/restaurant nearby)	−0.566 (0.073)*	−1.104 (0.178)*	−0.702 (0.147)*	−0.298 (0.168)	−0.372 (0.197)	−0.322 (0.162)*
Type of facility: (1 = part of gas/rest./store 2 = by itself)	−0.086 (0.072)	−0.157 (0.178)	−0.096 (0.146)	−0.114 (0.167)	−0.382 (0.199)	0.161 (0.162)
Type of information: (1 = tourist brochures 2 = computer system, no print)	−0.198 (0.072)*	−0.153 (0.178)	−0.325 (0.145)*	−0.160 (0.167)	−0.116 (0.201)	−0.291 (0.161)
Presence of travel counselor: (1 = counselors 8 a.m. - 5 p.m. 2 = no counselors available)	−0.280 (0.073)*	−0.309 (0.177)	−0.383 (0.148)*	−0.388 (0.168)*	0.020 (0.200)	−0.269 (0.162)
Type of Ownership: (1 = owned/operated by State 2 = privately owned/operated)	−0.319 (0.073)*	−0.072 (0.177)	−0.534 (0.146)*	−0.212 (0.168)	−0.461 (0.201)'	−0.243 (0.162)
Log Likelihood Constants only = [LL(0)]	−645.848	−124.847	−191.658	−116.151	−91.884	−120.855
Model Chi-square = 2*[LL(N)-LL(0)]	123.834	50.025	50.465	19.991	26.143	18.308
Chi-square p-value	0.000	0.000	0.000	0.003	0.000	0.006
McFaddens Rho-squared	0.096	0.200	0.132	0.086	0.142	0.076
Percent Correctly predicted	65.0%	74.3%	69.8%	63.7%	68.4%	64.8%

[1] = parameter estimate; [2] = standard error of estimate; * = significant at $\alpha = 0.05$

architectures to evaluate the appropriate number of nodes which should be included in the hidden layer (see Table 7). A training set was constructed that included approximately seventy-five percent (randomly selected) of the observations from survey data and the rest (25%) was used as a "test" data set. Six choice models were constructed based on the aggregated model and the locations of five tourist information centers. The results of the cross-validation process indicated a 6-6-1 BPNN architecture (six inputs, six hidden processing nodes, and one output) was most effective (considering training speed, efficiency and complexity of the models) in modeling respondent choice for each individual tourist information center. However, the results also indicated the overall BPNN model needed a substantially larger hidden layer (30 nodes) in order to accommodate the differences among visitors to the five tourist information centers.

As can be seen in Table 7, the BPNN models for the six welcome centers performed moderately well, ranging from a low of 62 percent classified correctly at Rend Lake to a high of 73 percent at Highland Silver Lake. Specifically, the model for Lake Forest Oasis consistently classified an average of 71 percent of the observations (71.4% on A and 71.0% on B) with R^2 value of 0.2. The Mississippi Rapids model averaged 67.1 percent (58.3% on A and 90.0% on B) with R^2 value of 0.2 ; the Rend Lake model averaged 62.1 percent classification rate (89.1% on A and 35.1% on B) with R^2 value of 0.12.; Highland Silver Lake model averaged 72.6 percent (58.6% on A and 86.7% on B) with R^2 value of 0.27; and, the Cumberland model averaged 63.7 percent (73.3% on A and 54.1% on B) with R^2 value. The best result found for the overall model included 30 nodes in the hidden layer and resulted in an average classification rate of 86.3% (76.6% on A and 96.1% on B) with an R^2 value of 0.15.

Comparison Between Logistic Regression and Back-Propagation Neural Networks Model

The results of the analyses using the logistic regression and the back-propagation neural network models showed that the neural network model performed as well as or better than the discrete choice model in terms of the goodness-of-fit (i.e., R^2) and classification rate (see Table 8). For the overall model, the neural network correctly predicted 89.2 percent on the training set (85.5% on testing), considerably better than the overall logistic regression (56.6%). However, four of the six neural network models did not provide a better prediction rate than the logistic regression models.

Comparison of the relative importance of the model attributes indicates that the neural network model provided similar results to the logistic regressions. *Service setting*, *highway accessibility*, and *type of ownership*

TABLE 7. Comparison of Predictive Accuracy of Back-Propagation Neural Network Model by Network Architecture

Network Input-Hidden-Output		Overall Model %	Lake Forest Oasis %	Mississippi Rapids %	Rend Lake %	Highland Silver Lake %	Cumberland %
6-6-1	Average	60.2[1] (61.8)	71.2 (86.2)	67.1 (61.8)	62.1 (55.9)	72.6 (60.5)	63.7 (63.4)
	Choice A	20.5 (23.6)	71.4 (78.6)	76.6 (77.1)	89.1 (80.0)	58.5 (44.4)	73.3 (73.9)
	Choice B	100.00 (100.00)	71.0 (93.8)	57.7 (46.4)	35.1 (31.8)	86.7 (76.5)	54.1 (52.9)
	R^2	0.0 (—)	0.2 (0.3)	0.2 (0.2)	0.1 (0.1)	0.3 (—)	0.1 (—)
6-30-1	Average	86.3 (83.9)	71.2 (86.2)	67.1 (61.8)	62.1 (55.9)	72.6 (60.5)	63.7 (63.4)
	Choice A	76.6 (74.0)	71.4 (78.6)	76.6 (77.1)	89.1 (80.0)	58.5 (44.4)	73.3 (73.9)
	Choice B	96.1 (93.8)	71.0 (93.8)	57.7 (46.4)	35.1 (31.8)	86.7 (76.5)	54.1 (52.9)
	R^2	0.2 (0.1)	0.2 (0.3)	0.2 (0.2)	0.1 (0.1)	0.3 (0.0)	0.1 (—)

1 = average percentage of correctly predicted of training set.
2 = average percentage of correctly predicted of testing set.

TABLE 8. Comparison of Importance Weightings Between Strategic Choice Model and Back-Propagation Neural Network Model by Tourist Information Centers

Model Parameter Estimate	Overall Model	Lake Forest Oasis	Mississippi Rapids	Rend Lake	Highland Silver Lake	Cumberland
Highway access: 1 = On frontage road 2 = within 1/3 mile of interstate)	11.9%[1] 20.9%[2]*	5.3% 6.4%	17.5% 12.1%	29.8% 31.8%*	31.9% 32.6%*	15.5% 22.2%*
Service setting: 1 = many gas/restaurants nearby 2 = no gas/restaurant nearby)	12.3% 30.9%*	44.2% 57.6%*	33.9% 30.2%*	21.1% 17.3%	18.8% 16.4%*	17.1% 19.5%*
Type of facility: 1 = part of gas/rest./store 2 = by itself	19.0% 4.7%	12.0% 8.2%	2.0% 4.1%	4.6% 6.6%	15.1% 16.8%	14.5% 9.7%
Type of information: 1 = tourist brochures 2 = computer system, no print)	19.2% 10.8%*	11.5% 8.0%	14.3% 14.0%*	13.1% 9.3%	10.5% 5.1%	18.6% 17.6%
Presence of travel counselor: (1 = counselors 8 a.m. - 5 p.m. 2 = no counselors available)	18.8% 15.3%*	19.4% 16.1%	11.8% 16.5%*	13.5% 22.6%*	3.5% 8.8%	19.0% 16.3%
Type of Ownership: (1 = owned/operated by State 2 = privately owned/operated)	18.7% 17.4%*	7.7% 3.8%	20.5% 23.0%*	17.9% 12.3%	20.2% 20.3%*	15.4% 14.7%
R^2	0.2[3] 0.1[4]	0.2 0.2	0.2 0.1	0.1 0.1	0.3 0.1	0.1 0.1
Prediction Rate	83.9%[5] 65.0%[6]	86.2% 74.3%	61.8% 69.8%	55.9% 63.7%	60.5% 68.4%	63.4% 64.8%

1 relative importance of attribute of neural network model
2 relative importance of regression coefficient of logistic regression
3 = Calculated R-square value for neural network model = $1 - (RMS^2/\text{variance of dependent variable})$
4 = McFaddens Rho-squared
5 = prediction rate of BPNN model based on the testing data set
6 = prediction rate of logistic regression
* = significant at p < 0.05

were considered to be important for both types of models. However, significant differences were also found. As can be seen in Table 8, the most significant difference was for the overall model and the Cumberland model. The most important attributes in the overall neural network model were *type of information* and *type of facility* whereas these two attributes were found to be the least important in the logistic regression model. For the Cumberland model, the results of neural network model showed the important attributes were *type of information* and *presence of travel counselor*; however, the results of the logistic regression model showed *highway accessibility* and *service setting* to be the most important.

CONCLUSIONS

Conventional discrete choice models are based on well established statistical theoretical foundations, can be easily calibrated and the results can be easily understood. Recently, neural network models have been developed which incorporate neuro-physiological theories with high speed computer technologies to provide another strategy for modeling choice behavior. These developments appear to offer several advantages for building models within the context of travel and tourism marketing. Most important, the incorporation of hidden layers within the neural network model provides more degrees of freedom and therefore offers substantially greater flexibility in building a complex model of human behavior. In addition, artificial neural network models are superior to the standard statistical analyses in terms of the modeling multiple dependent variables. Conventional models usually attempt to model a single choice (i.e. destination choice, etc.) and can not simultaneously consider a number of choice outcomes at one time. However, in a real world situation, decision makers are always facing the situation of multiple choices. Neural network models can easily incorporate a number of choice alternatives and therefore model the choice behavior in a more "real" world situation.

The flexibility of the neural network model offers substantial opportunity for building sophisticated models which can be used for marketing in the tourism industry. Recently, Mazanec (1992) used the neural network framework to conduct a segmentation analysis of Austrian tourists. Neural network models might also be developed to guide travel agents and tour operators in directing clients through the range of possible trips they offer. Advertising agencies can use neural network models to guide, for example, the development and placement of advertisements. The research on neural network models indicate they are a useful and reliable alternative for modeling tourist behavior and therefore offer the potential for wide application in the tourism industry.

There are, however, a number of important issues which limit the usefulness of ANNs. First, there is no error distribution theory associated with artificial neural networks; this limits the extent to which one can test the significance of model parameters and overall model performance. Second, the "learning" process when constructing a neural network model is difficult and open to interpretation. Two ways for selecting training data set for cross-validation learning process: one is a random selection, the other selects the representative patterns. In the random selection for a smaller data set it is problematic to split data into two sets without losing the representation of original data; and, it is difficult to obtain two identically distributed patterns of training and testing data sets. For the second method, there is no theoretical justification for researchers to find truly representative patterns and may result in invalid model estimation.

REFERENCES

Ahmad, S., Tesauro, G., & He, Y. (1990). Asymptotic Convergence of Backpropagation: Numerical Experiments. In D. S. Touretzky (Ed.). *Advances in Neural Information Processing Systems, 2.* Palo Alto, CA: Morgan Kaufmann Publishers, Inc.

Anderson, N. H. (1981). *Foundation of Information Integration Theory.* New York, NY: Academic Press.

Anderson, N. H. (1982). *Methods of Information Integration Theory.* New York, NY: Academic Press.

Anderson, N. H. (1990). *Contribution to Information Integration Theory.* New York, NY: Academic Press.

Batsell, R. R. & Louviere, J. J. (1991). Experimental Analysis of Choice. *Marketing Letters, 2,* 199-214.

Ben-Akiva, M., & Lerman, S. R. (1985). *Discrete Choice Analysis: Theory and Application to Travel Demand.* Cambridge, MA: MIT Press.

Bojanic, D. and Calantone (1990). Price Bundling in Public Recreation, *Leisure Sciences, 12, 1,* 67-78.

Carmichael, B. A. (1992). Using Conjoint Modelling to Measure Tourist Image and Analyze Ski Resort Choice, in P. Johnson and B. Thomas (Eds.), *Choice and Demand in Tourism,* New York: Mansell.

Castelaz, P. F. (1988) Neural Networks in Defense Applications. IEEE International Conference on Neural Networks, *2,* 473-480. San Diego, California.

Collins E., S. Ghosh & C. Scofield (1988). An Application of a Multiple Neural Network Learning System to Emulation of Mortgage Underwriting Judgements. IEEE International Conference on Neural Networks, *2,* 459-466. San Diego, California.

Dutta, S. & S. Skekhar (1988). Bond Rating: A Non-Conservative Application of Neural Networks. IEEE International Conference on Neural Networks, *2*, 443-450. San Diego, California.

Fesenmaier, D. R. (1990). Theoretical and Methodological Issues in Behavioral Modeling: Introductory Comments. *Leisure Sciences, 12*, 1-7.

Fesenmaier, D. R. (1994). Traveler Use of Visitor Information Centers: Implications for Development in Illinois. *Journal of Travel Research, 33*, 44-50.

Fesenmaier, D. R. & Vogt, C. A. (1993). Evaluating the Economic Impact of Travel Information Provided at Indiana Welcome Centers. *Journal of Travel Research, 31*, 33-39.

Fesenmaier, D. R., Vogt, C. A., & Stewart, W.P. (1993). Investigating the Influence of Welcome Center Information on Travel Behavior. *Journal of Travel Research, 31*, 47-52.

Garson, G. D. (1991). Interpreting Neural-Network Connection Weights. *AI Expert, 4*, 47-51.

Glass, G. V. & Hopkins, K. D. (1984). *Statistical Methods in Education and Psychology.* Englewood Cliffs, NJ: Prentice-Hall, Inc.

Golledge, R. G. & Timmermans, H. (1989). Applications of Behavioral Research on Spatial Problems I: Cognition. *Progress in Human Geography, 14*, 57-99.

Green, P. E., Carroll, J. D., & Goldberg, S. M. (1981). A General Approach to Product Design Optimization via Conjoint Analysis. *Journal of Marketing, 45*, 17-37.

Green, P. E. & Srinivasan, V. (1978). Conjoint Analysis in Consumer Research: Issues and Outlook. *Journal of Consumer Research, 5*, 103-123.

Haider, W. & Ewing, G. O. (1990). A Model of Tourist Choices of Hypothetical Caribbean Destinations. *Leisure Sciences, 12*, 33-47.

Hallsworth, A. G. (1988). Repertory Grid Methodology and the Analysis of Group Perception in Retailing. *International Journal of Retailing, 3*, 43-54.

Halperin, W. C. & Gale, N. (1984). Towards Behavioral Models of Spatial Choice: Some Recent Developments. In D. E. Pitfield (Ed.) *Logistic regressions in Regional Sciences* (pp. 88-102). London: Pion Publishing, Inc.

Hornik, K., Stinchcombe, M. & White, H. (1989). Multilayer Feedforward Networks Are Universal Approximators. *Neural Networks, 2.* 359-366.

Jost, A. (1993). Neural Networks: A Logical Progression in Credit and Marketing Decision System. *Credit World, 2*, 26-33.

Kim, S. I. (1988). *Evaluating Spatial Structure Effects In Recreation Travel Using a Gravity Type Model.* Unpublished Ph.D. dissertation, Texas A & M University, College Station.

Liber, S. R. & Fesenmaier, D. R. (1984). Modeling Recreation Choice: A Case Study of Management Alternatives in Chicago. *Regional Studies, 18*, 31-43.

Louviere, J. J. (1976). Information-Processing Theory and Functional Form in Spatial Behavior. In R. G. Golledge & G. Rushton (Ed.), *Spatial Choice and Spatial Behavior: Geographic Essays on the Analysis Preferences and Perceptions* (pp. 211-248). Columbus, OH: Ohio State University Press.

Louviere, J. J. (1988a). *Analyzing Decision Making: Metric Conjoint Analysis.*

Sage University Paper Series on Quantitative Applications in the Social Sciences, 67. Newbury, CA: Sage Publication, Inc.

Louviere, J. J (1988b). Conjoint Analysis Modelling of Stated Preferences: A Review of Theory, Methods, Recent Developments, and External Validity. *Journal of Transport Economics and Policy*, January, 93-119.

Louviere, J. J. & Hensher, D. A. (1983). Using Logistic Regressions with Experimental Design Data to Forecast Consumer Demand for a Unique Cultural Event. *Journal of Consumer Research, 10*, 348-361.

Louviere, J. J. & Woodworth, G. (1983). Design and Analysis of Simulated Consumer Choice or Allocation Experiments: An Approach Based on Aggregate Data. *Journal of Marketing Research, 20*, 350-367.

Louviere, J. J. & Timmermans, H. (1990). Stated Preferences and Choice Models Applied to Recreation Research: A Review. *Leisure Sciences, 12*, 9-32.

Lue, C., Crompton, J. and Stewart, W. (1994). Evidence of Cumulative Attraction in Multi-Destination Travel, typewritten.

Mazanec, J. A. (1992). Classifying Tourists into Market Segments: A Neural Network Approach. *Journal of Travel & Tourism Marketing*, 1, 1, 39-59.

Morgan, N. & Bourlard, H. (1990). Generalization and Parameter Estimation in Feedforward Nets: Some Experiment. In D. S. Touretzky (Ed.). *Advances in Neural Information Processing Systems, 2*. Palo Alto, CA: Morgan Kaufmann Publishers, Inc.

Morely, C. (1994a). Discrete Choice Analysis of the Impact of Tourist Prices, *Journal of Travel Research, 33*, 2, 8-14.

Morely, C. (1994b). Experimental Destination Choice Analysis, *Annals of Tourism Research, 21, 4*, 780-791.

Nelson, M. M. & Illingworth, W. T. (1991). *A Practical Guide to Neural Nets*. Reading, MA: Addison-Wesley Publishing, Co.

NeuralWare, Inc. (1993). *Reference Guide: Software Reference for Professional II/Plus and Neuralworks Explorer.* Pittsburgh, PA: NeuralWare, Inc.

Olshavsky, R. W. (1979). Task Complexity and Contingent Processing in Decision Making: A Replication and Extension. *Organizational Behavior and Human Performance, 24*, 300-316.

Payne, J. W. (1976). Task Complexity and Contingent Processing in Decision Making: An Information Search and Protocol Analysis. *Organization Behavior and Human Performance, 16*, 366-387.

Payne, J. W., J. R. Bettman, & E. J. Johnson (1992). Behavioral Decision Research: a Constructive Processing Perspective. *Annual Review of Psychology, 43*, 87-131.

Richards, M.G. & Ben-Akiva, M. E. (1975). *A Disaggregate Travel Demand Model*. Hants, England: Saxon House, D. C. Health Ltd.

Rumelhart, D.E., Hinton, G. E., & Williams, R. J., (1986). Learning Internal Representation by Error Propagation. In J. A. Anderson & E. Resenfield (Ed.) *Neurocomputing: Foundation of Research*, Chapter 41. (pp. 675-695). Cambridge, MA: MIT Press.

Roehl, W., Ditton, R., Holland, S. and R. Perdue (1992). Developing New Tourism Products: Sport Fishing in the Southeast United States, typewritten.

Schalkoff, R. J., (1992). *Pattern Recognition: Statistical, Structural and Neural Approaches.* New York, NY: John Wiley & Sons, Inc.

Simpson, P. K. (1990). *Artificial Neural Systems: Foundations, Paradigms, Applications, and Implementations.* Elmsford, NY: Pergamon Press, Inc.

Stein, R. (1993). Preprocessing Data for Neural Networks. *AI Expert*, March, 32-37.

Steinberg, D. & Colla, P. (1991). *LOGIT: A Supplementary Module for SYSTAT.* Evanston, IL: SYSTAT, Inc.

Stewart, W. P., Lue, C.C., Fesenmaier, D. R., & Anderson, B. S. (1993). A Comparison Between Welcome Center Visitor and General Highway Auto Travelers. *Journal of Travel Research*, *31*, 40-46.

SPSS Inc. (1993). *SPSS Base System Syntax Reference Guide, Release 6.0.* SPSS Inc. Chicago, IL.

Tierney, P.T. (1993). The Influence of State Traveler Information Centers on Tourist Length of Stay and Expenditures. *Journal of Travel Research*, *31*, 28-31.

Timmermans, H. (1982). Consumer Choice of Shopping Centre: An Information Integration Approach. *Regional Studies*, *16*, 171-182.

Timmermans, H. (1984a). Decompositional Multiattribute Preference Models in Spatial Choice Analysis: A Review of Some Recent Developments. *Progress in Human Geography*, *8*, 189-221.

Timmermans, H. (1984b). Decision Models for Predicting Preferences Among Multiattribute Choice Alternatives. In G. Bahrenberg, M. Fischer, & P. Nijamp (Ed.). *Recent Developments in Spatial Data Analysis* (pp. 337-354). Brookfield, VM: Gower Publishing Co.

Timmermans, H. (1984c). Logistic regressions versus Decompositional Multiattribute Preference Models: A Comparative Analysis of Model Performance in the Context of Spatial Shopping-Behavior. In D. E. Pitfield (Ed.) *Discrete Choice Models in Regional Sciences* (pp. 88-102). London: Pion Publishing, Inc.

Timmermans, H. & Golledge, R. G. (1989). Applications of Behavioral Research on Spatial Problems II: Preference and Choice. *Progress in Human Geography*, *14*, 311-354.

White, H. (1988). Economic Prediction Using Neural Networks: The Case of IBM Daily Stock Returns. IEEE International Conference on Neural Networks, *2*, 451-458. San Diego, California.

White, H. (1989). Neural-Network: Learning and Statistics. *AI Expert*, *12*, 48-52.

White, H. (1989). Some Asymptotic Results for Learning in Single Hidden-Layer Feedforward Network Model. *Journal of American Statistical Association*, *84*, 1003-1013.

Wiggins, V. L., Engquist, S. K., & Looper, L. T. (1992). *Applying Neural Networks to Air Force Personnel Analysis* (Report No. AL-TR-1991-0118). Brooks Air Force, TX: Human Resources Directorate Manpower and Personnel Research Division.

Yang, H., Kitamura, R., Jovanis, P. P., Vaughn, K. M. & Abdel-Aty, M. A. (1993). Exploration of Route Choice Behavior With Advanced Traveler Information Using Neural Network Concepts. *Transportation*, *20*, 199-223.

SURE Estimation
of Tourism Demand System Model:
U.S. Case

Sung Soo Pyo
Muzaffer Uysal
John T. Warner

SUMMARY. The purpose of this study is to build a tourism demand system model which incorporates inbound, outbound and domestic tourism of the U.S. The study utilizes the Seemingly Unrelated Regression (SURE) technique to investigate the international tourist flow between the U.S. and Canada, Japan, Mexico, United Kingdom, and inland European countries. Relevant marketing and policy implications for income and price elasticities are discussed. *[Article copies available from The Haworth Document Delivery Service: 1-800-342-9678. E-mail address: getinfo@haworth.com]*

INTRODUCTION

Tourism is a study of the temporary human movement to destinations outside of work and residential areas, of activities performed at the des-

Dr. Sung Soo Pyo is Department Head, Department of Tourism Management, Kyonggi University, Samhwan A. 1102 Dong 302 Ho, Imae-dong, Poondang-gu, Sungnam-city, 460-060, Korea. Dr. Muzaffer Uysal is Professor of Tourism, Department of Hospitality and Tourism Management, Virginia Polytechnic Institute and State University, 351 Wallace Hall, Blacksburg VA 24061-0429. Dr. John T. Warner is Professor of Economics, Department of Economics, Clemson University, Sirrine Hall, Clemson, SC, 29634.

Address correspondence to: Dr. Muzaffer Uysal, VPI, Department of Hospitality & Tourism Management, 351 Wallace Hall, Blacksburg, VA 24061-0429.

[Haworth co-indexing entry note]: "SURE Estimation of Tourism Demand System Model: U.S. Case." Pyo, Sung Soo, Muzaffer Uysal, and John T. Warner. Co-published simultaneously in *Journal of Travel & Tourism Marketing* (The Haworth Press, Inc.) Vol. 5, No. 1/2, 1996, pp. 145-160; and *Recent Advances in Tourism Marketing Research* (ed: Daniel R. Fesenmaier, Joseph T. O'Leary, and Muzaffer Uysal) The Haworth Press, Inc., 1996, pp. 145-160. Single or multiple copies of this article are available from The Haworth Document Delivery Service [1-800-342-9678, 9:00 a.m. - 5:00 p.m. (EST). E-mail address: getinfo@haworth.com].

tinations, of facilities which cater to tourist needs, and of the impacts that both man and industry have on the host socio-cultural, economic, and physical environments (Mathieson and Wall, 1984). This broad definition dramatizes the complex and multi-faceted aspects of tourism (Gunn, 1988).

Due to tourism's complexity and diversity, the study of tourism needs to utilize knowledge of various disciplines to expand and enhance the understanding of tourism phenomena and requires a systems approach. Of the many disciplines which contribute to the study of tourism, economics covers the rational behavior and market exchange of human activities (Hirshleifer, 1988). Specifically, tourism researchers examine tourism supply, demand, balance of payments, foreign exchange, employment, expenditures, development, multipliers, and other economic factors (Loeb, 1982; Crouch, 1991; Uysal and Crompton, 1984; Summary 1987; Witt and Martin, 1987). Most of this research has employed some sort of economic modelling based on economic theory. Understanding the nature of the effects that an independent variable of econometric models has on the dependent variable allows the user to estimate the change in demand for the given independent variable change (Uysal and Crompton, 1985; Smeral, 1988; Johnson and Ashworth, 1990; Calantone, Benedetto and Bojanic, 1987; Witt and Witt, 1992). However, the econometric models may suffer from multicollinearity, lack of accuracy, and relevance of data, variability of the parameter estimates, and problems caused by data aggregation (Sheldon and Var, 1985). Therefore, it is important to develop a model that will overcome some of the problems inherent in the econometric models. The purpose of this study is to build a U. S. Tourism demand systems model using the Seemingly Unrelated Regression (SURE) procedure.[1]

This application deals with the international tourist flow between the U.S. and eight other nations which were chosen for their relatively large market shares of international tourism and for data availability. Thus, the study analyzes inbound, outbound, and domestic tourism together in a tourism system.

VARIABLES AND SPECIFICATION OF THE MODEL

As classical economic theory suggests, the relative price of tourism in destination countries, prices in other countries as related goods, and income at the origin are the independent variables for explaining international tourism demand (Gray, 1970; Armstrong, 1972; Archer, 1980). Even though transportation cost is frequently included in various studies, this study did not consider this variable in the model because most studies which have extensively dealt with U.S. international tourism suggest not using a transportation cost variable in the model. The one exception is the study by Stronge (1982). In a study by Keintz (1971) exploring the demand for international travel to and from the United States, the travel cost results revealed that the variable was not significant in many equations. Sami (1971) has experienced similar results in his study investigating the determinants of United States demand for tourism. Loeb (1982) eliminated the travel cost variable from analysis of international travel to the United States due to the difficulty of obtaining accurate data on transportation costs, and insignificant statistical results of travel costs in previous studies. Some studies (Anastasopoulou 1984; Artus, 1972; Fujii and Mak, 1985) have found a high (negative) correlation between the airfare and income variables, which cause difficulty evaluating the effects of both income and travel costs on international tourism demand. As a result, the model without the transportation cost variable was used in this study.

In defining the model, tourists are assumed to maximize their travel experience under individual budget constraints. Consequently, the demand for tourism is a function of income and prices (Abu-Ghazaleh, 1985). Also, consumer theory suggests that only real income and relative prices enter the demand function (Silberberg, 1978). It is assumed that the cross elasticity between the demand for international travel and demand for other goods in the origin country is zero. In other words, a portion of time and income for foreign travel is already allocated irrespective of price of home goods and services.

Thus, the demand function for the international inbound and outbound tourism could be specified as:

$$X_{ij} = f\{Y_j, (P_i/P_j), (P_k/P_j)\}. \tag{1}$$

where, x = quantity index of travel goods and services sold,
Y = per capita real income in U.S. dollars,
P = price adjusted by the exchange rates,
i = destination country,
j = origin country, and
k = all other relevant countries.

The function indicates that the quantity of travel goods sold (X) in country i to tourists from country j is a function of the real income of the origin country (Y_j), and relative prices of various countries including destination (P_i) compared to the origin ($_j$).

The quantity index of travel goods sold calculated from expenditures was used as the dependent variable since the number of tourists does not correctly indicate the quantity of tourist goods and services sold. Also, the bed nights do not include nights spent in homes of friends and relatives and may exclude data of supplementary accommodations such as non-registered lodging facilities (Barry and O'Hagan, 1972). However, the expenditure terms indicate the volume of tourist goods sold whether tourists stay in commercial accommodations or not.

If the nominal expenditure is divided by a price index, the result becomes real expenditure or the quantity index of travel goods sold (Sami, 1971). Because tourist money is spent in destinations, the quantity index was obtained by deflating the nominal expenditure with the price index of a destination. Further, the own price elasticity of demand is for the price of destinations; the price elasticity of demand is calculated from the nominal expenditure, the prices which are going to be cancelled out are the destination prices. Therefore, the tourist expenditure should be deflated by the price index of the destination.

All income was calculated in terms of U.S. dollars. To calculate per capita GNP, GNP was divided by population. Per capita GNP was further divided by the destination price index to make real terms. The value of the income elasticity of tourism is useful in determining the relative merits of tourism as an avenue of production diversification (Joseph and Jud, 1973; Jud and Joseph, 1974).

At the approximation of the relative price of tourist goods and services, the Consumer Price Index (CPI) was utilized. Even though the U.S. has a travel price index, only CPIs were used for consistency because other countries do not have a travel price index. In addition, the CPI was further adjusted toward a common price by multiplying per unit price in the origin currency using U.S. dollars. Exchange rates between foreign countries were not considered, since it is assumed that the U.S. has very limited control in exchange rates between other countries, and, therefore, only exchange rates directly related to the U.S. have important policy implications. Estimates of the price elasticity of tourism exports are meaningful in the determination of future foreign exchange policies and in the calculation of gains and losses from future currency devaluation (Joseph and Jud, 1973).

Only the prices of Canada and Mexico are considered in the domestic tourism equation since they are closely related to the domestic tourism due to their proximity to the U.S. The functional form for the U.S. domestic tourism is:

$$X = \{Y, (TPI/CPI), (Pc/TPI), (Pm/TPI)\}. \tag{2}$$

where, X = quantity index of domestic tourist goods sold,
Y = per capita real GNP in the U.S.
TPI = travel price index of the U.S.
CPI = consumer price index of the U.S.,
Pc = consumer price index of Canada, and
PM = consumer price index of Mexico.

SPECIFICATION AND INTERPRETATION OF THE MODEL

One functional form of each demand equation, which originates with Abu-Ghazaleh (1984) and Anastasopoulos (1984), is the linear specification:

$$X = a_1 + a_2Y_j + a_3(P_i/P_j) + a_k(P_k/P_j) + \varepsilon. \tag{3}$$

For convenient elasticity estimation, an alternative specification is the log-linear:

$$\ln X = a + B\ln Y_j + Y_i \ln(P_i/P_j) + Y_k \ln(P_k/P_j) + \varepsilon. \tag{4}$$

By performing a logarithmic manipulation, the log-linear demand function becomes:

$$\ln X = a + B\ln y_j + Y_i \ln P_i + Y_k \ln P_k - (Y_i + Y_k) \ln P_j + \varepsilon. \tag{5}$$

The sign of income elasticity is expected to be positive, since as income increases, the propensity of travel increases. One can obtain the income elasticity of demand by differentiating (1.21) in terms of Y_j:

$$\partial \ln X_i / \partial Y_j = \partial \beta in Y_j / \partial Y_j. \tag{6}$$
$$(1/X_i)(\partial X_i \partial Y_j) = \beta / Y_j. \tag{7}$$
$$(Y_j/X_i)(\partial X_i/\partial Y_j) = \beta. \tag{8}$$

Therefore, the income elasticity of demand is β. The income elasticity of demand indicates the percentage change of the tourism product quality demanded as income changes by one percent, other variables holding constant. If income elasticity is less than one, the goods and services are called necessities. If it is greater than one, they are classified as luxuries. If it has a negative sign, they are inferior goods and services (Clarke, 1978).

The elasticity of demand for travel is expected to be greater than one; thus, tourism goods and services can be classified as a luxury. This assumption is justified since the percentage change of discretionary income, a part of which is the travel budget, is greater than that of total income (Pyo, Uysal and McClellan, 1991). However, this assumption may not hold in certain market segments (Uysal and Crompton, 1984; Witt and Martin, 1985).

The expected sign of the price elasticity of demand for travel y_i is negative since as the price of the destination increases, the demand for travel decreases. The price elasticity of demand indicates the percentage change in tourism product quantity demanded as the destination price changes by one percent, other factors held constant. The price elasticity of demand is y_i, because:

$$\partial \ln X_i / \partial P_i = Y_i \, (\partial \ln P_i \partial P_i). \tag{9}$$
$$(1/X_i) \, (\partial X_i / \partial P_i) \, (\partial X_i / \partial P_i) = Y_i / P_i. \tag{10}$$
$$(P_i/X_i) \, (\partial X_i / \partial P_i) = Y_i. \tag{11}$$

The expected sign of own price elasticities are negative. However, the sign of cross elasticities (y_i) is not decisive. The signs of the y_k can be either positive or negative. If the sign is the same as y_i (negative), tourism of country k is complementary to that of country i. If foreign tourism in country i increases, the complementary country tourism also improves. If the sign is different (positive), they are substitutes, and competing against each other for international tourism. If the prices in country k increase, tourists move to a less expensive country i, instead of travelling in country k. The elasticity of substitution indicates the percentage change of the country's tourism product quantity demanded in destination i as one percent price change in k-th destination, if other countries are the same. The *elasticity* substitution is:

$$\partial \ln X_i / \partial P_k = Yk \, (\partial \ln P_k / \partial P_k). \tag{12}$$
$$(1/X_i) \, (\partial X_i / \partial P_k) = Y_k / P_k. \tag{13}$$
$$(P_k/X_i) \, (\partial X_i / \partial P_k) = Y_k. \tag{14}$$

The effect of exchange rate on income and prices can be computed as an analogy of the income elasticity of demand, own price elasticity of demand and elasticity of substitution. They are β, y_i, and y_k, respectively. The elasticities of exchange rate indicate the percentage change of tourism goods sold due to a one percent change of the exchange rate. The elasticity effect due to exchange rate change on income and price is the same as the elasticity of income and price since:

$$Pk = (CPI_k) \, (\text{Exchange Rate}_k) \tag{15}$$

$$\ln P_k = \ln(CPI_k) + \ln(Exchange\ Rate_k). \tag{16}$$

DATA ANALYSIS

Tourism expenditure data were obtained from the *Survey of Current Business* (United State Department of Commerce, 1973 to 1986). The data, covering eighteen years from 1968 to 1985, included eight nations: Canada, Mexico, Japan, United Kingdom, Germany, France, Italy, and the Netherlands. Data on gross national product (GNP = consumption expenditure), population, consumer price index (CPI) and exchange rate were compiled from the *International Financial Statistics Yearbook* (International Monetary Fund, 1988). Data for the domestic tourism were acquired from the US Travel Data Center (1989).

The last three years of France's GNP, one year of Mexico's GNP, and the first four years of domestic travel sales amounts were not available. Those missing GNPs were calculated by taking GNP and Gross Domestic Product (GDP) ratios for the last two years, and multiplying by GDP. The travel sales amounts were extrapolated by considering two years (1972 to 1974) changes in real sales amounts. If the Travel Price Index (TPI) is 100 in 1967, the TPI in 1972 is 123 (Goeldner and Duea, 1984). The average annual change was adjusted with TPI (1980 = 100). Nominal domestic tourism expenditures were calculated by considering the real travel sales amount and TPI.

Multicollinearity

In the screening process to build a tourism demand systems model, it was found that relative price variables were highly correlated with each other. This result indicates that there are close economic relationships between certain country groups. Such groups of countries are four nations in Europe (France, Germany, Italy, and the Netherlands) and two countries in North America (Canada and the U.S.). To resolve the problem of linear dependency, data of the four European nations were aggregated, and labeled as "inland European countries" because the majority of those countries are located in inland Europe. This data aggregation reduces the number of equations from seventeen (8 nations * 2 + 1 for domestic tourism) to eleven. The expenditure data of the four nations were generated by adding the corresponding four tourist expenditures. Income and price index were calculated by weighting them according to the travel expenditure share.

Autocorrelation

The model was first estimated by OLS. Even though there was no equation with the Durbin-Watson d statistic below the lower boundary, the equations with the statistic below the upper boundary were transformed by using the Cochrane-Orcutt and Prais-Winston procedures and were estimated. The autocorrelation coefficient (p) was estimated by subtracting the half of the Durbin-Watson d statistic from one since:

$$\text{Durbin-Watson d} \cong 2(1 - p). \tag{17}$$

The first observation (the Prais-Winston method case) was transformed by:

$$x^*_1 = \sqrt{}\,(1 - p^2)x_1. \tag{18}$$

The other observations, either Cochrane-Orcutt or Prais-Winston methods, were transformed by:

$$x^*_t = x_t - px_{t-1}. \tag{19}$$

When the number of data points is relatively small, an equation with the Durbin-Watson d statistic below the upper boundary tends to have the autocorrelation problem. However, there is no reason to believe that every equation with such a Durbin-Watson d statistic has an autocorrelation problem. Furthermore, if R^2 is too low, and F and t scores are not significant, the model may not be useful for the demand analysis. Therefore, this study compared parameter estimates with raw data and transformed data due to autocorrelations, and chose better estimates in terms of R^2 and significance of F and t scores.

The Prais-Winston method estimation performed better in the models of the U.S. to Canada and U.K. travel, and with U.S. domestic tourism over the estimation with the original data. The significance of F scores and R^2 were improved. Therefore, only those equation estimations were compared by transformation methods.

During the data transformation, the Cochrane-Orcutt method misses one observation, and thereby loses one degree of freedom. Since the number of data points of this study is small (eighteen) and the number of independent variables was relatively large (six for the international and four for the domestic tourism), losing one degree of freedom is not desirable. Consequently, all models with the Prais-Winston transformation perform better in the significance statistics than those models with the Cochrane-Orcutt transformation.

For the SURE estimation, the Durbin-Watson d statistic was obtained from the original data analysis. If the statistic was lower than the upper boundary, the correspondent data were transformed by using the Prais-Winston method. By comparing those two results, first, the decision to use either original data or transformed data was made. Second, by using appropriate data, another parameter estimation was performed. Finally, by comparing all estimations, the final model was obtained. As a result, the demand system used transformed data for the U.K. to the U.S., the U.S. to Canada, and the domestic tourism equations. Tables 1 and 2 depict the results of the final tourism demand system model for inbound and out-bound tourism. However, in the following section, the discussions on the study findings were simultaneously provided.

FINDINGS AND MARKETING IMPLICATIONS

Income Elasticity

Income elasticities with positive signs ranged from 0.499 (US to Canada) to 3.827 (US to inland European countries). Two income elasticities of border country travel are almost unitary (Mexico to US = 1.080) or inelastic (US to Canada = 0.499). Income elasticities of other border country travel have "wrong signs" (Canada to US and US to Mexico). And, the income elasticity of domestic tourism is inelastic (0.889). This finding suggests that visits and/or tours to neighboring countries may be necessities. Classification of border country tourism as a necessity can be further justified, since a large portion of border traffic is composed of shopping (Canada to the US and Mexico to the US). Also, tourism in Canada and Mexico is relatively less expensive than that in the U.S. due to exchange rate differentials. Relatively high income elasticities to overseas countries suggest that travel to overseas countries can be considered as luxury goods whose customers are usually high income people. This income elasticity difference may be explained by income effects on travel costs.

Price Elasticity

The price elasticities of demand ranged from -0.560 (US to UK) to -4.282 (Japan to US). This elasticity indicates the percentage change of the tourism goods sold in the destination due to a one percent change in the destination price.

The most price sensitive markets are the inland European and Japanese

TABLE 1. Seemingly Unrelated Regression Equation (SURE) Estimation of Inbound Tourism

Canada to US D-W – 1.766

	Intercept	Income	Pus/Pc	Pm/Pc	Pj/Pc	Puk/Pc	Pe/Pc
Coefficient	7.485	-0.302	-2.107	0.135	0.320	0.441	0.201
Significance	0.004	0.357	0.007	0.205	0.202	0.003	0.332

Mexico to US D-W – 1.310

	Intercept	Income	Pus/Pm	Pc/Pm	Pj/Pm	Puk/Pm	Pe/Pm
Coefficient	-0.882	1.080	1.550	-1.597	0.567	0.514	-0.590
Significance	0.647	0.012	0.198	0.165	0.227	0.098	0.146

Japan to US D-W = 1.864

	Intercept	Income	Pus/Pj	Pc/Pj	Pm/Pj	Pj/Puk	Pe/Pj
Coefficient	-13.693	2.544	-4.282	4.350	0.449	0.892	0.590
Significance	0.000	0.000	0.000	0.000	0.053	0.001	0.198

U.K. to US D-W = 0.963

	Intercept	Income	Pus/Puk	Pc/Puk	Pm/Puk	Pj/Puk	Pe/Puk
Coefficient	0.690	0.743	2.794	-3.007	0.109	0.405	0.498
Significance	0.047	0.353	0.060	0.053	0.664	0.468	0.383

France, Germany, Italy, and Netherlands to US D-W = 2.694

	Intercept	Income	Pus/Pe	Pc/Pe	Pj/Pe	Pm/Pe	Puk/Pe
Coefficient	-4921	2.687	-2.559	2.499	-1.535	-0.416	1.808
Significance	0.002	0.000	0.018	0.040	0.000	0.000	0.000

Note: Weighted Mean Square Error = 0.865 (d.f. = 123). Weighted R square = 0.99. The equations for the U.K. to the US used data transformed by the Prais-Winston method. The Durbin-Watson statistics of the equation came from the SURE estimation of the original data. Pus = price of the US, c = Canada, m = Mexico, J = Japan, uk = U.K., e = inland European countries, TPI = travel price index, and CPI = consumer price index.

TABLE 2. Seemingly Unrelated Regression Equation (SURE) Estimation of Outbound Tourism and Domestic Tourism

US to Canada
D-W = 1.493

	Intercept	Income	Pc/Pus	Pm/Pus	Pj/Pus	Puk/Pus	Pe/Pus
Coefficient	0.332	0.499	0.255	0.107	-0.012	-0.198	-0.181
Significance	0.064	0.011	0.513	0.196	0.945	0.046	0.335

US to Mexico
D-W = 1.811

	Intercept	Income	Pm/Pus	Pc/Pus	Pj/Pus	Puk/Pus	Pe/Pus
Coefficient	22.163	-3.024	0.272	4.616	0.336	-0.494	1.149
Significance	0.030	0.080	0.433	0.003	0.669	0.177	0.129

US to Japan
D-W = 1.727

	Intercept	Income	Pj/Pus	Pc/Pus	Pm/Pus	Puk/Pus	Pe/Pus
Coefficient	-16.495	3.407	0.363	0.380	-0.207	-0.228	-1.393
Significance	0.066	0.034	0.524	0.657	0.383	0.366	0.017

US to U.K.
D-W = 1.446

	Intercept	Income	Puk/Pus	Pc/Pus	Pm/Pus	Pj/Pus	Ps/Pus
Coefficient	-11.846	2.811	-0.560	-0.459	-0.110	0.141	-0.352
Significance	0.022	0.004	0.003	0.396	0.497	0.687	0.250

US to France, Germany, Italy, and Netherlands
D-W = 1.505

	Intercept	Income	Pe/Pus	Pc/Pus	Pm/Pus	Pj/Pus	Puk/Pus
Coefficient	-18.433	3.827	-1.624	-0.127	-0.185	-0.144	-0.249
Significance	0.002	0.001	0.000	0.799	0.192	0.655	0.101

Domestic Tourism

US Domestic
D-W = -0.932

	Intercept	Income	TPI/CPI	Pc/TPI	Pm/TPI
Coefficient	0.380	0.889	-2.061	-0.499	-0.029
Significance	0.000	0.000	0.001	0.027	0.462

Note: Weighted Mean Square Error = 0.865 (d.f. = 123). Weighted R Square = 0.990. Equations for the US to Canada, and the US domestic tourism used data transformed by the Prais-Winston method. The Durbin-Watson statistics of those equations came from the SURE estimation of the original data. Pus = Price of the US, c = Canada, M = Mexico, j = Japan, uk = U.K., e = inland European countries, TPI = travel price index, and CPI = consumer price index.

tourists to the U.S. since most of the price variables are significant in those equations. The least price sensitive segment is Mexican tourists to the U.S. None of the prices in the equation are significant at the 0.05 probability level. Therefore, price strategies to inland European and Japanese markets can be effective. But the strategy may not be useful in enticing Mexican tourists to the U.S.

Cross Price Elasticity and Market Strategy

Expenditures from Canadian tourism in the U.S. are sensitive to price changes in the U.S. (own price elasticity = -2.107). Thus, price strategies can be effective in attracting Canadian tourism in the U.S. All countries are competing against the U.S. for Canadian tourist dollars (positive signs), especially the U.K. Marketing strategies rendering benefits for visiting the U.S. instead of the U.K. need to be developed to attract potential Canadian U.K. visitors to the U.S.

Mexican tourism in the U.S. has almost unitary income elasticity (1.080). This almost unitary income elasticity may be due to the characteristics of the Mexican tourist market which is composed of only a small number of affluent Mexicans, and thus, per capita GNP change in Mexico does not induce much change in tourism quantity demanded. The unitary income and (insignificant) price elasticities may indicate that the Mexican market is stable. Also, they tend to travel to Canada when they travel to the U.S. (insignificant cross elasticity = 1.597). However, the spillover effect is not strong. Also, when Mexican tourism in the U.S. increases, these tourists' trips to inland European countries increase (negative sign). Since the price effects are not significant enough, other marketing efforts (for example, promoting favorite destinations for Mexicans) can be more effective than the price strategy in this market segment.

To attract Japanese tourism in the U.S., targeting high income people (income elasticity = 2.554) with price-appealing messages (price elasticity = -4.282) is a good strategy. All countries compete for the Japanese tourism market. The competition between the U.S. and Canada is especially keen (cross price elasticity = 4.350). Concurrent with a one percent Canadian price increase, Japanese tourism in the U.S. increases by 4.340 percent.

The income of U.K. people does not significantly affect their tourism to the U.S. However, the U.S. price significantly influences U.K. tourism in the U.S. Tourists from the U.K. to the U.S. also tend to travel to Canada (cross price elasticity = -3.007). Therefore, developing package tours including the U.S. and Canada can be the first step to sell more U.S. tourist goods to the U.K. visitors. The offerings of this package should be attractive enough to compete with Mexico, Japan and the inland countries in Europe (positive sign).

As with Japanese tourism, the income and price elasticities of the inland European country tourism in the U.S. are relatively large (income elasticity =2.687 and price elasticity = − 2.559). Therefore, the target market in the region is high income people, and a price strategy also can be effective. Canada and the U.K. are competing against the U.S. for those tourists (positive sign). For a one percent price hike in Canada and the U.K., tourist goods sold to the inland European people in the U.S. increase by 2.499% and 1.808% respectively. On the other hand, there is a spillover effect revealing multiple destination behavior, with Mexico in particular as another concurrent destination (negative sign).

The Americans consider travel to Canada a necessity (income elasticity = 0.499), and they are less sensitive to the tourism price in Canada (insignificant price elasticity = 0.255). These elasticities may be due to the relatively stronger purchasing power of U.S. dollars compared to Canadian dollars. Consequently, Canada's tourism promotion to attract the U.S. general public with appropriate themes can be more effective than price strategies. Mexico tends to compete against Canada for U.S. tourism (positive sign). As tours by Americans in Canada increase, travel by U.S. tourists in the U.K. also expands.

Mexico competes against all countries for U.S. tourism except for the U.K. The competition between Mexico and Canada is especially keen. If tourism in Canada becomes more expensive, Americans will tend to change their destinations from Canada to Mexico. Specifically, as the price in Canada increases by one percent, the U.S. tourism in Mexico increases by 4.616%.

To attract the U.S. tourists to Japan, high income people are the target market (income elasticity of demand = 3.407), and a favorite tourism product marketing emphasis is better than the price promotion since the price variable is not significant. Japan and Canada are competing for U.S. tourism. However, as tourism quantities demanded by the U.S. tourists in other countries increase, tourism by the U.S. tourists in Japan improves (negative sign).

High income people of the U.S. tend to visit the U.K. (income elasticity = 2.811). The U.S. tourists are not sensitive to the tourism product price sensitivity (price elasticity = − 0.56). High income people of the U.S. tend to visit inland European countries (income elasticity of demand = 3.827), and they are relatively price sensitive (price elasticity of demand =   1.624). Income and price variables should be considered in promoting U.S. visitors to those countries. The U.S. tourism in other countries shows the same trend as tourism in the four European nations by U.S. visitors (negative sign).

The U.S. domestic travel is a necessity and responds sensitively to the price change (income elasticity = 0.889, and price elasticity = −2.081). Therefore, promoting to the general public with price strategies can be suggested. Domestic tourism and travel to Canada and Mexico are complementary (negative sign). Thus, as domestic tourism improves, tourism to Canada and Mexico also increases.

CONCLUDING REMARKS

The most severe competitor of the U.S. for foreign tourism is Canada, especially for Japanese and inland European tourism. On the other hand, strong cooperation between the U.S. and Canada can be recommended to attract U.K. tourists to North America. If Canada loses price competitiveness, Mexico benefits greatly from it.

The marketing implications can be used for national and regional level international tourism promotion. Since a destination as a whole appeals to tourists, national or regional level tourism promotion is necessary. Also, this promotional activity may be more cost effective than promotion by segments of tourism components such as airlines and hotels. The U.S. Travel and Tourism Administration (USTTA) or regional tourism organizations can be a catalyst or facilitator for such tourism promotion.

It is hoped that this model will be applied to other countries with more observations. Analyses with micro data is also recommended. If the results are compared, literature related to tourism analyses can be enriched and, thus, advancement of the tourism demand systems model can be made.

NOTE

1. SURE is a technique for explaining the complex phenomena of tourism by considering correlations between disturbance terms (unexplained variance) of a systems model. All variables relevant to tourism cannot be entered in a model. Therefore, the unexplained variance of an equation can be related with the residuals of other equations in a system. By considering correlations between residuals, the SURE technique proves a marginal gain in efficiency over the single ordinary least square (OLS) equation estimation (Maddala, 1988).

REFERENCES

Abu-Ghazaleh, M. (1985). Economics of Tourism in Jordan. *Dissertation Abstract International*, 46(8), 2371-A.

Anastasopoulos, P.G. (1984). Interdependencies in International Travel: The Role of Relative Prices. A Case Study of theMediterranean Region, *Dissertation Abstract International*, 45(5), 1480-A.

Archer, B.H. (1976). Demand Forecasting. Wales: University of Wales Press.

Archer, B.H. (1980). Forecasting Demand: Quantitative and Intuitive Techniques. *Tourism Management*, 1(1), 5-12.

Armstrong, G.W.G. (1972). International Tourism: Coming or Going, The Methodological Problems of Forecasting. *Futures*, (June), 115-125.

Artus, J.R. (1972). An Econometric Analysis of International Travel. *International Monetary Fund Staff Papers*, 19(3), 579-614.

Barry, K. and O'Hagan, J. (1972). An Econometric Study of British Tourist Expenditure in Ireland. *Economic and Social Review*, 3(2), 6869-A.

Calantone, R.J., Benedetto, C.A.D., and Bojanic, D. (1987). A Comprehensive Review of the Tourism Forecasting Literature. *Journal of Travel Research*, 26 (2), 28-39.

Clarke, C.D. (1978). An Analysis of the Determinants of Demand for Tourism in Barbados. *Dissertation Abstract International*, 49(11), 6869-A.

Crouch, G. (1991). Determinant of International Tourist Flows: Findings from 30 Years of Empirical Research. *TTRA Conference Proceedings*, pp. 45-46.

Crouch, G. (1992). Effect of Income and Price on International Tourism. *Annals of Tourism Research*, 19(4), 643-664.

Fujii, E.T. and Mak, J. (1981). Forecasting Travel Demand When the Explanatory Variables are Highly Correlated. *Journal of Travel Research*, 18(4), 31-34.

Fujii, E.T. and Mak, J. (1981). Forecasting Travel Demand; Some Methodological Issues. *The Annals of Regional Science*, 15(2), 72-82.

Goeldner, C. R. and Duea, K.P. (1983). *Travel Trends in the United States and Canada*. Colorado: University of Colorado.

Gray, H. Peter. (1970). International Travel Internation Trade. Lexington: Health Lexington Books.

Gunn, C. A. (1988). *Tourism Planning* (2ns ed.). New York: Taylor and Francis.

Hirshleifer, J. (1988). *Price Theory and Applications* (4th ed.). New Jersey: Prentice-Hall Inc.

International Monetary Fund. (1988). *International Financial Statistics Yearbook*. Washington, D.C.: International Monetary Fund.

Johnson, P. and J. Ashworth (1990). Modeling Tourism Demand: A Summary Review. *Leisure Studies*, (9) 145-160.

Joseph, H. and Jud, G.D. (1973). Estimates of Tourism Demand: Latin American In W. Krause, G.D. Jud, and H. Joseph, *International Tourism and Latin American Development* (25-42). Texas: University of Texas at Austin.

Jud, G.D. and Joseph, H. (1974). International Demand for Latin American Tourism. *Growth and Change*, 5(1), 25-31.

Keintz, R.M. (1971). The Demand for International Travel to and from the United States. *Dissertation Abstract International*, 32(1), 62-A.

Loeb, P.D. (1982). International Travel to the United States: An Econometric Evaluation. *Annals of Tourism Research*, 9(1), 7-20.

Maddala, G.S. (1988). *Introduction to Econometrics*. New York: Macmillan Publishing Company.

Mathieson, A. and Wall, G. (1984). *Tourism: Economic, Physical and Social Impacts* (3rd impression). New York: Longman Group Limited.

Pyo, S., Uysal, M. and R. McLellan (1991). A Linear Expenditure Model for Tourism Demand. *Annals of Tourism Research*, 18(3), 443-454.

Quayson, J. and Var, T. (1982). A Tourism Demand Function for the Okanagan, BC. *Tourism Management*, 3(2), 108-115.

Sami, M. (1978). The Determinants of the United States Demand for Tourism. *Dissertation Abstract International*, 32(6), 2891-A.

Sheldon, P.J. and Var, T. (1985). Tourism Forecasting: A Review of Empirical Research. *Journal of Forecasting*, 4, 183-195.

Silberberg, E. (1990). *The Structure of Economics: A Mathematical Analysis.* New York: McGraw-Hill Book.

Smeral, E. (1988). Tourism Demand, Economic Theory and Econometrics: An Integrated Approach. *Journal of Travel Research*, Spring 38-43.

Stronge, W. (1982). The Overseas Demand for Tourism in the United States. *The Review of Regional Studies*, 12 (3), 40-53.

Summary, R. (1987). Estimation of Tourism Demand by Multivariable Regression Analysis. *Tourism Management*, 8 (2), 317-322.

United States Department of Commerce (1973 to 1986). *Survey of Current Business.* Bureau of Economic Analysis of the U.S. Department of Commerce.

US Travel Data Center. (1989). *The 1988-89 Economic Review of Travel in America.* Washington, DC: US Travel Data Center.

Uysal, M. and Crompton, J.L. (1984). Determinants of Demand for International Tourist Flows to Turkey. *Tourism Management*, 5(4): 288-297.

Uysal, M. and Crompton, J.L. (1985). An Overview of Approaches Used to Forecast Tourism Demand. *Journal of Travel Research*, 23(4), 7-15.

Witt, S.F. and Martin, C.A. (1985). Forecasting Future Trends in European Tourist Demand. *Tourist Review*, 40(4), 12-20.

Witt, S.F. and Martin, C.A. (1987). Econometric Models for Forecasting International Tourism Demand. *Journal of Travel Research*, 25(3), 23-30.

Witt, S. and C. Witt (1992). Modeling and Forecasting Demand in Tourism. *Academic Press.*

Leisure Market Segmentation:
An Integrated
Preferences/Constraints-Based Approach

Marcus P. Stemerding

Harmen Oppewal

Theo A. M. Beckers

Harry J. P. Timmermans

SUMMARY. Traditional segmentation schemes are often based on a grouping of consumers with similar preference functions. The research steps, ultimately leading to such segmentation schemes, are typically independent. In the present article, a new integrated approach to segmentation is introduced, which incorporates elements of traditional approaches, albeit in a new and innovative way. The new methodology and its potential managerial and policy relevance is illustrated using the Dutch initiative of reducing car use for leisure trips as an example. *[Article copies available from The Haworth Document Delivery Service: 1-800-342-9678. E-mail address: getinfo@haworth.com]*

Marcus P. Stemerding is a PhD candidate, Harmen Oppewal is Assistant Professor, and Harry J. P. Timmermans is Professor of Urban Planning, Eindhovn University of Technology, Urban Planning Group, postvak 20, P.O. Box 513, 5600 MB Eindhoven, The Netherlands. E-mail: M.P.Stemerding@bwk.tue.nl. Harry Timmermans is also holder of the Carthy Foundation Chair of Marketing, at the University of Alberta, Edmonton, Canada. Theo A. M. Beckers is Professor of Leisure Studies, Tilburg University.

This research project is financially supported by the Co-operation Centre, Tilburg and Eindhoven Universities (SOBU).

[Haworth co-indexing entry note]: "Leisure Market Segmentation: An Integrated Preferences/ Constraints-Based Approach." Stemerding et al. Co-published simultaneously in *Journal of Travel & Tourism Marketing* (The Haworth Press, Inc.) Vol. 5, No. 3, 1996, pp. 161-185; and *Recent Advances in Tourism Marketing Research* (ed: Daniel R. Fesenmaier, Joseph T. O'Leary, and Muzaffer Uysal) The Haworth Press, Inc., 1996, pp. 161-185. Single or multiple copies of this article are available from The Haworth Document Delivery Service [1-800-342-9678, 9:00 a.m. - 5:00 p.m. (EST). E-mail address: getinfo@haworth.com].

161

INTRODUCTION

One of the central issues in tourism marketing concerns the identification of target groups. Effective segmentation schemes are considered to be of utmost importance for successfully marketing tourism products or implementing tourism-related policies. In methodological terms, segmentation research has typically followed either of the following two strategies. Market segments can be derived by clustering respondents on the basis of their socio-economic characteristics or overt behavior. Alternatively, segmentation can be based on individuals' preferences for various products.

The latter approach usually involves various steps. First, the attributes influencing tourism-related decisions are elicited. A variety of methods, ranging from factor listing to repertory grid analyses, is available to identify these influential attributes. Once these attributes have been identified, some kind of preference or choice model is used to describe individuals' preference functions. Especially, conjoint and compositional preference models have found ample application in tourism research. The estimated preference functions are then used to identify groups of individuals which are homogeneous in terms of their underlying preference functions.

Although these methodologies are easy to use and have resulted in many interesting and actionable segmentation schemes, they nevertheless have some obvious shortcomings. First, the preference approach described above involves a series of truly independent steps. Often, the sample responding to the attribute elicitation task is different from the sample of respondents involved in the conjoint experiment. While this may be acceptable practice if the focus is on generalizability, it prevents one from segmenting respondents on individual information regarding both the kind of attributes and the nature of the preference function. Of course, this is the direct result of the fact that the two steps are not fully integrated. Secondly, this approach is based on preference only, and does not take constraints on behavior explicitly into consideration. Constraints such as lack of time or money, or pressure imposed by the presence of children, may hinder individuals to choose a preferred alternative, or to participate more often. Consequently, the most valid results would be obtained if one could successfully differentiate between constraints and preferences.

In this paper, a new methodology that has been developed to avoid some of these shortcomings is introduced. It is based on the integrated use of a series of tasks that allows one to elicit the attributes influencing the choice process of interest, classify these attributes into rejection-inducing and hence constraint-type of attributes and trade-off attributes, and estimate a preference function, which can then be used to group respondents into segments. Some elements of this new suggested methodology are common with traditional approaches, but it differs in terms of the specific combination of tasks and elements. The goals of this paper are to outline the new methodology and illustrate its application in the context of a tourism policy program in the Netherlands to reduce car use for leisure trips.

To this end, the paper is structured as follows. First, the background of the application will be outlined. Then, we will sketch the theoretical framework underlying the analyses. Next, the new integrated method will be introduced and discussed. This method was developed to elicit the factors and constraints influencing leisure consumers' choice behavior, and on this basis of this, to derive consumer segments. Then the results of the analyses are reported on, describing the market segments identified. As a result the possible marketing strategies for each of the identified market segments are discussed, with particular attention to constraints to behavior. The paper concludes with a discussion of the results and design of the study, and suggestions for further research.

BACKGROUND OF THE STUDY

One of the tourism policy issues in the Netherlands is a reaction to the increased awareness that in many densely populated areas in Western Europe, tourists and recreation participants have contributed significantly to an immense mobility growth. On holidays and summer weekends, roads serving the major leisure/tourist sites suffer from traffic congestion and inadequate parking capacity. This in turn has caused poor accessibility of those sites, poor environmental quality, and tourists' annoyance. Total mobility figures show that leisure travel is substantially larger than commuter traffic. Concern about this growing problem has led local planning authorities, transport companies and the leisure industry to propose initiatives to reduce car use to leisure sites. In the Netherlands, some experiments have recently been implemented which attempt to stimulate non-car travel for recreational day trips. These involved the introduction of shuttle bus services from railway stations and large car parks to the leisure sites, and the planning of new leisure sites near major public transport facilities. Furthermore, existing non-car options were promoted by advertising and offering discounts on combined train and entrance tickets. Although these experiments did succeed in increasing the use of public transport to the leisure sites, evaluation research indicated that they did not result in a decrease in motorcar travel. Thus, empirical evidence seems to suggest that the experimental measures have not been very effective in influencing people's mode choice behavior. Assuming that there is a wide variety of individual demands and desires for leisure travel, the effectiveness of programs for reducing car mobility seems largely dependent on one's success in targeting the leisure consumer. In terms of the process of decision making, leisure travel is not different from any other kind of travel: individuals or households choose leisure destinations on the basis of the utility they derive from such destinations, given the constraints they face to realize their preferences. These utilities or preferences in turn are a function of the attributes of the destinations and the transport modes that may interact with household characteristics and context variables. Hence, it may be that the introduction of the discount tickets allows a particular market segment to make additional trips, rather than changing their transport mode choice. Thus, if one wishes to assess the potential impact of these programs, it is important to understand the choice process of leisure consumers, the nature of their preference functions, the constraints that are influencing their behavior, and the elasticity aspects of leisure travel. A market segmentation approach that incorporates these aspects may assist in optimizing the impact of such car mobility reducing programs.

CONCEPTUAL FRAMEWORK

The theoretical basis for the present study can be viewed as an extension of the framework, previously outlined in Timmermans (1982), and applied to other studies of recreational choice (e.g., Lieber & Fesenmaier, 1984). This framework assumes that leisure destination choice is the result of a cognitive decision process. Based on individual characteristics and decision criteria, individuals (or households) perceive the alternatives in their choice set and derive part-worth utilities from the attributes describing the alternatives. Individuals' perceptions are not necessarily true, nor are individuals familiar with all alternatives. Individuals are assumed to subjectively perceive a subset of choice alternatives and subsequently arrive at an overall preference judgment of the alternative by integrating the separate evaluations of these attributes. In other words, the overall utility of the alternative is a function of the part-worth utilities of its attributes. This process of integration is highly subjective. Individuals are assumed to use certain combination rules to weigh the attributes of the choice alternatives. Combination rules can be either compensatory or noncompensatory. Compensatory rules describe a compensatory decision making process in that a low appraisal of one specific attribute can be compensated, at least partially, by a high score on one or more other attributes. The use of noncompensatory combination rules implies that a low appraisal cannot be compensated, and will therefore induce the rejection of the choice alternative. Finally, individuals are assumed to arrive at a choice, given their overall preference for the alternative in their choice set, by implementing a choice rule. For example, one can assume that individuals will invariably choose the alternative with the highest overall preference.

In the original conceptual framework, constraints to behavior were not explicitly taken into consideration. In contrast, constraints were seen as operating through some of the other components of the conceptual model. For example, constraints related to personal or household characteristics were seen to operate through the background variables and influence the perception and evaluation of the choice alternatives. Similarly, temporal and spatial constraints were implicitly viewed as exogenous factors influencing the size and composition of individuals' choice sets.

Because the issue of constraints is very pertinent in the present study, it may be relevant to elaborate the original conceptual framework and explicitly incorporate different kinds of constraints. Following Henderson (cf. Jackson, 1988) and Jackson and Searle (1985), we differentiate between intervening and antecedent constraints (see Figure 1). Intervening constraints operate between the individual's preferences and the actual choice. Antecedent constraints prevent an individual to consider an alternative and thus influence his/her choice. The latter type of constraints thus influence the perception, evaluation of the attributes and the combination rule. Another distinction that is useful here is between blocking and inhibiting constraints (cf. Jackson & Searle, 1985: 598). Constraints of the first type induce immediate rejection of the alternative and would be indicative of a noncompensatory combination rule. The latter just make an alternative less preferable or complicate participating; compensation with other (highly preferred) features, or adaptation of the individual is eventually possible. Constraints may cover a latent demand for a certain alternative. Given a valid identification of (the nature of) constraints, the potential demand can be measured.

AN INTEGRATED APPROACH

It is critical to the present analyses to (i) measure the attributes influencing the respondents' leisure travel (destination and transport mode) decisions, (ii) identify the role these attributes play in the decision making process (constraints/rejection inducing attributes or trade-off attributes), (iii) derive a preference function that allows us to position leisure destinations on a preference scale, and (iv) to use these results to identify consumer segments. To this end, we developed a method that is derived from elements of the Repertory Grid methodology, the Decision Plan Nets approach and a choice-based scaling model. It differs from these traditional approaches in that these elements are used in a new, integrated fashion.

The Repertory Grid methodology has been applied to consumer choice problems before, especially in transportation (e.g., Timmermans et al., 1982a) and retailing (e.g., Timmermans et al., 1982b, 1984; Hallsworth, 1988; Coshall, 1985; Hudson, 1980; Opacic & Potter, 1986) and the Decision Plan approach has also been applied in recreation research previously (e.g., Timmermans & Van der Heijden, 1987), but to the best of our knowledge, the integrated method developed for the present study is new.

The Repertory Grid method as originally developed by Kelly (1955) in clinical psychology explores individuals' perceptions by identifying the characteristics by which individuals distinguish between objects. In a Repertory Grid interview, respondents are presented a list of triads of choice alternatives. They are requested to name the features that differentiate one alternative from the other two. That is, they are prompted to name the attributes by which the two choice alternatives are similar and thereby different from the third. Respondents are asked to name these attributes or personal constructs using new triads until no new constructs are mentioned. This results in a list of perceived characteristics the respondents apparently use to discriminate between the presented choice alternatives. These attributes are then assumed to influence individuals' destination choices. The major advantage of this method over other methods is that the task is relatively uncomplicated and that it controls for interviewer bias (cf. Stemerding et al., 1992).

To elicit a valid list of attributes, it is vital to have the respondent consider a diverse set of alternatives. In fact, the number of alternatives is unlimited but not all features of all alternatives are equally important. In this respect, a conventional Repertory Grid method is not very efficient as the triads are generated at random. Therefore, in this study we used a different approach, which is based on choice sets that are constructed according to the principles of the design of statistical experiments.

This new method involves the following steps. First, the potential destinations have to be classified into types. For each type, N destinations are selected. Alternatively, one can use real-world destinations directly. Next, these destinations are placed into choice sets, using the principles of the statistical design of experiments to create choice sets. Each set thus consists of a combination of selected destinations, one for each type. Respondents are then requested to identify the most as well as the least preferred destination in each choice set, and to name attributes that generated this response. This will result in a list of explicitly positive and explicitly negative aspects of the destinations.

Hence, our method has in common with conventional repertory grid analysis that subjects are requested to elicit the constructs or attributes they use to differentiate between choice alternatives. It differs in that choice sets, constructed according to experimental design principles, rather than randomly generated triads are used to generate these responses.

Having elicited the attributes influencing leisure destinations choice, the next step involves identifying the specific role of each of these attributes in the respondents' decision making process. This step is based on the Decision Net approach, which traditionally has been applied for this purpose, but as a stand-alone method. Our application thus differs from previous studies in this respect in that the output of the adjusted Repertory Grid method or attribute elicitation task is used as input to the Decision Plan Net (cf. Stemerding et al., 1993).

The Decision Plan Net method (Bettman, 1970, 1979; Park & Lutz, 1982) was originally designed to represent individual decision making processes. Basically, decision nets involve a structured interview in which respondents are invited to list the attributes influencing their decision making. Note that in our application, this step is replaced by the suggested attribute elicitation method. Having listed the influential attributes, respondents are requested to explicate the conditions under which they would no longer consider the choice alternative. Such attributes are called rejection inducing dimensions and refer to noncompensatory combination rules. An alternative will be rejected if a particular attribute does not meet an individual's set of conditions. Such attributes are indicative of constraints in the process. Alternatively, an individual may still consider the choice alternative if this attribute is compensated by better levels of one or more of the other attributes. These trade-off dimensions refer to compensatory combination rules. Finally, relative preference dimensions may be identified. These make the alternative more desirable. Acceptance or rejection of the alternative, however, does not depend on such an attribute. Thus, elements of a decision net approach may be used to identify the kind of constraints that were discussed in the conceptual model.

The attribute elicitation task generates choice frequencies for the destinations included in the choice sets. These frequencies can be aggregated across respondents, which can serve as the input of a scaling model that allows one to position the destinations on a preference scale. If orthogonal designs are used, the experimental design fulfills the sufficient and necessary conditions to estimate a multinomial logit model. Hence, a MNL model can be used to derive the preference scale. Note that this is not a separate step in the analysis, but follows directly from the adopted method.

Finally, rather than focusing on the preference function, which describes the positioning of the destinations on an overall preference scale without taking constraints into account, the choice frequencies observed across the designed choice sets may be used as input for a clustering algorithm to group the respondents into segments according to their choice patterns as observed under experimental conditions. Any clustering algorithm or other appropriate grouping technique may be used to derive the segments. Note again, that these results are obtained simultaneously as part of the integrated measurement approach. The application of the suggested methodology will be illustrated next, using the Dutch policy of reducing car mobility for leisure trips as an example.

STUDY DESIGN

Data

The data for the present study were collected in the summer of 1993 as part of a survey among 150 randomly selected households in the Eindhoven/Tilburg region in the Netherlands. Respondents were initially contacted by phone and asked a series of questions about their leisure travel activities. Those who said they were frequently involved in leisure activities were invited to participate in a follow up home interview. The average interview took approximately 1 hour to complete, and involved detailed questions about the respondents' perception of leisure destinations, their evaluations, and a structured interview to elicit and identify the nature of their decision making process for leisure travel. Finally, information about their leisure experience and personal background variables was collected.

Analyses and Results

Following the measurement approach described previously, first the potential destinations were classified into four types: zoo, amusement park (family theme park), museum, and beach site. For each type, four destinations were selected (see Table 1). All these destinations were within a distance range of 100 miles (160 kms) of the study area, and were assumed to be well known. The alternatives were presented to respondents not as destinations, but as comprehensive leisure trips, including transport mode, journey both ways and a few hours stay at the destination. To force respon-

TABLE 1. Selected Destinations

(ZO) Zoos:	Zoo Antwerpen, Antwerp,
	Belgium Burgers' Bush, Zoo and Safari,
	Arnhem Artis Zoo, Amsterdam
	Beekse Bergen safaripark
(MU) Museums:	Rijksmuseum Amsterdam
	Open Air museum, Arnhem
	Railway museum, Utrecht
	Kröller-Müller, National Park Hoge Veluwe
(AP) Amusement Parks/Theme Parks:	Efteling, Kaatsheuvel
	Land van Ooit, Drunen
	Madurodam, The Hague
	Walibi, Belgium
(BE) Beaches:	Hoek van Holland
	Scheveningen
	Domburg, Walcheren
	Renesse/Haamstede

dents to explicitly consider attributes of the transport mode, we invited them to perform the same choice/attribute identification task twice. The first series of choice sets represented trips to be made by public transport, the second series was similar and represented trips to be made by car. Consequently, respondents had to take public transport attributes (e.g., complexity and length of trip, accessibility), in combination with the site's specific features, into consideration. Likewise, in the second series of choice sets, car trip attributes (e.g., parking facilities, traffic jam probability) and the site's specific features were jointly considered.

These trip/destination descriptions were varied according to an experimental design. Because we identified four sites for each destination type, and each type can be absent, all combinations of destination types involve a 5^4 full factorial design. Two orthogonal fractions of this design, involving 25 sets were constructed, one for trips by public transport, and one for leisure trips by car. Thus, choice sets varied in size and composition. The maximum size involves one destination for each of the four types of leisure destinations. Choice sets can be smaller if one or more of the destination types is not available. To avoid fatigue, respondents were asked to respond to only 15 choice sets, which were drawn at random. Respondents were requested to identify the most as well as the least preferred destination in each set of alternatives, and to name attributes that generated this response. This resulted in a list of attributes the respondents used to discriminate between the destinations.

The pattern of choices across the choice sets served as input for a hierachical clustering algorithm to group the respondents into segments. In general, if an orthogonal fractional factorial design is used and all respondents express their choices for the same choice sets, the responses to all choice sets can be used directly as input for the clustering routine. In some applications, such as this one, the number of choice sets may be too large, and consequently, the reliability of the responses may be at risk. To avoid fatigue and patternized response patterns, one can construct a fraction of the factorial. If one is willing to assume that pairwise choice probabilities are independent from the existence of any other alternative in the choice set, then the aggregated choice frequencies for each destination can still be used as input for the clustering algorithm. If, as in our case, a randomization procedure has been used to select the choice sets that are presented to respondents, one no longer has strict control over the number of times a particular destination is presented to respondents. The proportion of times a destination is chosen, given the number of times it has been presented, is a more reliable measure to perform the segmentation. This option was chosen in the present study. Because respondents were requested to make choices for each of the 16 leisure sites when travelling by public transport and when travelling by car separately, their adjusted response patterns to 32 profiles were used as input for the cluster analysis. The *average linking within groups* method was used to group the respondents. This method groups respondents such that the average Euclidean distance between all members of the resulting cluster is as small as possible.

Four segments resulted from this procedure. First, we described each segment in terms of the personal characteristics of their members, and their average use of the destinations types. For each segment separately, a multinomial logit choice model was also estimated, which positioned each of the leisure sites on a preference scale. This analysis was conducted twice, once for the public transport scenario and once for the car scenario. The aggregated choice frequencies were used as the dependent variable of the choice model, the leisure sites were represented by a set of dummy variables. Iterative reweighted least squares analysis was used to estimate the preference scales.

The results of these analyses are presented in Tables 2 and 3. These tables indicate that the market segments can be characterized as follows:

Segment #1 (N = 40): Members of this segment are attracted to zoos and the amusement park *De Efteling*, and have recently made relatively

TABLE 2. Preference Results for the 4 Different Segments

SEGMENT #1 (N = 40)

PUBLIC TRANSPORT

	par. value	std. error
1. ap efteling	2.38**	.26
2. zo burgers'	2.22**	.26
3. zo antwerp	1.99**	.26
4. zo beekse bergen	1.83**	.25
5. zo artis	1.75**	.25
6. be scheveningen	1.13**	.26
7. ap madurodam	0.87**	.28
8. ap land va ooit	0.74*	.28
9. be hoek v.holland	0.26	.30
10. mu railway	0.18	.30
11. mu rijksmuseum	0.15	.27
12. ap walibi	0.00	
13. be walcheren	-0.09	.28
14. mu open air	-0.15	.32
15. be renesse	-0.55	.35
16. mu kröller-müller	-1.07*	.45

CAR TRIP

	par. value	std. error
1. ap efteling	1.28**	.23
2. zo burgers'	0.92**	.21
3. zo antwerp	0.89**	.21
4. zo beekse bergen	0.22	.19
5. zo artis	0.21	.20
6. ap walibi	0.00	
7. ap madurodam	-0.13	.21
8. mu open air	-0.26	.29
9. ap land van ooit	-0.34	.23
10. be scheveningen	-0.66**	.25
11. be walcheren	-0.93**	.26
12. be hoeke v.holland	-1.03**	.25
13. be renesse	-1.04**	.26
14. mu rijksmuseum	-1.19**	.29
15. mu kröller-müller	-1.56**	.30
16. mu railway	-1.95**	.28

SEGMENT #2 (N = 21)

PUBLIC TRANSPORT

	par. value	std. error
1. ap efteling	1.83**	.32
2. ap madurodam	1.34**	.30
3. ap land van ooit	1.03**	.30
4. zo burgers'	0.99**	.29
5. mu kröller-müller	0.31	.30
6. mu railway	0.22	.30
7. zo beekse bergen	0.21	.31
8. ap walibi	0	
9. mu open air	-0.15	.32
10. zo artis	-0.18	.31
11. be scheveningen	-0.40	.33
12. be hoeke v.holland	-0.41	.36
13. zo antwerp	-0.65*	.35
14. mu rijksmuseum	-1.17*	.33
15. be walcheren	-1.85*	.39
16. be renesse	-1.78**	.52

CAR TRIP

	par. value	std. error
1. ap efteling	307**	.58
2. ap madurodam	0.68*	.28
3. ap land van ooit	0.68*	.29
4. mu open air	0.55	.36
5. ap walibi	0	
6. mu kröller-müller	-0.18	.31
7. zo beekse bergen	-0.33	.28
8. zo burgers'	-0.66*	.32
9. zo antwerp	-0.72*	.34
10. mu railway	-0.89**	.29
11. zo artis	0.99**	.32
12. be renesse	-1.08**	.35
13. be walcheren	-1.22**	.36
14. be scheveningen	-1.45**	.35
15. be hoeke v.holland	-1.81**	.41
16. mu rijksmuseum	-2.10**	.48

* denotes significance at the .1 level   ** denotes significance as the .01 level

TABLE 2 (continued)

SEGMENT #3 (N = 26)

PUBLIC TRANSPORT	par. value	std. error	CAR TRIP	par. value	std. error
1. be walcheren	3.48**	.43	1. be walcheren	2.34**	.34
2. be hoek v.holland	2.69**	.41	2. be scheveningen	1.89**	.32
3. be renesse	2.57**	.42	3. be renesse	1.52**	.32
4. be scheveningen	2.43**	.40	4. mu open air	1.25*	.37
5. ap efteling	2.32**	.43	5. ap efteling	1.16**	.35
6. zo beekse bergen	2.25**	.42	6. be hoek v.holland	0.83**	.32
7. mu kröller-müller	1.92**	.43	7. zo beekse bergen	0.67*	.31
8. zo antwerp	1.54**	.43	8. mu rijksmuseum	0.31	.35
9. zo burgers'	1.36**	.44	9. ap walibi	0.00	
10. mu open air	1.10**	.41	10. ap madurodam	−0.05	.36
11. mu rijksmuseum	1.04*	.46	11. zo antwerp	−0.07	.37
12. zo artis	0.92*	.42	12. zo burgers'	−0.16	.38
13. ap madurodam	0.74	.49	13. mu kröller-müller	−0.28	.38
14. mu railway	0.34	.52	14. mu railway	−0.62	.37
15. ap walibi	0.00		15. zo artis	−0.77	.41
16. ap land van ooit	−0.20	.58	16. ap land van ooit	−1.57*	.50

SEGMENT #4 (N = 63)

PUBLIC TRANSPORT	par. value	std. error	CAR TRIP	par. value	std. error
1. mu rijksmuseum	4.32**	.41	1. mu kröller-müller	3.57**	.28
2. mu open air	3.66**	.41	2. zo antwerp	2.63**	.28
3. mu kröller-müller	3.59**	.41	3. mu open air	2.59**	.30
4. zo burgers'	3.28**	.40	4. zo burgers'	2.53***	.27
5. zo antwerp	3.14**	.41	5. mu rijksmuseum	2.52**	.27
6. zo artis	2.99**	.41	6. ap efteling	2.48**	.29
7. ap efteling	2.87**	.41	7. mu railway	1.97**	.26
8. mu railway	2.71**	.41	8. ap madurodam	1.67**	.28
9. ap madurodam	2.38**	.42	9. be walcheren	1.23**	.30
10. zo beekse bergen	2.24**	.42	10. zo beekse bergen	1.16**	.29
11. be scheveningen	2.07**	.42	11. zo artis	1.15*	.27
12. be walcheren	1.47**	.44	12. be scheveningen	1.13**	27
13. ap land van ooit	0.77*	.47	13. be renesse	1.00**	.30
14. be hoek v.holland	0.30	.50	14. ap land van ooit	0.35	.32
15. ap walibi	0.00		15. be hoek v.holland	0.22	.33
16. be renesse	−0.45	.60	16. ap walibi	0.00	

*denotes significance at the .1 level

**denotes significance at the .01 level

TABLE 3. Number of Destinations from the Choice Set Visited Over the Past Two Years

	Mean	Standard Deviation	Zoo	Museum	Amusement Park	Beach
Total Sample (N = 150)	3.41	2.2	.81	.61	.89	1.11
Segment #1 (N = 40)	3.42	2.1	1.17	.23	1.03	1.00
Segment #2 (N = 21)	3.05	2.7	.62	.43	1.29	.71
Segment #3 (N = 26)	2.92	1.9	.62	.27	.77	1.27
Segment #4 (N = 63)	3.73	2.2	.71	1.05	.71	1.25

many trips to these sites. The group's preference for museums is low. The 30-39 age group is overrepresented, as are families with children. The education level of the respondents is below average; the income level is in the median group.

Segment #2 (N = 21): Amusement park fans. Compared to the first segment, this group is even more strongly oriented to amusement parks. The socio-demographic profile of this segment is quite similar to that of segment #1; only age and income are slightly lower.

Segment #3 (N = 26): Beach fans. They are exclusively attracted to beach locations, which is reflected in their behavior. The education level of this segment is below average.

Segment #4 (N = 63): A large group of culture enthusiasts. They love museums, and to a lesser degree, zoos. Families with children are underrepresented, while income is above average, and education levels are well above average. Seventy-six percent of the segment (compared with 57 percent of the total sample) is over 40 years of age, while 43 percent (35 total sample) is over 50.

As illustrated by Table 2, the segments differ in terms of preference for the leisure destinations. One would assume that the distinguished segments should be more homogeneous than the sample as a whole in terms of their preferences. Therefore, some additional analyses to test this hypothesis were performed. A first test involved running separate choice models. If the segments have different preference functions, a model incorporating segment-specific constants should perform better than the preference models for the total sample. A model with a segment-specific constant would of course still assume that the form of the preference function would be the same. Therefore, we also estimated a third model that allows the preference scales for the leisure sites to differ between market segments. Models were estimated for the public transport and car options separately.

The results are presented in Table 4. It demonstrates that adding segment-specific constants significantly improves the fit of the model for both the car and public transport options. The market segments differ significantly in terms of preference (see also Table 5). The model with segment-varying preference functions performs even better, as indicated in Table 4. Thus, these results suggest that the derived market segments exhibit different preference structures.

Another test is related to the consistency of the derived preference scales. We assumed that respondents belonging to the same segment would be more homogeneous than the total sample in terms of their preference for a particular type of leisure destination. Hence, we hypothesized that similar destinations will have similar positions on the derived preference scales. One way of testing this assumption is to examine the patterns of preference rankings for each type of leisure destination. In the ideal case, the first four rankings would all relate to the same type of destination, the second set of four rankings to another type, etc. That is, we are

TABLE 4. Model Comparisons with Their Associated Statistics

		$G2$[1]	DF[2]	# Choice Sets
PUBLIC TRANSPORT	model 1, without segmentation	637	15	96
	model 2, segment specific constants	723	18	96
	model 3, segment specific preference scales	2456	60	96
CAR	model 1, without segmentation	495	15	100
	model 2, segment specific constants	598	18	100
	model 3, segment specific preference scales	2147	60	100

[1]$G2 = -2[LL(0)-LL(B)]$; likelihood ratio test statistic, chi square distributed
[2]Degrees of Freedom (# of parameters) with G2

TABLE 5. Segment Significance, Compared with Segment #4 (Model 3)

	PUBLIC TRANSPORT		CAR	
	t-statistic	Probability $(Z > |t|)$[1]	t-statistic	Probability $(Z > |t|)$[1]
Segment #1	−4.966	.0000	−6.971	.0000
Segment #2	−7.424	.0000	−8.355	.0000
Segment #3	−2.788	.0053	−2.481	.0131

[1] The probability that the parameter values of the segment constants differ from segment #4.

testing whether our segmentation is primarily driven by the type of destination. Therefore, a simple measure of consistency would be to take the observed total difference in preference rankings between all destinations belonging to a particular type, and express this as a proportion of the maximum range. In the present study, the minimum total difference between preference rankings of the destinations of the same type is 10, and hence 40 for the total set of destinations. A completely inconsistent pattern would result in a value of 160 for the total set of destinations; for one type (4 destinations in a table of 16) this maximum value is 58.

The consistency values for the four segments and the total sample are presented in Table 6. It clearly demonstrates that the segments are more consistent than the sample as a whole. Segment #1 is the most consistent. A separate analysis of the leisure types shows that the segments' preferences are primarily consistent for the high ranking types. All preferences on the less preferred types are less consistent, which may suggest that the segments indeed are primarily based on type of destinations, and that trade-offs between type of destination and other attributes are more common for the less preferred type of destinations. Alternatively, the lower consistency of the less preferred types may also suggest some degree of indifference toward these types.

The derived segment can be a useful marketing tool as it identifies the consumer preference and their socio-demographic characteristics. One could argue that this segmentation scheme provides information about the latent demand for each of the identified destination types and the selected sites. Having identified these segments and their preference structures, the question then becomes whether this latent demand can actually be realised given the constraints the consumers are facing. In order to identify the

TABLE 6. Consistency of Preference Patterns

		zoo[1]	museum[1]	amus.pk[1]	beach[1]	total[2]
whole sample (N = 150)	public transport	0.21	0.33	0.83	0.13	0.60
	car	0.35	0.56	0.83	0.25	0.80
segment #1 (N = 40)	public transport	0.00	0.23	0.50	0.44	0.50
	car	0.00	0.31	0.31	0	0.25
segment #2 (N = 21)	public transport	0.42	0.42	0.25	0.17	0.50
	car	0.06	0.63	0.06	0.00	0.30
segment #3 (N = 26)	public transport	0.19	0.25	0.52	0.00	0.38
	car	0.31	0.56	0.44	0.13	0.58
segment #4 (N = 63)	public transport	0.19	0.25	0.38	0.15	0.38
	car	0.48	0.21	0.50	0.19	0.55

[1] for single type maximum difference = 58
[2] for all types maximum difference = 160

impact of constraints, the next step of the analysis involved identifying the specific role of each of the elicited attributes in the respondents' decision making process, using the Decision Net approach. That is, the elicited attributes were used as input in a decision net task. Respondents were requested to explicate the conditions under which they would no longer consider the destination. In addition, they were requested to name compensating attributes or attribute levels, or identify the attributes as a relative preference dimension.

The dimensions derived from the Decision Plan Net task were used to identify constraints within market segments. Rejection inducing dimensions were viewed as conditions which need to be satisfied to accept a destination. In other words, a trip that does not feature a particular rejection-inducing attribute at the acceptable level, will not be made. Because the Decision Nets were constructed for public transport and car trips separately, we were able to identify the specific rejection inducing dimensions for public transport trips, and hence evaluate the car use reducing policy. This enabled us to demonstrate whether certain mode change strategies are feasible for a particular market segment.

In principle, a constraints analysis can be performed at the level of individual attributes. Such an analysis would highlight the idiosyncracies of the respondents. For the present article, we decided to categorize the attributes into eight types, as listed in Table 7: personal taste, accessibility by public transport and car, situational aspects, specific requirements for children, costs, experience and time/distance. In order to compare the findings between the car and public transport scenarios, and between respondents, travel time, cost and number of transfer (in the public transport option), were introduced into the Decision Nets a priori. This categorization was used because the impact of policy schemes and marketing strategies will vary by constraint. Constraints originating from personal taste and aspirations are the least likely to be influenced, whereas a lack of time or money, or special requirements for children can possibly be overcome by policy measures.

Constraints analysis then involves whether consumer preferences can actually be realized. That is, one first has to determine whether a particular attribute is a rejection-inducing dimension, and then, if it is, whether the conditions pertaining to a particular leisure sites act as a constraint, preventing consumers from choosing that particular destination. In this article, we first consider the responses on the travel time and number of transfers attributes. Respondents have explicated their maximum acceptable values. These individual threshold values were compared against the

TABLE 7. Categories of Attributes Relevant to the Destination and Transport Mode Choice

1	personal taste specifically related to the site
2	accessibility by public transport
3	accessibility by car
4	situational aspects
5	special requirements for children
6	cost aspects
7	experience with the trip
8	aspects of time and distance

objective attribute values of the top four destinations of the segment that individual belongs to (Table 8a). These real travel time values were obtained from the official public transport time tables, measured between the public transport terminal closest from the respondent's home and the leisure site. Thus, allowing for driving or taking a taxi to the first major railway station, travel time and transfers to reach this station from home were not accounted for initially. The 'unlikely' label was for all trips that would not allow for one extra transfer or 30 minutes to reach the closest railway station from home. A trip that could not be realized within the maximum travel time or number of transfers as suggested by the respondent's decision net, was considered to be 'impossible.'

Among the four market segments, considerable differences occur in the ability to reach the favorite destinations by public transport. Segment #3 has expressed the highest relative demands for public transport trips. However, due to their expressed constraints, the top four preferred trips, all to beach locations, are all impossible to reach within the limits provided by the respondents. Consequently, the favorite trips are possible for only half the segment. Furthermore, when in addition the maximum number of transfers (see Table 8b) is also taken into consideration, this proportion drops even further: only a third of the segment can make the trips. Similar trends can be observed for the other market segments, although in these cases, the absolute levels of the proportions are higher, often because the favorite leisure sites are located closer to the study area.

When travelling by car, few constraints are relevant, as is indicated by Table 8c. To account for possible delays caused by traffic jams and parking problems, we considered a trip as unlikely within a margin of 30 minutes from the threshold value. As Table 8c shows, travel-time related constraints have far less impact on leisure trips by car. Again, segment #3 scores lowest, but still higher than the highest of the public transport scenarios. Whereas nearly all respondents are not constrained in time to make their favorite trips by car, a considerable number is constrained to make the most preferred trips by public transport.

The segments' results on other rejection inducing dimensions generally confirm the findings derived for the travel time and transfer attributes. Again, segment #3 (the beach lovers) emerge as the most constrained. The highest average number of rejection inducing dimensions is reported for this segment (see Table 9). This group scores high on the attributes of the public transport facilities (more than half of the segment reports rejection inducing dimensions on this category), and on time and distance aspects. A noteworthy proportion of segment #1 reports constraints related to children's requirements. A relatively large proportion of segment #4 mentions rejection inducing dimensions that specifically relate to the site.

MARKET SEGMENT STRATEGIES

The derived knowledge of the relevant preferences, constraints and background profiles of the segment members enables one to suggest relevant, segment specific marketing strategies. These can be expressed in terms of the appropriate planning or marketing and promotion initiatives to change mode choice behavior in favor of public transport. As Tables 1 and 2 show, destinations well accessible by public transport tend to rank higher on the public transport list, while unaccessible destinations tend to perform better

TABLE 8a. Feasibility of Preferred Leisure Trips by Public Transport: Travel Time

	Top 4 of Trips	Impossible	Unlikely[1]	Possible	Possible/Total
segment #1	1. ap efteling	0	1	39	0.98
(N = 40)	2. zo burgers'	6	7	27	0.68
	3. zo antwerp	6	7	27	0.68
	4. zo beekse bergen	1	3	36	0.90
segment #2	1. ap efteling	0	0	21	1.00
(N = 21)	2. ap madurodam	5	3	13	0.62
	3. ap land van ooit	0	3	18	0.86
	4. zo burgers'	5	1	15	0.71
segment #3	1. be walcheren	14	1	11	0.42
(N = 26)	2. be hoek van holland	13	1	12	0.46
	3. be renesse	15	2	9	0.35
	4. be scheveningen	8	6	12	0.46
segment #4	1. mu rijksmuseum	11	8	44	0.70
(N = 63)	2. mu open air	11	8	44	0.70
	3. mu kröller-müller	19	5	39	0.62
	4. zo burgers'	9	5	49	0.78

[1]unlikely: maximum of 30 minutes from home to station

TABLE 8b. Feasibility of Preferred Leisure Trips by Public Transport: Travel Time and Transfers

	Top 4 of Trips	Impossible	Unlikely[1]	Possible	Possible/Total
segment #1	1. ap efteling	0	4	36	0.90
(N = 40)	2. zo burgers'	10	8	22	0.55
	3. zo antwerp	9	9	22	0.55
	4. zo beekse bergen	1	5	34	0.85
segment #2	1. ap efteling	0	2	19	0.90
(N = 21)	2. ap madurodam	5	5	11	0.52
	3. ap land van ooit	1	5	15	0.38
	4. zo burgers'	7	2	12	0.57
segment #3	1. be walcheren	18	1	7	0.27
(N = 26)	2. be hoek van holland	14	2	10	0.38
	3. be renesse	18	2	6	0.23
	4. be scheveningen	9	7	10	0.38
segment #4	1. mu rijksmuseum	12	15	36	0.57
(N = 63)	2. mu open air	14	12	37	0.59
	3. mu kröller-müller	27	6	30	0.48
	4. zo burgers'	13	8	42	0.67

[1] unlikely: maximum of 30 minutes from home to station, or no interchange between home and station

TABLE 8c. Feasibility of Preferred Leisure Trips by Car: Travel Time

	Top 4 of Trips	Impossible	Unlikely[1]	Possible	Possible/Total
segment #1	1 . ap efteling	0	0	40	1.00
(N = 40)	2. zo burgers'	0	2	38	0.95
	3. zo antwerp	0	0	40	1.00
	4. zo Artis	1	2	37	0.93
segment #2	1. ap efteling	0	0	21	1.00
(N = 21)	2. ap madurodam	1	1	19	0.90
	3. ap land van ooit	0	0	21	1.00
	4. mu open air	0	5	15	0.76

	Top 4 of Trips	Impossible	Unlikely[1]	Possible	Possible/Total
segment #3	1. be walcheren	2	4	20	0.77
(N = 26)	2. be scheveningen	2	1	23	0.88
	3. be renesse	2	4	20	0.77
	4. mu open air	1	1	24	0.92
segment #4	1. mu kröller-müller	0	6	57	0.90
(N = 63)	2. zo antwerp	0	0	63	1.00
	3. mu open air	0	3	60	0.95
	4. zo burgers'	0	3	60	0.95

[1]unlikely: margin of 30 minutes

on the car option table. The segments show some differences on this point. While segment #1 does not differentiate that much between the two transport options, segments #3 and #4 do distinguish more clearly between the public transport and car options. Again, it should be noted that deviations on the high ranking destinations are the most important; the respondents demonstrated an indifference toward the other, less preferred sites.

Using such results, the following strategies can be suggested for the segments. Segment #1, the group of zoo enthusiasts, primarily require capacity to accommodate families comfortably, because half of the constraints reported by this segment related to children, whereas only a third of this segment reports the attribute travel time as rejection inducing. As far as segment #2 is concerned, Table 9 suggests that the four selected categories of rejection inducing dimensions are equally important to this small group of amusement park fans. As this group is largely similar to segment #1, the same strategy may apply. However, travel time is more important, as 43 percent of the group considers this as rejection inducing.

Segment #3, the beach fans, reports the highest number of rejection inducing dimensions. They have high demands for the public transport mode itself, and for travel time. Members of this segment have visited relatively few of the selected sites over the past two years. For this group, public transport connections with beach locations should not be complicated, easy to find and as direct as possible. Because of the relatively large distance from the respondents' homes to the beaches, a public transport experiment with this market segment will be difficult to implement. There is discrepancy between the public transport and car options, and a high proportion has rejection inducing dimensions on the second category. This

TABLE 9. Rejection Inducing Dimensions, Public Transport Option

	mean N of rejection inducing dimensions (RID)	% of respondents score RID on categories.[1]			
		1: personal taste	2: accessibility by public transport	5: requirements for children	8: time, distance
segment #1	3.4	75	40	50	32
segment #2	3.1	62	43	43	43
segment #3	4.4	77	58	38	58
segment #4	3.5	84	38	29	32

[1]: see TABLE 8

suggests that inaccessible locations will not be traveled by public transport.

Finally, segment #4 is the highly active group of well-off cultural seniors. Few constraints are reported, the most important of which are the site specific (taste) attributes. However, the group does make a clear distinction between the public transport and car options (cf. Table 2, the ranking of *Rijksmuseum* in Amsterdam). It suggests that destinations well accessible by public transport, are more likely to be visited by public transport. The appropriate promotion of these sites may support this result.

DISCUSSION

Market segments can be considered as target groups to whom the appropriate marketing mix of promotion, measures and other initiatives need to be applied. Programs are likely to have dissimilar effects on different types of leisure participants. Some of this variation may be explained by households' socio-economic characteristics, but leisure preference and constraints are likely to vary across socio-economic groups (e.g., Loker & Perdue, 1992; Spotts & Mahoney, 1991; Finn & Louviere, 1990). Therefore, we require segmentation into subgroups with coherent patterns of behavior, to be targeted efficiently by specific (marketing) strategies. In this study, we therefore identified clusters of potential visitors of specific leisure destinations. The resulting segments are then described in terms of constraints and their demand of leisure trips by non-car transport. In addition, personal and socio-economic profiles of the segments support the development of marketing strategies.

In this study, market segments were formed on the basis of a new integrated approach which simultaneously allows one to identify the attributes influencing leisure trip decisions, identify the nature of each of these attributes in general, and constraints in particular, position leisure destinations on a preference scale, and cluster respondents into market segments. The suggested methodology can replace a series of independent steps, based on unrelated methods. The findings of the present study and the experience obtained with administering the new method suggest that it potentially offers a reliable and valid alternative to currently applied methods. It is also is easy to administer and easy to use. Unlike the repertory grid method, it has the additional advantage that the elicited attributes are directly based on choices rather than perceptual dimensions. Consequently, the elicited attributes are likely more valid.

It should be emphasised however that the suggested method can be improved. For example, the clustering of the respondents is still based on preferences. Constraints are used to describe the segments. Alternatively, one could develop a clustering algorithm that would take both preferences and constraints into consideration simultaneously. This might improve the managerial or policy relevance of the market segments as one would have segments that would be more homogeneous not only in terms of preferences but also in terms of constraints. Furthermore, the preference scaling model is based on first choice only. The suggested approach however also yields information about the least preferred alternative. Future research therefore will examine how this additional information might be analysed to derive preference funcions.

In order to maximize the impact of car reducing initiatives, it is necessary to develop different strategies for the target groups. Therefore, having considered the socio-economic backgrounds of the segment members and their leisure practices, suggestions for separate strategies for the segments were outlined. Because the segments' preferences discriminate between the four selected leisure types, the strategies imply some relevant measures to be taken at the destinations. These involve fast and direct connections to museums. For public transport connections with amusement parks and zoos, accomodation for families (children, luggage) needs to be accounted for. Zoos located in well accessible cities have far better chances of attracting visitors by public transport. Since all market segments contain more unconstrained individuals than the modal split suggests (more people could travel by public transport than in the present situation), a promotion of the exisiting public transport alternatives may already achieve good results. The results of this study do not present measures to be taken at beach sites. The segment of beach devotees within our sample (region of Eindhoven/Tilburg), were most constrained by the relatively great distance to the beach locations. We consider this as a local problem; those beach fans who live closer to the shores are probably less constrained to travel by public transport, assuming that they would express equivalent thresholds.

REFERENCES

Bettman, J.R. (1970). Information Processing Models of Consumer Behavior. *Journal of Marketing Research* Vol. vii: 370-76.

Bettman, J.R. (1979). *An Information Processing Theory of Consumer Choice.* Reading, Mass.: Addison-Wesley.

Coshall, J. (1985). The Form of Micro-Spatial Consumer Cognition and Its Congruence with Search Behaviour. *Tijdschrift voor Econ. en Soc. Geografie*, 76 No.8: 345-55.

Finn, A. & J. Louviere (1990). Shopping-Center Patronage Models: Fashioning a Consideration Set Segmentation Solution. *Journal of Business Research*, vol.21: 259-75.

Hallsworth, A.G. (1988). Repertory Grid Methodology and the Analysis of Group Perceptions in Retailing. *International Journal of Retailing* 3, 4: 43-54.

Hudson, R. (1980). Personal Construct Theory, the Repertory Grid Measure and Human Geography. *Progress in Human Geography*, 4: 346-59.

Jackson, E.L. (1988). Leisure Constraints: a Survey of Past Research. *Leisure Sciences* vol.10: 203-15.

Jackson, E.L. & M.S. Searle (1985). Recreation Participation and Barriers to Participation: Concepts and Models. *Loisir et Société* 8: 693-707.

Kelly, G.A. (1955). *A Theory of Personality, the Theory of Personal Constructs.* New York: Norton.

Lieber, S. & D. Fesenmaier (1984). Modelling Recreation Choice: A Case Study of Management Alternatives in Chicago. *Regional Studies 18*, 31-43.

Loker, L.E. & R.R. Perdue (1992). A Benefit-based Segmentation of a Nonresident Summer Travel Market. *Journal of Travel Research*, Summer: 30-35.

Opacic, S. & R. Potter (1986). Grocery Store Cognitions of Disadvantaged Consumer Groups: A Reading Case Study. *Tijdschrift voor Econ. en Soc. Geografie*, 77 No. 4: 288-98.

Park, C. Whan & R. Lutz (1982). Decision Plans and Consumer Choice Dynamics. *Journal of Marketing Research* Vol. xix: 108-15.

Spotts, D.M. & E.M. Mahoney (1991). Segmenting Visitors to a Destination Region Based on the Volume of their Expenditures. *Journal of Travel Research* vol. 29, spring: 24-31.

Stemerding, M.P., H. Oppewal, A.W.J. Borgers & H.J.P. Timmermans (1992). *The Identification of Attributes and Constraints Influencing Recreational Travel Behaviour.* Paper presented at the Joint Conference of LSA and VVS. Tilburg, The Netherlands, 10-12 December 1992.

Stemerding, M.P., H. Oppewal, Th.A.M. Beckers & H.J.P. Timmermans (1993). *The Application of Qualitative Methods to Identify Attributes and Constraints of Leisure Travel Decisions.* Paper presented at the 1993 NRPA Leisure Research Symposium. San Jose, California, USA, 21-23 October 1993.

Timmermans, H.J.P. (1982). Consumer Choice of Shopping Centre: An Information Integration Approach. *Regional Studies* 1982, vol. 3: 171-82.

Timmermans, H., R. van der Heijden & H. Westerveld (1982a). The Identification of Factors Influencing Destination Choice: An Application of the Repertory Grid Methodology. *Transportation* 11: 189-203.

Timmermans, H., R. van der Heijden & H. Westerveld (1982b). Cognition of Urban Retailing Structures: A Dutch Case Study. *Tijdschrift voor Econ. en Soc. Geografie*, 73 No.1: 2-12.

Timmermans, H., R. van der Heijden & H. Westerveld (1984). Decision-Making Experiments and Real-World Choice Behavior. *Geografiska Annaler* 66B 1: 39-48.

Timmermans, H. & R. van der Heijden (1987). Uncovering Spatial Decision-Making Processes: A Decision Net Approach Applied to Recreational Behavior. *Tijdschrift voor Econ. en Soc. Geografie*, 78 No. 4: 297-304.

Conjoint Analysis of Downhill Skiers Used to Improve Data Collection for Market Segmentation

Barbara A. Carmichael

SUMMARY. A review of academic and government sources suggested that six key attributes of ski resort attractiveness were: variety of runs, snow conditions, value for money, lift lines, staff friendliness and access to home. As part of a larger study in Victoria, B.C., Canada, a sample of 100 skiers completed personal interviews in which they were asked to rank order 29 resort profiles in terms of preference. Seventy skiers ranked the profiles for both short trips and long trips, with an additional 18 skiers evaluating short trips (total = 88 skiers), and an additional 12 skiers evaluating short trips (total = 82 skiers). Using conjoint analysis, the relative importance of the six attributes to ski resort choice was computed for both scenarios. Skiers were clustered, using these importance values from conjoint analysis. They were also grouped using demographic data, information on skier ability and motivation. Analysis of variance was used to test for significant differences between the groupings and analyse the validity and usefulness of the segmentation criteria. *[Article copies available from The Haworth Document Delivery Service: 1-800-342-9678. E-mail address: getinfo@haworth.com]*

Dr. Barbara A. Carmichael is Assistant Professor, Department of Geography, Central Connecticut State University, 1615 Stanley Street, New Britain, CT 06050-4010.

[Haworth co-indexing entry note]: "Conjoint Analysis of Downhill Skiers Used to Improve Data Collection for Market Segmentation." Carmichael, Barbara A. Co-published simultaneously in *Journal of Travel & Tourism Marketing* (The Haworth Press, Inc.) Vol. 5, No. 3, 1996, pp. 187-206; and *Recent Advances in Tourism Marketing Research* (ed: Daniel R. Fesenmaier, Joseph T. O'Leary, and Muzaffer Uysal) The Haworth Press, Inc., 1996, pp. 187-206. Single or multiple copies of this article are available from The Haworth Document Delivery Service [1-800-342-9678, 9:00 a.m. - 5:00 p.m. (EST). E-mail address: getinfo@haworth.com].

INTRODUCTION

The downhill ski market is a large and growing market and one of the most popular outdoor recreation activities in North America. The trend in skier visits showed an annual growth rate of 8.6% during the period 1977/78 to 1987/88 (Goeldner, 1989) and continues to increase. Within British Columbia, in Canada, skier visits totalled 3,629,000 skiers for the 1988-89 season and showed a ten percent increase on the previous season. Such a large group of skiers are unlikely to be uniform in the benefits which they seek either in the tangible and perceived attributes of the ski resort product or in the intangible and internal personal benefits of the skiing experience. Therefore, market segmentation may provide a useful tool to define markets more precisely and to understand the differing needs of subgroups or segments within markets. Kotler (1972 p. 166) defined market segmentation as "the subdividing of a market into homogeneous subsets of consumers where any set may conceivably be selected as a market target to be reached with a distinct marketing mix." In this paper, different methods of market segmentation are compared and examined for their usefulness in targeting skier markets.

A number of studies have used market segmentation of tourism markets with varying degrees of success. Early segmentation studies in tourism were based on geographic and socio-demographic methods of segmentation, for example, Goeldner (1978) segmented Colorado skiers in terms of in state or out of state residence; Mills, Couturier and Snepenger (1986) segmented Texas snow skiers according to heavy or light expenditure on skiing and related these groups to other socio-demographic data. Stynes and Mahoney (1980) segmented the ski market in Michigan according to frequency of participation in skiing. These studies were limited in that they did not consider the tangible and intangible benefits sought by skiers. Indeed, this drawback was highlighted in the Texas study in the statement, "Future studies should incorporate benefits sought and other relevant variables thought to provide a more meaningful segmentation" (Mills, Couturier and Snepenger, 1986 p. 23). As these benefits are likely to influence skier choice behavior, segmenting skiers according to benefits sought will assist managers in a more focused advertizing strategy.

Figure 1 outlines some of the variables which have potential as segmentation criteria. They include socio-demographics, behavioral factors and benefits sought either within the ski resort attributes or within the ski experience itself. In addition, ski market groupings, in terms of these segmentation variables, will probably be different according to the situation context. Previous research by the author has shown that the length of trip planned is an important factor which influences the relative impor-

FIGURE 1. Skier Segmentation Variables

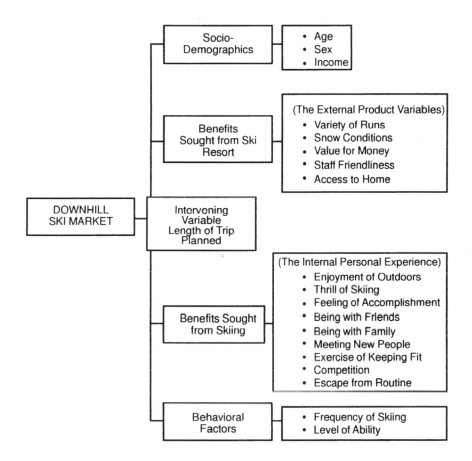

tance of ski resort attributes (Carmichael, 1991, p. 72). Therefore, in Figure 1, "length of trip" planned is conceptualized as an intervening variable and useful as an initial step in segmenting markets.

It is realised that this list of benefits sought within the skiing experience, as shown in Figure 1, is not exhaustive but represents some of the domains used in the much more extensive measurement scales used by Driver in the Recreation Experience Preference Scales which describe the benefits of leisure (Driver, Tinsley and Manfredo, 1991, p. 276). Benefits refer to a change that is viewed to be advantageous (an improvement in condition or a gain to an individual skier). Previous research on the North American ski market suggested that the most important motivations of Canadian skiers are related to the benefits of enjoying nature during the winter season, experiencing skiing's thrills and challenges, improving one's physical abilities and socialising (Williams, 1986, p. 26). In addition, a telephone survey of 1504 adult skiers selected from eleven cities in North America, which represent the eleven largest markets for British Columbian ski destinations, revealed the importance of eight basic reasons for skiing. These benefits were enjoyment of the outdoors (67% reporting), being with friends (54%), thrill of skiing (53%), exercise and keeping fit (49%), being with family (40%), feeling of accomplishment (29%), meeting new people (16%) and competition (5%), (Campbell Goodall and Associates, 1989). These eight basics include psychological, aesthetic, physical and sociability benefits and they were included in the present study since they were relevant to the British Columbia ski market and apply to 1989-90 conditions.

In this paper, the author will examine alternative methods of segmenting skier markets using sample data collected in Victoria, British Columbia, Canada during the 1989-1990 ski season. As part of a larger study, 100 personal interviews were completed and data were collected using conjoint analysis on the relative importance of ski resort attributes in decision making for either a short trip (1-3 days skiing) or a long trip (4 or more days skiing). Additional data were collected on socio-demographics, behavioral characteristics and skier motivation defined by benefits sought from the skiing experience. These variables were combined in different ways to explore the relationships between them and to suggest meaningful segmentation criteria for the skier market.

In former studies, two strategies form the basis for research design in market segmentation: factor cluster segmentation and a priori segmentation. Factor cluster segmentation produces market segments analytically in a two step process. The first step involves the definition of important characteristics of the segments through factor analysis of a large number of descriptive variables. These characteristics are then used to cluster individuals into statistically homogeneous segments (Smith, 1989). This approach was used in a number of tourism market segmentation studies (Jurowski, Usyal and Noe, 1993, Calantone and Johar, 1984, Smith and Smale, 1982) in contrast a priori segmentation is a procedure in which the researcher selects the basis for defining the segments. Once this basis is defined, a second step is to profile the predetermined segments with respect to selected descriptions. These are many examples of a priori segmentation of tourism markets (Woodside and Jacobs, 1985, McQueen and Miller, 1985, Anderson and Langmeyer, 1982).

In the present study, two different approaches were taken to segment skiers. The first was a hybrid or combination of the two approaches described above. The basis for selecting skiers to market segments was decided priori by using data from conjoint analysis. It was hypothesised that the importance which skiers place on ski resort attributes in the decision making process of choosing between resorts was a sound basis for skier segmentation. Skiers were clustered on the importance which they placed on ski resort attributes as revealed by conjoint analysis. The segments were then compared on demographic behavorial and motivation (benefit) variables. The second approach used in this study was a traditional a priori approach with market segments identified in terms of personal characteristics. The segments were compared on the importance which they placed on ski resort attributes in resort choice decision making. The hybrid and a priori methods of skier segmentation were compared on how effectively they described meaningful market segments.

RESEARCH DESIGN

Figure 2 outlines the steps in the research design of this segmentation study. The key attributes of ski resort choice were identified and skiers were asked to rank order hypothetical destinations. Conjoint analysis was used to measure the relative importance of ski resort attributes to destination choice. Two segmentation methods were used. First, skiers were segmented according to the importance that the resort attributes meant to their choice behavior (hybrid cluster approach). Second, they were segmented according to demographic, motivation and behavioral variables (a priori approach).

1. Identifying the Key Attributes of Ski Resort Choice

This first step was probably one of the most important according to Claxton who stated that "the identification of attributes that consumers are asked to evaluate is part of the problem definition process, the cornerstone of research design" (Claxton, 1987, p. 466). An analysis of published research both from academic and government sources showed that certain attributes were frequently mentioned as being important in resort evaluation (as shown in Table 1). The attributes most commonly chosen to measure resort attractiveness were size, access, price and lift line variables. In this study, the attributes chosen were based on the finding of past research and included snow conditions, variety of runs, lift lines, value for

FIGURE 2. Research Design

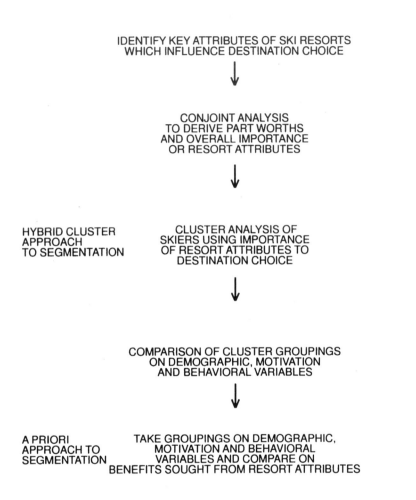

money, staff friendliness and access to home. This choice reflected the physical, experiential and accessibility aspects of ski resorts which influence their attractiveness. Size of resort was operationalized by "variety of runs," micro-climate by "snow conditions," crowding by "lift lines," service quality by "staff friendliness" and accessibility by "access to home." Price was replaced by "value for money." The number of attributes was limited to six as past studies have shown that respondents have

TABLE 1. Attributes of Ski Resorts Used in Previous Studies

Academic and Government Literature	Size	Snow	Price	Access	Staff Friendliness	Lift Lines
Market Facts (1978)	x	x	x			
Where Do the Trails End? (1986)	x	x		x		
B.C. Skier Survey (1982)		x		x		
B.C. Skier Survey (1988)	x	x	x	x	x	x
Echelberger & Shafer (1970)	x			x		
Elsner (1971)	x		x	x		x
Johnson & Elsner (1972)	x		x	x		x
McAllister & Klett (1976)	x			x		x
Ewing & Kulka (1979)	x					x
Wetstein & McKeele (1980)			x			
Morey (1987)	x					
Walsh & Davitt (1983)			x	x		
Dilley & Pozihun (1986)	x				x	x
Goodall & Bergsma(1990)	x	x	x	x		x

difficulty in evaluating large numbers of variables at once (Miller, 1956). The median number of attributes previously used in conjoint analysis was seven (Cattin and Wittink, 1984); and Green and Shrinivasan (1978) have suggested that individuals have difficulty evaluating objects defined on more than six attributes at a time because of information overload.

2. Conjoint Analysis

Conjoint measurement is used in choice situations to provide an index of the relative value of attributes or partworths of attributes in influencing preference. Separate partworths are estimated for each level of each attribute. These values represent the relative importance of each attribute and its associated level in terms of its overall attractiveness to any particular choice (Smith, 1989).

One hundred personal interviews were used to collect data for conjoint analysis. Skiers were presented with twenty-nine ski resort profiles and asked to rank order them in terms of preference, either for a short 1-3 day break or for a longer 4-7 day vacation. Seventy of the one hundred skiers were asked to evaluate a second context. In total eighty-eight skiers ranked the cards for a short trip and eighty-two skiers ranked the cards for a longer trip. This method used for data collection was the full profile approach, which is the most commonly used method in conjoint analysis (Cattin and Wittink, 1989, p. 47). A minimum of twenty-five hypothetical ski resort profiles were needed to estimate the main effects of the six attributes at four levels. The twenty-five profiles were generated by the OPLAN program of the SPSS Categories Statistical Package so that respondents were presented with an orthogonal design which represented a range of profiles with combinations of attributes at different levels. Also, four hold out cards were generated making twenty-nine cards in total.

The ranking of the twenty-five resorts was used as data for ordinary least squares regression analysis. The partworth scores indicated the influence of each attribute (independent variable) on the respondents' preference for a ski resort profile (dependent variable). The details of the model used to estimate partworths may be generally described by Formula 1 below.

$$V_h \notin \sum_{i=1}^{6} \sum_{k=1}^{4} V_{ik} \cdot X_{ik}^{(h)} \tag{1}$$

Where V_h represents the evaluation of profile h (h = 1, 2, ... 25)
V_{ik} is the part worth (regression coefficient) associated with level k (k = 1, 2, 3, 4) of attribute i (i = 1, 2, . . . 6)
$X_{ik}^{(h)}$ is the variable of level K of attribute i that corresponds to profile h and

---

(Source: Based on Akaah and Korgaonkar, 1988, p. 41)

More details of this method are described in previous publications (Carmichael, 1991, Carmichael, 1992). As a result of the orthogonal design matrix for the independent variables the computed partworth scores (raw regression coefficients) were all expressed in a common unit. This meant that these partworth scores could be added together to give the total utility or image of a particular combination of attributes within a ski resort profile, as was used in a previous study in predictive choice modelling (Carmichael, 1991). The partworths could also be combined to show the overall importance for each attribute in terms of its contribution to resort preference. These importance values were standardized scores. They were found by examining the range in the partworth utilities for each attribute and standardizing the value by dividing by the total range in value of all partworths. Formula 2 below summarizes this procedure.

$$W_i = \frac{\{\max_k (V_{ik}) - \min_k (V_{ik})\}}{\sum_{i=1}^{6} \{\max_k (V_{ik}) - \min_k (V_{ik})\}} \qquad (2)$$

where W_i denotes the relative importance of attribute i (i = 1, 2, . . . 6) and k is level of each attribute. V_{ik} is the part worth utility for attribute i, level k

(Source: Based on Akaah and Korgaonkar, 1988, p. 41)

SKIER SEGMENTATION: HYBRID CLUSTER APPROACH

The overall importance scores of ski resort attributes to destination choice was used as a basis of cluster analysis so that skiers could be grouped into market segments following the macro approach suggested by Crompton. Cluster analysis is a classification tool used to separate the sample into mutually exclusive groups based on similarities among cases and has been used in a number of tourism segmentation studies (Mazanek, 1984, Davis and Sternquist, 1987). In this study, hierarchical cluster analysis identified six clusters as the best solution for the short trip scenario and six clusters for the long trip scenario. Hierarchical cluster analysis requires that the number of the cluster is specified by the researcher. A number of solutions were explored but solutions of less than six clusters were inappropriate because the resultant sample sizes within each cluster solution were either too small to warrant separate marketing strategies or too large to be meaningful.

1. Short Trip Situation (1-3 Days Skiing)

The six clusters showed how differing groups emphasized different importance values for the ski resort attributes (Table 2). Some of the clusters obtained from this analysis were very small and therefore making generalizations about ski markets from these results should be treated with caution. Therefore, comparisons of the cluster groupings were made using demographic, motivation and behavioral variables for both a six cluster solution and alternatively, for the two largest size clusters–cluster 1 (n = 50) and cluster 2 (n = 19), within the six cluster solution.

One way analysis of variance tests were used to investigate differences between cluster groups on the socio-demographic, behavioral or motivation descriptors. This technique is concerned with differences between

TABLE 2. Importance of Ski Resort Attributes to Clusters Short Trip Situation (1-3 Days Skiing)

RESORT ATTRIBUTES	CLU 1 N = 50	CLU 2 N = 19	CLU 3 N = 8	CLU 4 N = 6	CLU 5 N = 4	CLU 6 N = 1	TOTAL N = 88
VARIETY OF RUNS	16.03	18.95	6.40	4.01	<u>48.64</u>	1.30	16.28
SNOW CONDITIONS	<u>29.68</u>	<u>47.21</u>	16.08	<u>57.57</u>	19.98	13.40	<u>33.50</u>
LIFT LINES	9.72	18.56	12.08	3.93	17.34	19.33	11.90
VALUE FOR MONEY	17.11	4.80	9.38	<u>19.14</u>	4.43	17.07	13.31
STAFF FRIENDLINESS	5.66	3.03	3.48	3.24	3.53	<u>45.62</u>	5.09
ACCESS TO HOME	21.96	7.44	<u>52.57</u>	12.11	6.11	3.28	20.00
IMPORTANT FACTOR	SNOW ACCESS	NOW VARIETY LIFT LINES	ACCESS	SNOW	VARIETY	STAFF	SNOW

The figures in the cells represent the mean relative importance of the ski resort attribute to resort choice for the skiers within that cluster. Underlined figures represent the attribute which is of the greatest importance to skiers within that cluster. The final column gives the mean relative importance of the ski resort attributes for all skiers considering a short trip (as computed by formula 2).

samples as classes to summarize their characteristics. However, the procedure emphasizes sum of squares rather than differences of means (Clark
and Hoskins 1986, p. 266). No statistically significant differences were
found with any of the variables. When the two largest clusters were
compared only one variable, feeling of accomplishment, showed a statistically significant difference between the groups (F ratio 4.6870, F prob
0.0342). Group 1 had a stronger need for accomplishment than Group 2.
Therefore, for the short trip situation no meaningful segmentation was
achieved by this method.

Longer Trip Situation (4 or More Days Skiing)

In a similar manner to the short trip analysis, hierarchial cluster analysis
was used to create clusters of skiers who were grouped on the importance
which they placed on the six resort attributes when deciding to take a long
trip. As with the short trip situation, solutions with less than six clusters
showed one large group and a number of very small groups. Table 3 shows
the six cluster solution. Cluster 1 skiers placed snow conditions, value for
money and variety of runs with approximately equal weighting; Cluster 2
were mainly interested in snow conditions and variety of runs; Cluster 3
were 'value for money' conscious; whereas Cluster 4 felt that access was
most important; Cluster 5 needed excellent snow conditions and Cluster 6
felt that lift lines were most important in their resort choice.

Despite the small sample sizes for some of the clusters one way analysis of
variance was used to test for statistically significant differences between the
cluster groups on the socio-demographic and motivation variables. Only age (F
= 3.2402, F prob = .0108) and the need to be with family (F = 3.2463, F prob =
.0109) showed statistically significant differences between the clusters.

Because of the small number of skiers in some of the clusters, the one
way analysis of variance was repeated to compare Clusters 1, 2 and 5.
They showed significant differences in age (F = 4.0785, F prob = .0223)
and ability (F = 3.5117, F prob =.0367). Skiers in Group 2 had higher
levels of ability and were more interested in variety of runs (F ratio
4.4075, F prob = .0168).

With these results, it was felt that the hybrid cluster method of segmenting skiers was unsuccessful in this context as there were so few differences
noted between clusters on the socio-demographic or motivation variables.

SKIER SEGMENTATION: A PRIORI APPROACH

The importance values from conjoint analysis for individual skiers were
used as clustering variables in the hybrid cluster approach. This method

TABLE 3. Importance of Ski Resort Attributes to Clusters (Long Trip Situation—4 or More Days Skiing)

RESORT ATTRIBUTES	CLU 1 N = 33	CLU 2 N = 19	CLU 3 N = 5	CLU 4 N = 4	CLU 5 N = 19	CLU 6 N = 2	TOTAL N = 82
VARIETY OF RUNS	21.09	36.48	13.72	9.18	9.49	8.82	20.64
SNOW CONDITIONS	24.18	42.29	18.57	15.38	50.14	26.63	33.20
LIFT LINES	12.46	7.65	18.45	6.99	13.91	39.94	12.49
VALUE FOR MONEY	22.42	6.51	47.08	13.11	15.41	8.09	17.81
STAFF FRIENDLINESS	6.91	2.65	3.60	4.70	4.42	5.19	4.99
ACCESS TO HOME	11.83	4.42	6.44	50.65	6.63	11.35	10.46
IMPORTANT FACTOR	SNOW VALUE VARIETY	SNOW VARIETY	VALUE	ACCESS	SNOW	LIFT	SNOW

The figures in the cells represent the mean relative importance of the ski resort attributes to resort choice for the skiers within that cluster. Underlined figures represent the attribute which is of the greatest importance to skiers within that cluster. The final column gives the mean relative importance of the ski resort attributes for all skiers considering a long trip (as computed by formula 2).

produced groups which did not seem particularly meaningful in terms of the other skier descriptors. Therefore, a second approach, building up from the demographic and motivation groups, to compare the groups on the benefits sought in ski resort attributes was developed and this approach achieved greater success in segmenting skiers. One way analysis of variance tests were used to test for differences between groups on benefits sought in ski resort attributes under different situations of ski resort choice. Duncan multiple range tests (the alpha level was set at .05) were used to determine which means were significantly different. Table 4 summarises the significant results from the short trip and Table 5 summarises the results from the long trip situation. On both tables the means represent the mean value of the importance of ski resort attribute to the skiers segments. The number of market segments varies according to the method of a priori market segmentation.

1. Short Trip Situation (1-3 Days Skiing)

When skiers were segmented by skier ability, novices were found to have greater concern over access to home for the short trip whereas advanced skiers had greater need for variety of runs. The youngest and oldest age groups also placed greater importance on variety of runs.

When skiers were segmented by sex, males placed more importance on

TABLE 4. Profile of the Short Trip Skiers (1-3 Days Skiing) by Demographic and Motivation (Benefit) Variables

Segmentation by skiing ability
1 = novice, 2 = intermediate, 3 = advanced

	mean	F ratio	F prob
access	Gp 1 41.9333 Gp 2 20.0433 Gp 3 18.0826	3.3253	.0409
variety	Gp 1 5.2600 Gp 2 12.9200 Gp 3 24.0515	10.0182	.0001

access Gp 1 significantly different from Gp 2 and 3.
variety Gp 3 significantly different from Gp 1 and 2.

Segmentation by age
1 = 15-18, 2 = 19-24, 3 = 25-34, 4 = 35-44, 5 = 45-54, 6 = 55-64, 7 = 65+

	mean	F ratio	F prob
variety	Gp 1 22.9646 Gp 2 19.8470 Gp 3 18.1147 Gp 4 10.1626 Gp 5 16.7630 Gp 6 38.9900	3.5777	.0058

variety Gp 4 significantly different from Gp 2, 3 and 6.

Segmentation by sex
1 = male, 2 = female

	mean	t Statistic	2 Tail sig.
staff	Gp 1 6.14 Gp 2 3.70	1.94	.056

TABLE 4 (continued)

Segmentation on Motivation Variables:
1= highly ranked, 2 = moderately ranked, 3 = poorly ranked

1) feeling of accomplishment

	mean	F ratio	F prob
variety	Gp 1 20.4606 Gp 2 18.8510 Gp 3 9.9076	4.2998	.0172

variety, – Gp 3 significantly different from Gp 1 and 2.

2) need to escape from routine

	mean	F ratio	F prob
value	Gp 1 15.2429 Gp 2 12.5581 Gp 3 7.4253	3.1200	.0501

value, Gp 3 significantly different from Gp 1.

3) exhilaration, thrill of skiing

	mean	F ratio	F prob
snow	Gp/1 36.0594 Gp/2 26.8747 Gp/3 32.5078	3.1223	.0500

snow, Gp 1 significantly different from GP 2 and 3.
Duncan's Multiple Ranges Test Results, alpha level set at 0.05.

staff friendliness although for both males and females staff friendliness was relatively unimportant compared with other resort attributes. In the case of sex, with two group means, a t-test was used rather than analysis of variance.

The skiers were segmented on the motivation variables but the rankings were collapsed from 1-9 with 3 groups (1-3, 4-6, 7-9) so that the number of skiers in each group would be large enough for analysis and there would be no missing categories. Groups identified on the feelings of accomplishment benefit or motivation, were statistically significantly different in the importance which they placed on variety of runs. Those with the highest need for accomplishment also evaluated variety of runs with greater importance. Segmentation on the basis of the need to escape from routine showed that skiers who placed little emphasis on the need to escape, placed less importance on value of money. Finally, exhilaration or thrill of skiing showed a statistically significant relationship with snow conditions. The greater the need for exhilaration and thrills, the greater the importance of snow conditions. For the short trip situation, segmentation on the variables, age, income, need for competition and need for exercise and keep-

TABLE 5. Profile of the Long Trip Skiers (4 or More Days Skiing) by Demographic and Motivation (Benefit) Variables

Segmentation by ability
1= novice, 2 = intermediate, 3 = advanced

	mean	F ratio	F prob
variety	Gp 1 14.2467 Gp 2 18.0341 Gp 3 26.2792	3.9280	.0239

variety, Gp 2 significantly different from Gp 3.

Segmentation by sex
1= male, 2 = female

	mean	t statistic	2 tail sig
lift	Gp 1 14.6229 Gp 2 10.3554	2.08	.04

Segmentation on Motivation Variables
1= highly ranked, 2 =moderately ranked, 3 = poorly ranked.

1) need for competition

	mean	F ratio	F prob
variety	Gp 1 15.2400 Gp 2 36.3740 Gp 3 20.1632	4.3104	.0171

variety, Gp 2 significantly different from Gp 1 and 3.

TABLE 5 (continued)

2) need to escape

	mean	F ratio	F prob
staff	Gp 1 4.4347 Gp 2 6.6816 Gp 3 2.7888	5.2986	.0072
variety	Gp 1 18.9906 Gp 2 18.7788 Gp 3 28.3053	3.7087	.0294

staff, Gp 2 significantly different from Gp 3 and Gp 1.
variety, Gp 3 significantly different from Gp 2 and Gp 1.

3) need to be with family

	mean	F ratio	F prob
variety	Gp 1 20.4905 Gp 2 16.1211 Gp 3 27.4394	3.8807	.0252

* variety, Gp 2 significantly different from Gp 3.

4) need for exhilaration, thrill of skiing

	mean	F ratio	F prob
access	Gp 1 7.0213 Gp 2 13.6784 Gp 3 16.9933	4.5162	.0142
snow	Gp 1 37.3652 Gp 2 27.6442 Gp 3 26.5078	4.0401	.0218

access Gp 1 significantly different from Gp 2 and 3.
snow Gp 2 significantly different from Gp 1.
Duncan's Multiple Ranges Test, alpha level set at 0.05.

ing fit showed no significant differences between the groups on the importance placed on ski resort attributes.

2. Long Trip Situation (4 or More Days Skiing)

When skiers were grouped on ability, advanced skiers placed greater importance on variety for the longer trip, whereas on the short trip they were satisfied with a more local product. T-test results for groupings by sex showed that lift lines were a more important factor in decision making for males than females (who it appears from these results may be more tolerant of queuing).

Groupings using the motivation variables also produced interesting findings. As with the short trip data, the motivation rankings were collapsed from nine categories (1-9) into three (1-3, 4-6, 7-9) to avoid the problem of missing categories. When skiers were segmented by the need for competition, those ranking competition as moderately important showed the highest need for variety of runs. Similarly, those ranking the need to escape as moderately important showed the greatest need for staff friendliness. Those with less need to escape showed more importance of variety of runs, which seems the reverse of what is expected intuitively. Where less emphasis is placed on the need to be with family, the importance of variety of runs in destination choice is greater. In addition, skiers with the greatest need for exhilaration and the thrill of skiing place less emphasis on access for the longer trip and more importance on snow conditions.

DISCUSSION

Cluster analysis of skiers according to their ski resort choice behavior and the importance which they place on ski resort attributes did not produce meaningful market segments either for the short trip or the long trip situation. This is not to imply that the approach is invalid only that in this context the a priori method produced more easily identifiable segments. There are a number of criteria which are useful to assess the quality of market segmentation. Firstly, the target market should be accessible and easily be able to be reached from information channels. Because the clusters showed little relationship to the easily identifiable socio-demographic and behavioral variables it would be difficult to target the cluster groups.

Secondly, the segments must be of sufficient size to make them economical to reach. A solution of many small segments may make statistical sense but could be meaningless in practical terms. One of the drawbacks of this study relates to the constraints on sample size of the personal interview method. Unfortunately, cluster solutions smaller than six revealed one large cluster and a number of much smaller clusters.

A third criteria for effective segmentation is measurability and the segments should be defined in such a way that information is available on marketing behavior. In this study, the segments were measurable since data was available on ski choice behavior as well as skiers being described on all of the variables shown in Figure 1. However, this hybrid cluster approach, starting with benefits sought in resorts and then moving backwards to identify the skiers by other descriptors revealed few statistically significant differences between the segments on these descriptors.

Much more successful was the traditional a priori approach. For both short trip and long trip scenarios significant differences were found between segments. For the short trip, four meaningful segments were identified:

1. VARIETY LOVERS: YOUNGER, HIGHER SKIING ABILITY, STRONG NEED FOR ACCOMPLISHMENT
2. VALUE LOVERS: NEED TO ESCAPE FROM ROUTINE
3. SNOW LOVERS: NEED TO ENJOY THE THRILL OF SKIING
4. ACCESS LOVERS: LOWER SKIING ABILITY

For the longer trip, two segments were identified:

1. VARIETY LOVERS: ADVANCED SKIERS, MODERATE NEED FOR COMPETITION, STRONG NEED TO ESCAPE, LITTLE NEED TO BE WITH FAMILY
2. SNOW LOVERS: NEED TO ENJOY THE THRILL OF SKIING

In conclusion, it should be emphasized that, overall, snow conditions was the most important attribute for the majority of skiers for both the short trip and the long trip. However, other attributes are important in the trade off situation of the decision making process. In the short trip situation the largest cluster (n = 50), found by the hybrid cluster approach showed the need for snow and access whereas in the longer trip situation, the largest cluster (n = 33) was concerned with snow, value and variety. While these remain preliminary findings of an exploratory nature they do provide some guidelines for ski resort managers who are considering how to segment the skier market.

When designing brochures, managers need to focus on their resort attributes. For example, small ski resorts which are well placed to serve a nearby urban market could focus on their ease of access and snow or snow making benefits. Resorts wishing to target longer distance travel need to emphasize variety and snow conditions. If variety within a single resort is lacking then combining with other resorts and offering a regional package is a useful tactic which also may satisfy a value for money image. Given the importance of snow conditions to all skiers, it is important to invest in snow making, where necessary, to ensure snow quality. Also, it is vital to make sure that skiers know how much the resort has to offer with improved snow making ability.

This exploratory analysis shows that there are a number of relationships between the segmentation variables which can be used to describe ski market segments in a meaningful way. However, the a priori approach in this study proved to be a more useful tool for analysis than the hybrid cluster approach. In both approaches data from conjoint analysis was used in the segmentation process. Conjoint measurement provides an exciting opportunity to understand market segments in the tourism industry, not just for skiers, but within other contexts and for other recreation activities.

BIBLIOGRAPHY

British Columbia Skier Survey, (1982) British Columbia Ministry of Tourism, Recreation and Culture, Victoria, B.C., Canada.

British Columbia Skier Survey, (1988) British Columbia Ministry of Tourism, Recreation and Culture, Victoria, B.C., Canada.

Carmichael, B.A. (1992) "Using Conjoint Modelling to Measure Tourist Image and Analyze Ski Resort Choice": P. Johnson and B. Thomas, (eds.) *Choice and Demand in Tourism,* New York: Mansell.

Carmichael, B.A. (1991) *Tourist Image and Ski Resort Choice: An Analysis of the Victoria, B.C. Skier Market,* Unpublished Doctoral Dissertation, University of Victoria, B.C., Canada.

Cattin, P. and Wittink, D.R. (1982) "Commercial Use of Conjoint Analysis: A Survey," *Journal of Marketing,* 46(2): 44-53.

Clark W.A.V. and Hoskins P.L. (1986) *Statistical Methods for Geographers.* New York John Wiley & Sons.

Claxton, J.D. (1987) "Conjoint Analysis in Travel Research, A Manager's Guide." In J.R.B. Ritchie and C.R. Goeldner, (eds.), *Travel Tourism and Hospitality Research, A Handbook for Managers and Researchers* (pp. 459-469). New York: John Wiley and Sons Inc..

Crompton, J. (1983) "Selecting Target Markets – A Key to Effective Marketing," *Journal of Park and Recreation Administration* 1(1): 7-26.

Davis, B.D. and Sternquist, B. (1987) "Appealing to the Elusive Tourist: An Attribute Cluster Strategy," *Journal of Travel Research* 25(4): 25-31.

Dilley, R.S. and Pozihun, P. (1986) "Skiers in Thunder Bay, Ontario: Perceptions and Behavior," *Recreation Research Review,* 12(4): 27-32.

Echelberger, H.E. and Shafer, E.L. (1970) "Snow + "x" = Use of Ski Slopes," *Journal of Market Research* 7(2): 388-392.

Elsner, J.H. (1971) "A Regression Method for Estimating the Level of Use and Market Area of a Proposed Large Ski Resort," *Journal of Leisure Research* 3(3): 160-167.

Ewing, G.O. and Kulka, T. (1979) "Revealed and Stated Preference Analysis of Ski Resort Attractiveness," *Leisure Sciences* 2(3/4): 249-275.

Goeldner, C.R. et al. (1989) *Economic Analysis of North American Ski Areas,* Boulder, University of Colorado, Business Research Division, Graduate School of Business Administration.

Goodall, B. and Bergsma, T. (1990) "Destinations as Marketed in Tour Operator's Brochures." In G. Ashworth, and B. Goodall, (eds.) *Marketing Tourism Places*(170-192).London: Routledge.

Green, P. and Shrinivasan, V. (September 1978) "Conjoint Analysis in Consumer Research, Issues and Outlook," *Journal of Consumer Research* 5(3): 103-123.

Haley, R.I. (1984) "Benefit Segmentation Backwards and Forward," *Journal of Advertising Research*, 24(1): 19-25.

Johnson, W.E. and Elsner, G.H. (1972) "Variability in Use Among Ski Areas: A Statistical Study of the Californian Market Region," *Journal of Leisure Research* 4(4): 43-49.

Kotler, P. (1972) *Marketing Management, Analysis Planning and Control,* 2nd Edition, Englewood Cliff, N.J., Prentice Hall.

Mazanek, J.A. (1984) "How to Detect Travel Market Segments: A Clustering Approach," *Journal of Travel Research* 23(1): 17-21.

McAllister, D.M. and Klett, F.R. (1976) "A Modified Gravity Model of Regional Recreation Activity with An Application to Ski Trips," *Journal of Leisure Research* 8(1): 21-35.

Miller, B.A. (1956) "The Magic Number Seven Plus or Minus Two: Some Limits on Our Capacity for Processing Information," *The Psychological Review*, 63(2): 81-97.

Mills, A., Couturier, H., Snepenger, D.J. (1986) "Segmenting Texas Snow Skiers," *Journal of Travel Research*, 25(2): 19-23.

Morey, E.R. (1981) "The Demand for Site Specific Recreation Activities: A Characteristic Approach," *Journal of Environment Economics and Management* 8: 345-371.

Smith, S.L.T. (1989) *Tourism Analysis a Handbook*, Harlow, U.K.: Longman Group, U.K.

Stynes, D.J. and Mahoney, E.M. (1980) *Michigan Downhill Ski Market Study: Segmenting Active Skiers*, Agricultural Experiment Station Report no. 391, East Lansing, MI: Michigan State University.

Walsh, R.G. and Davitt, G.J. (1983) "A Demand Function for Length of Stay on Ski Trips to Aspen," *Journal of Travel Research* 21(4): 25-29.

Wetstein, M.E. and McNeely, T. G. (November 1980) "Specification Errors and Influence in Recreation Demand Models," *American Journal of Agricultural Economics*, 63(4): 798-800.

Willims, P. (1986) *"Where Do the Trails Lead,"* A Focus on the Canadian Ski Market, National Ski Industries Association and Tourism Canada.

Performance-Importance Analysis of Escorted Tour Evaluations

Charles R. Duke

Margaret A. Persia

SUMMARY. As an addition to the manager's set of tools, performance-importance analysis can provide insight into tourist evaluations on critical issues. On a performance-importance grid, the interaction of performance perceptions with the importance for an evaluation crite ria permits managers to grasp the relative success of tour features. An illustration is used plotting tourist pre-trip expectations, post-trip satisfactions, and importances of each on a performance-importance grid to consider potential decisions for escorted tours design. Changes in evaluations (expectations-to-satisfactions) demonstrated the flexibility of the grid in adapting to different measures. *[Article copies available from The Haworth Document Delivery Service: 1-800-342-9678. E-mail address: getinfo@haworth.com]*

Consumer evaluations of performance have been recognized as critical to the success of service industries such as tourism (cf. Cronin and Taylor, 1992; Um and Crompton, 1991). However, the tools developed to measure and analyze these evaluations have not been easily adapted for use by industry due to either troublesome theory or specialized mathematical sys-

Charles R. Duke is Assistant Professor, Department of Marketing, Clemson University, Box 341325, Clemson, SC 29634-1325. Margaret A. Persia is Instructor, Department of Hospitality Management, East Stroudsburg University, East Stroudsburg, PA 18301-2999.

[Haworth co-indexing entry note]: "Performance-Importance Analysis of Escorted Tour Evaluations." Duke, Charles R., and Margaret A. Persia. Co-published simultaneously in *Journal of Travel & Tourism Marketing* (The Haworth Press, Inc.) Vol. 5, No. 3, 1996, pp. 207-223; and *Recent Advances in Tourism Marketing Research* (ed: Daniel R. Fesenmaier, Joseph T. O'Leary, and Muzaffer Uysal) The Haworth Press, Inc., 1996, pp. 207-223. Single or multiple copies of this article are available from The Haworth Document Delivery Service [1-800-342-9678, 9:00 a.m. - 5:00 p.m. (EST). E-mail address: getinfo@haworth].

tems (cf. Babakus and Boller, 1992; Ditton, Graefe, and Fedler, 1981). Translating consumer measurements into action may be hampered by (1) management's lack of understanding of the practical significance of sophisticated statistics as well as by (2) the use of only performance or only importance instead of both sides of the question (cf. Martilla and James, 1977). Attempts continue to be made to distill consumer attitude and opinion into single scales or measures using performance and importance evaluations (Ennew, Reed, and Binks, 1993). A more popular approach with theoretical development has been aimed at universal service factors such as SERVQUAL applications and its variants (cf. Cronin and Taylor, 1992) along with other universal evaluation attempts (cf. Um and Crompton, 1992). These universal, factor-analytic-styled models require consistency across companies and industries if a single model is to be used by analysts to evaluate either a single company or the position of that company in a marketplace (cf. Um and Crompton, 1991; Parasuraman, Zeithaml, and Berry, 1988). However, a lack of consistency across industries and segments casts doubt on the application of the basic theory used to develop the models. The broad tourism industry varies in its offerings and the appropriate criteria for use in evaluation (cf. Duke and Persia, 1993). Thus the application of a universal evaluation model with standard questions provides less than optimum managerial information and leads to the search for other techniques more useful for managerial analysis.

As a result, managers have been perplexed over the appropriateness of various measures of consumer attitudes and opinions including expectation, satisfaction, and preferences (cf. Cote, Foxman, and Cutler, 1989). One attempt to reestablish performance and importance analysis in service quality suggested that generalized indexes of quality could be calculated (cf. Ennew, Reed, and Binks, 1992), but these are difficult for managers to use in operations. Indexes of quality, expressed as supply and demand indicators, do not adequately express managerial issues. Additionally, multiplicative models (performance × importance = contribution to an attitude or feeling) often do not resemble either the original performance ratings or the original importance ratings.

A need appears to exist for practical tools based on sound behavioral principles that help managers understand and use consumer evaluations. Operational managers, pressed for time and without access to sophisticated software, need to have easy-to-use methods that do not require a computer or statistical skills needed in factor analysis, discriminant analysis, or multidimensional scaling. Useful tools should reflect the information needed to support common management decisions such as promotion effectiveness, product delivery, operational effectiveness, service level approval, and intent to repurchase or recommend to others. Effective tools are often presented visually so that the results can be relayed to higher management quickly and with greater impact. Tools should be flexible and versatile so that they can be used with a wide variety of inputs to obtain different decision support information. That is, the same techniques should be able to be applied to several different issues or constructs.

Although no technique is without fault, analysis tools currently suggested by academics tend to be specialized and to require sophisticated statistical understanding and software. Perhaps additional choices of techniques are needed to increase the managerial usefulness of consumer evaluations. Less statistically demanding techniques such as qualitative responses to open-ended questions are useful but lack validity in computations and are not likely to be representative of the general market place. Listings of raw data ratings (such as expectation or satisfaction) give good information on performance levels but do not quickly relay the impact of evaluation-importance interactions. Quantitative techniques such as factor analysis and discriminant analysis can produce groupings of issues and underlying dimensions or can indicate the degree of change needed in response to consumer needs. However, these techniques require sophisticated hardware and software as well as specialized training, neither of which are necessarily available to the tour designer or manager.

PERFORMANCE-IMPORTANCE ANALYSIS

To fill the need for effective managerial information, easy to use methods, high impact visual presentation, and flexibility in uses, tour managers should consider analysis techniques used and proven in the past. Performance-importance grid analysis (cf. Martilla and James, 1977) was considered to be an effective management tool but lost favor when more quantitative methods became practical with computerization. These grids are not intended to replace statistical or mathematical analysis, but rather to augment currently used information and to provide information more useful for managerial decisions. The axis of the grids use the scales or scores provided from customers to place each variable (or combination of variables) in position. The choice of axis for either performance or importance is left to the personal preference of the manger or analyst. For convenience in this article, performance variables were placed on the horizontal (x) axis and importance measures were placed on the vertical (y) axis (Figure 1).

Interpreting the performance-importance grid into action is a fairly straightforward exercise. Each quadrant can be summarized into specific

FIGURE 1. Performance-Importance Grid Example[1]

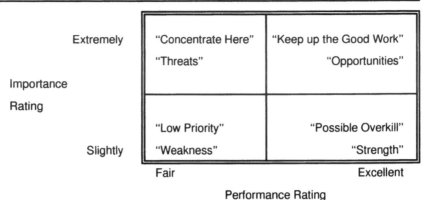

[1] Adapted from Martilla and James (1977) and Gates and Amarani (1992).

directions for management (Figure 1). Issues of importance to consumers that show excellent performance by the tour operator indicate that consumers are pleased with the work performed ("Keep Up The Good Work") and may be "Opportunities" for the tour to promote. Important issues not being handled well demand immediate attention ("Concentrate Here") and may be "Threats" to the tour's survival. Issues of lesser importance that are performed well might be considered for less emphasis ("Possible Overkill"), but this may also be a "Strength" on which to build new customers. In the last quadrant, low performance on unimportant issues may receive little more effort ("Low Priority"), or might be a "Weakness" that another firm might exploit.

Alternative Performance Measures

Performance measures may include expectation, satisfaction, preference levels, or others depending on the managerial purpose or decision needed. Although individual data may be plotted, it is more likely that appropriate segment or group means for individual criteria may be most beneficial for analysis. Then the manager can analyze customer concerns or evaluations by inspection and inference. The grids can be used in conjunction with standard statistical tests (such as t-tests of significant differences between groups) to illustrate important issues of concern. Whereas evaluation levels suggest performance concerns, the importance levels suggest priorities for customers. Performance measures may include expectations, performance, satisfactions, changes on any of these over time, or comparisons among these for the same time frame.

Expectations: These evaluative scores relate to managerial decisions on issues that deal with tour preparation by the customer. Managerial issues to be considered by these scores include design and execution of promotions, advertising, features highlighted in pre-tour communications, reception services just prior to trips, as well as other issues.

Preferences: These evaluations relate to alternatives and tradeoffs that the customer makes, especially in choice of destinations, attractions, or features (Babakus and Boller, 1992). The design of a tour is most prevalent in this evaluation. The timing of preference evaluations may alter the style of information obtained (cf. Cote, Foxman, and Cutler, 1989).

Satisfactions: These evaluations indicate the impression of the customer on the accomplishment of the goals of the tour (cf. Duke and Persia, 1993). Also considered here is intent to repurchase or intent to relay positive recommendations to others. This relates to design of the tour but also indicates a short-term operational assessment of how well a specific tour was executed.

Changes: For those able to collect information consistently over time or to use different evaluative questions, differences in evaluations indicate trends in customer attitude over time or differences among segments of consumers. One example of changes can be developed as consumers evaluate their expectations prior to a tour and then rate their satisfaction afterward. This may indicate learning on the part of the consumer and changes of importance over the experience of the trip. It could also show the effect of group dynamics or interaction during the tour. Perhaps it could show changes from an expectation of meeting minimum criteria to one of value added services in satisfaction (cf. Zeithaml, Berry, and Parasuraman, 1993). Aside from the changes in evaluation, changes in importance ratings may show more about the priorities of customers before, during, and after a tour than any single raw evaluation score (cf. Persia and Gitelson, 1993).

PERFORMANCE-IMPORTANCE ANALYSIS ILLUSTRATION

Illustration Objective

The objective of this exercise is to reconsider the use of performance-importance grids in tourism management and to illustrate these ideas by applying the technique to the results of a national tour survey. This national survey evaluated the performance of escorted tours and provided information on promotional aspects as well as design and operations assessments.

Design

A prior study using a national survey, performed to explore customer evaluations as well as satisfaction theory, provided data on expectations, satisfactions, and importances for escorted tour participants (Duke and Persia, 1993). Pre-tour and post-tour evaluation issues and criteria were developed in an exploratory study. Pre-tour expectation evaluations were then obtained on multiple items from a national sample of escorted tour purchasers. After completing their travels, respondents provided post-tour satisfaction ratings on the same issues. Means for each item measured were plotted on a performance-importance grid.

Sampling

The original study procedure asked travel agencies and tour operators from throughout the United States for assistance in data collection (Duke and Persia, 1993). Agencies were selected randomly from a list of those approved by the Airline Reporting Corporation, the widest sample frame available. Tour operators were selected randomly from a list of members of the National Tour Association (NTA). Firms were asked to distribute surveys to escorted tour clients booked on upcoming tours. Post-tour data was requested from each of the pre-tour participants. For this application of performance-importance grids, completed questionnaires from 149 pre-tour evaluations and 89 post-tour evaluations were used. Respondent characteristics, shown in Table 1, were similar to those for domestic escorted tours (cf. Longwoods, 1990). The majority of respondents were female, and most participants were between the ages of 61 and 75. Education level was relatively high. Respondents reported that they were experienced group travelers with a large majority having participated in previous escorted tours. European tours outnumbered all other foreign destinations which included a highly diverse set of destinations. Approximately one-third of the respondents indicated that they had visited their tour destination before. Tours occurred in every month of the year except January. Respondents resided in a number of different states.

Instrument

The evaluation statements in the original study were derived from an exploratory study of escorted tour participants. Specific statements from

TABLE 1. Tour Dimension Evaluation Study Respondent Characteristics

Variables	Pre-Tour Evaluation		Post-Tour Evaluation	
	Number	Percent	Number	Percent
Gender:				
Male	49	36.8	37	41.6
Female	84	63.2	52	58.4
Age: 20-40	8	6.0	6	6.7
41-60	21	15.8	14	15.7
61-65	27	20.3	17	19.1
66-70	40	30.1	29	32.6
71-75	23	17.3	13	14.6
76-85	14	10.5	10	11.2
Education:				
<High School	12	9.0	3	3.4
High School	37	27.8	29	32.6
Vo/Tech	9	6.8	6	6.7
Some College	31	23.3	17	19.1
Bachelor Degree	27	20.3	19	21.3
Graduate Degree	17	12.8	15	16.9
Tour Experience:				
Never Toured	5	3.7	5	5.6
1-3 Tours	32	24.1	20	22.5
4 or More Tours	96	72.2	64	71.9
Destination:				
Domestic (U.S.)	62	46.6	39	43.8
Foreign:				
Canada/Mexico	18	13.5	10	11.2
Europe	27	20.3	19	21.3
Other "Overseas"	26	19.6	21	23.7
Total Foreign:	71	53.4	50	56.2
Month of Tour:				
January	0	0.0	0	0.0
February	3	2.3	1	1.1
March	4	3.0	2	2.2
April	1	.8	1	1.1
May	5	3.7	3	3.4
June	32	24.0	24	27.0
July	19	14.3	12	13.5
August	7	5.3	5	5.6
September	33	24.8	23	25.8
October	16	12.0	14	15.7
November	4	3.0	2	2.2
December	9	6.8	2	2.2

the exploratory study reflected consumer concerns in their own terminology (cf. Peter and Ray, 1984). Issues of concern noted in this exploratory study included many of those found in prior studies such as itinerary, personal satisfaction, social interaction, services provided, and scenery. After content analysis and industry researchers' review for reasonability, the final statements (Table 2) were again pretested and considered appropriate by consumers who were a part of the target group but not a part of final data collection. Subjects responded to the statements by completing Likert scales rating pre-tour expectations and post-tour satisfactions (+2 = strongly agree, −2 = strongly disagree) as well as itemized

TABLE 2. Tour Dimension Study Evaluation Statements Developed from Exploratory Study

- I expect the scenery will be a source of enjoyment on this tour.
- I expect to be treated as a special person.
- I expect the tour escort in particular to make this tour enjoyable.
- I expect to be comfortable on this tour.
- I expect to make friends with other passengers on this tour.
- I expect the atmosphere among the group to be friendly.
- I don't expect to be alone often.
- I expect to learn new things about myself on this tour.
- I expect to get my money's worth on this tour.
- I expect to relax on this tour.
- I expect this tour will be the best way I personally could visit this destination.
- I expect I won't have to make major decisions on this tour.
- I expect to do what I couldn't do alone on this tour.
- I expect we will see as much as possible.
- I expect this tour to be adventurous.
- I expect never to be bored on this tour.
- I expect that stops at interesting places will be long enough to see what is important.
- I expect to be shown the most important attractions during this tour.
- I expect this tour to be educational.
- I expect to be safe from harm or injury on this tour.

scales rating pre- and post-tour importance (+2 = very important, +1 = important, 0 = neutral, − 1 = unimportant).

ANALYSIS USING PERFORMANCE-IMPORTANCE GRIDS

Means for pre-trip expectations and importances (Table 3) provided plot points for a pre-trip grid (Figure 2). Plot points are identified by the statement number used to list each expectation criteria in Table 3. Because respondents tend to overrate satisfactions and other evaluations on many scales (cf. Peterson and Wilson, 1992), the ratings here show only positive importance and positive expectations. Arbitrary quadrants can be devised using the approximate midpoint of this plot (cf. Martilla and James, 1977). Since expectations do not indicate low performance, it is reasonable that no ratings were dramatically off the diagonal from lower-right to upper-left. The only unimportant and low expectation issue was "learning about myself." Modest expectations and importances involved relaxation, adventure, education, friendly passengers, as well as not being alone, bored, or special. All other issues fell into the upper quadrant of "opportunities" where "good work" on the part of the tour provider was expected. This might indicate that a base level of performance is needed to cover the basic concrete itinerary issues first. These issues should be stressed in pre-trip communications and used in promotions (ads, brochures, travel agent interfaces, telephone booking, reception, etc.).

Post-trip satisfactions and importances (Table 4) were used to plot evaluations after respondents returned from their tours (Figure 3). Plot points are identified by the statement number used to list each satisfaction criteria in Table 4. Similar evidence of over-rating is present, and a similar arbitrary quadrant division of about mid-scale can be used to evaluate the satisfaction grid ratings. Whereas "learning about myself" is still in the "low-priority" quadrant, fewer issues fall into the modest ranges around the scale mid-points including adventure, education, and not being alone. All other issues were rated in the "keep up the good work" quadrant. This result appears to indicate good performance since no critical issues were rated with lower satisfaction ("threats" or "concentrate here"), and no high satisfaction issue was low in importance ("overkill"). This might indicate a need for not only itinerary issues but also social interaction issues to be used in tour design ensuring that tour features as well as the tour leader perform as needed.

Changes in the pre- to post-trip evaluations (Table 5) and importances (Table 6) add another dimension to the usefulness of performance-importance grids in managerial decisions. Tests for significant differences in the

TABLE 3. Pre-Trip Expectations and Importance for All Respondents (n = 133)[1]

Statement: (n = 133)	Pre-Trip Expectations (mean)	(s.d.)	Pre-Trip Importance (mean)	(s.d.)
1. to be shown the most important attractions	1.64	.58	1.81	.84
2. the scenery will be a source of enjoyment	1.63	.61	1.66	.64
3. stops long enough to see what's important	1.55	.62	1.71	.63
4. to be comfortable on this tour	1.52	.56	1.68	.86
5. we will see as much as possible	1.51	.69	1.61	.73
6. to be safe from harm or injury	1.49	.67	1.66	.97
7. tour will be the best way I could personally visit this destination	1.47	.83	1.62	.98
8. to get my money's worth on this tour	1.46	.63	1.72	.90
9. atmosphere among group to be friendly	1.40	.59	1.54	.65
10. to do what I couldn't do alone on this tour	1.37	.88	1.44	.83
11. escort to make this tour enjoyable	1.36	.73	1.58	.72
12. I won't have to make major decisions	1.25	.85	1.21	.95
13. to relax on this tour	1.08	.91	1.04	1.03
14. this tour to be adventurous	1.06	.85	.89	1.07
15. to make friends with other passengers	1.03	.72	.83	1.20
16. (not) to be alone often	.97	.88	.50	1.17
17. this tour to be educational	.97	.84	.67	1.11
18. to never be bored on this tour	.92	1.00	.90	.98
19. to be treated as a special person	.90	1.00	.88	1.11
20. I will learn new things about myself	.30	.90	.16	1.21

[1] Listed in order of highest expectation
(+2 = Strongly Agree; −2 = Strongly Disagree).

FIGURE 2. Pre-Trip Evaluations: Expectations and Importance

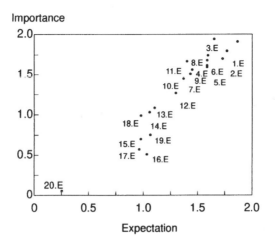

pre- to post-trip measures from respondents completing both question-naires indicated changes in evaluations (satisfactions versus expectations) as well as importances. Because a grid showing all of the points would be too cluttered for this illustration, only some of the significant changes were plotted (Figure 4). Plot points are indicated by the statement number used in the listing of the criteria. This grid shows interesting differences in evaluations across the trip experience. Satisfaction ratings with seeing important attractions (1), long enough stops (3), comfort (4), and seeing as much as possible (5) were significantly less than expectation ratings. This issue is captured by the tests of significance, but the grid quickly illustrates the drop along with the apparent stability of the importance ratings (with the exception that "comfort" became significantly more important). Other issues such as enjoyable escorts, not making decisions, relaxation, and friendly passengers show large changes in both importance and evalua-tion. The decreased satisfaction with attractions and time available might indicate that concrete itinerary issues may never be fully satisfied. The social aspects rose dramatically, and the importance ratings of many issues were higher. This information might be used in tour design to be aware of how people change (concrete issues to social issues) and how this transi-tion must be effected from pre-trip communications through the end of the trip experience itself.

TABLE 4. Post-Trip Satisfactions and Importance[1]

Statement: (n = 89)	Post-Trip Satisfactions (mean)	(s.d.)	Post-Trip Importance (mean)	(s.d.)
1. I was shown the most important attractions	1.49	.79	1.81	.39
2. the scenery was a source of enjoyment	1.73	.51	1.71	.54
3. stops were long enough to see what's important	1.22	.87	1.79	.43
4. was comfortable on this tour	1.35	.96	1.71	.46
5. saw as much as possible	1.29	.93	1.55	.67
6. was safe from harm or injury	1.58	.77	1.73	.59
7. tour was the best way I could personally visit this destination	1.49	.79	1.64	.62
8. got my money's worth on this tour	1.22	1.05	1.74	.44
9. atmosphere among group was friendly	1.49	.75	1.63	.55
10. did what I couldn't do alone on this tour	1.33	.92	1.42	.89
11. escort made this tour enjoyable	1.36	.99	1.80	.43
12. didn't have to make major decisions	1.49	.75	1.42	.84
13. relaxed on this tour	1.18	.95	1.39	.85
14. this tour was adventurous	1.02	.82	.90	.92
15. made friends with other passengers	1.43	.65	1.20	.81
16. (was not) alone often	1.24	.79	.61	1.13
17. this tour was educational	1.23	.65	.81	1.02
18. was never bored on this tour	1.18	.86	1.18	.93
20. learned new things about myself	.49	.75	.06	1.15

[1] Listed in order of highest pre-trip expectation for convenience of comparison
(+2 = Strongly Agree; − 2 = Strongly Disagree).

CONCLUSION

Performance-importance analysis can be used to quickly view and comprehend the tourist's perception of critical tour elements. The interaction between the evaluation of each critical element and its importance permits managers to grasp the relative success of the tour on each feature rated by

FIGURE 3. Post-Trip Evaluations: Satisfactions and Importance

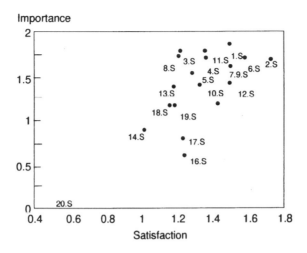

the customer. The general approach includes the following steps: critical elements are identified; ratings are obtained on both the performance of the tour on each element and the importance of the element; means are obtained for a specified group; means are plotted on appropriately scaled grids; grids are analyzed by inspection to consider managerial implications. Variations of the analysis approach can be used to illustrate changing evaluation ratings over time to detect shifts in the taste or preferences of the target market. Comparisons of various measures (such as expectations and satisfactions used here) are possible if the situation permits. The grids may be used to illustrate the differences among groups (for example, foreign versus domestic travelers, males versus females, or agency bookings versus tour operator bookings).

Limitations of performance-importance charts include its lack of statistical significance testing ability and its sensitivity to the section of scale used in the visual presentation. As illustrated in this article, performance-importance charts are meant to augment, not replace, statistical comparisons of critical issues. The charts may help to indicate or to highlight issues not previously considered, but conventional statistical tests must be used to determine significance. Additionally, the scale segments used in the charts may exaggerate or hide certain changes. That is, when the full scale is used in the example shown here, the changes will appear less dramatic. On the other hand, when a very small portion of the scale is used

TABLE 5. Attributes Ratings: Expectation (Pre-Trip) versus Satisfaction (Post Trip) for Post-Trip Respondents Only[1]

Statement: (n = 89)	Pre-Trip Expectation	Post-Trip Satisfaction	t-value	prob.
1. to be shown the most important attractions	1.69	1.49	1.87	.07[3]
2. the scenery will be a source of enjoyment	1.65	1.73	1.15	.25
3. stops long enough to see what's important	1.58	1.22	3.38	.001[2]
4. to be comfortable on this tour	1.52	1.35	1.43	.16
5. we will see as much as possible	1.52	1.29	2.29	.02[2]
6. to be safe from harm or injury	1.52	1.58	.64	.53
7. this tour will be the best way I personally could visit this destination	1.37	1.49	1.11	.27
8. to get my money's worth on this tour	1.53	1.22	2.53	.01[2]
9. atmosphere among group to be friendly	1.38	1.49	1.34	.18
10. to do what I couldn't do alone on this tour	1.31	1.33	.09	.93
11. escort to make this tour enjoyable	1.34	1.36	.20	.84
12. I won't have to make major decisions	1.24	1.49	2.48	.02[2]
13. to relax on this tour	1.05	1.18	1.06	.29
14. this tour to be adventurous	1.02	1.02	.00	1.00
15. to make friends with other passengers	.94	1.43	5.38	.000[2]
16. (not) to be alone often	.99	1.24	2.40	.02[2]
17. this tour to be educational	.92	1.23	3.79	.00[2]
18. to never be bored on this tour	.94	1.16	1.79	.08[3]
19. to be treated as a special person	1.01	1.18	1.52	.13
20. I will learn new things about myself	.24	.49	2.75	.007[2]

[1] Listed in order of highest expectation
(+2 = Strongly Agree; − 2 = Strongly Disagree).
[2] Significant (alpha = .05).
[3] Marginal significance (alpha = .06 to .10).

TABLE 6. Attributes Importance Ratings: Expection (Pre-Trip) versus Satisfaction (Post-Trip) for Post-Trip Respondents Only[1]

Statement: (n = 89)	Pre-Trip Expectation	Post-Trip Satisfaction	t-value	prob.
1. to be shown the most important attraction	1.76	1.81	.75	.45
2. the scenery will be a source of enjoyment	1.67	1.71	.44	.44
3. stops long enough to see what's important	1.75	1.79	.50	.62
4. to be comfortable on this tour	1.60	1.71	1.73	.09[3]
5. we will see as much as possible	1.58	1.55	.41	.68
6. to be safe from harm or injury	1.66	1.73	.83	.41
7. this tour will be the best way I personally could visit this destination	1.48	1.64	1.64	.10[3]
8. to get my money's worth on this tour	1.72	1.74	.31	.76
9. atmosphere among group to be friendly	1.55	1.63	1.15	.25
10. to do what I couldn't do alone on this tour	1.43	1.42	.10	.92
11. escort to make this tour enjoyable	1.64	1.80	2.47	.02[2]
12. I won't have to make major decisions	1.26	1.42	1.39	.17
13. to relax on this tour	1.07	1.39	2.92	.004[2]
14. this tour to be adventurous	.74	.90	1.47	.15
15. to make friends with other passengers	.70	1.20	3.96	.000[2]
16. (not) to be alone often	.51	.61	.71	.48
17. this tour to be educational	.56	.81	2.32	.02[2]
18. to never be bored on this tour	.97	1.19	2.08	.04[2]
19. to be treated as a special person	1.01	1.18	1.57	.12
20. I will learn new things about myself	.06	.06	.00	1.00

[1] Listed in order of highest expectation (+2 = Strongly Agree; −2 = Strongly Disagree).
[2] Significant (alpha = .05).
[3] Marginal significance (alpha − .06 to .10).

FIGURE 4. Changes in Evaluations and Importance

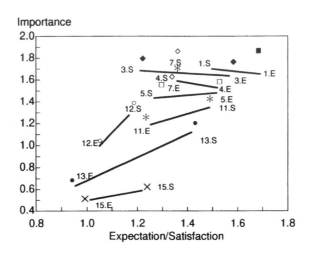

to produce the charts, small changes may be exaggerated in scope. The scale section chosen for charting should be illustrative of the issues, defendable on some research basis, and appropriate for the audience involved.

In the illustration used here, escorted tour designers can infer from this analysis that certain expectations can be used to enhance promotions and develop a base of customer purchases. Satisfaction can illustrate how well a particular tour was handled as well as indicate significantly good or bad features that deserve attention. During a tour, emphasis on itinerary issues should be adequate, but customers are likely to always be left unsatiated. However as seen from the grids, significant attention to social and personal issues in tour design can demonstrably improve customer evaluations and repurchase intent.

Performance-importance grids are simple and effective tools that can be used to analyze critical issues in customer evaluations. They can be adapted for varied purposes and changed by the type of questions asked. This makes them flexible and adaptable for the manager who may want to learn only one type of analysis and apply it to many situations or decisions needed.

REFERENCES

Babakus, E. and Boller, G.W. (1992). "An Empirical Assessment of the SERVQUAL Scale." *Journal of Business Research*, 24 (3, May), 253-268.

Cote, J.A., Foxman, E.R., and Cutler, B.D. (1989). "Seeking an Appropriate Standard of Comparison for Post-Purchase Evaluations." In *Advances in Consumer Research*, 16, T.K. Srull, ed., Provo, UT: Association for Consumer Research, 502-506.

Cronin, J.J., Jr. and Taylor, S.A. (1992). "Measuring Service Quality: A Reexamination and Extension." *Journal of Marketing*, 56 (July), 55-68.

Ditton, R.B., Graefe, A.R., and Fedler, A.J. (1981). "Recreational Satisfaction at Buffalo National River: Some Measurement Concerns." In *Some Recent Products of River Recreation Research*, GTR NC-63, St. Paul, MN: USDA Forest Service, North Central Forest Experiment Station 61.

Duke, C.R. and Persia, M.A. (1993). "Foreign and Domestic Escorted Tour Expectations of American Travelers." *Journal of International Consumer Marketing*, 6 (3), 61-77.

Ennew, C.T., Reed, G.V., and Binks, M.R. (1993). "Importance-Performance Analysis and the Measurement of Service Quality." *European Journal of Marketing*, 27 (2), 59-70.

Gates, R.A. and Amarani, S. (1992). "Incorporating the Voice of the Customer into the Product Management Process." In *Managing Product Development: Winning in the 90s*, Feldman, P.P., Hustad, T.P., and Page, A.L., eds, Indianapolis, IN: Product Development Management Association. 101-112.

Longwoods Travel (1990). *National Tour Foundation Group Travel Report*, Longwoods International, USA.

Martilla, J.A. and James, J.C. (1977). "Importance-Performance Analysis." *Journal of Marketing*, 41 (January), 77-79.

Parasuraman, A., Zeithaml, Valerie A., and Berry, Leonard L. (1988). "SERVQUAL: A Multiple- Item Scale for Measuring Consumer Perceptions of Service Quality." *Journal of Retailing*, 64 (Spring), 12-43.

Persia, M.A. and Gitelson, R.J. (1993). "The Differences Among Travel Agency Users in the Importance Ratings of Agency Service Features." *Journal of Travel & Tourism Marketing*, 2 (3), 77-98.

Peter, J.P. and M.L. Ray (1984). *Measurement Readings for Marketing Research*, Chicago: American Marketing Association.

Peterson, R.A. and Wilson, W.R. (1992). "Measuring Customer Satisfaction: Fact and Artifact." *Journal of the Academy of Marketing Science*, 20 (1), 61-71.

Um, S. and Crompton, J.L. (1991), "Development of Pleasure Travel Attitude Dimensions." *Annals of Tourism Research*, 18 (4), 500-504.

Zeithaml, V.A., Berry, L.L., and Parasuraman, A. (1993), "The Nature and Determinants of Customer Expectations of Service." *Journal of the Academy of Marketing Science*, 21 (1), 1-12.

Importance-Performance
and Segmentation:
Where Do We Go from Here?

Jerry J. Vaske
Jay Beaman
Richard Stanley
Michel Grenier

SUMMARY. This paper examines how optimizing resource allocation is influenced by the existence of user segments with different attitudes. In particular, it concentrates on how the attributes of a service or destination area, their importance to clients, and the clients' perceptions of performance can be used to incrementally guide decisions toward more optimal resource allocation. Results are based on simulating behavior at a hypothetical day use area by four user groups. Findings highlight the need for client segmentation prior to importance-performance (IP) analysis. IP analyses without segmentation are likely to result in user displacement of some segments giving a false impression of valid decisions. It is argued that even

Jerry J. Vaske is Associate Professor, Human Dimensions in Natural Resources Unit, Colorado State University, Fort Collins, CO. Jay Beaman is Research Advisor, Strategic Research and Analysis, Department of Canadian Heritage, Ottawa, Ontario, Canada. Richard Stanley is Head, Economics Group, Strategic Research and Analysis, Department of Canadian Heritage, Ottawa, Ontario, Canada. Michel Grenier is Analyst, Parks Canada, Department of Canadian Heritage, Ottawa, Ontario, Canada.

Direct all correspondence to: Jerry J. Vaske, Department of Natural Resource Recreation & Tourism, Colorado State University, Fort Collins, CO 80523.

[Haworth co-indexing entry note]: "Importance-Performance and Segmentation: Where Do We Go from Here?" Vaske et al. Co-published simultaneously in *Journal of Travel & Tourism Marketing* (The Haworth Press, Inc.) Vol. 5, No. 3, 1996, pp. 225-240; and *Recent Advances in Tourism Marketing Research* (ed: Daniel R. Fesenmaier, Joseph T. O'Leary, and Muzaffer Uysal) The Haworth Press, Inc., 1996, pp. 225-240. Single or multiple copies of this article are available from The Haworth Document Delivery Service [1-800-342-9678, 9:00 a.m. - 5:00 p.m. (EST). E-mail address: getinfo@haworth.com].

with improved analysis methods, the ad hoc model behind IP makes its use risky. As continuing rapid development of decision modeling allows, IP should be replaced with decision models that allow a more solid foundation for decisions in economic, social and statistical theory. *[Article copies available from The Haworth Document Delivery Service: 1-800-342-9678. E-mail address: getinfo@haworth.com]*

INTRODUCTION

Importance-performance (IP) has emerged as a popular analytical tool in fields as diverse as health care, marketing, banking, education, and sport psychology (Alberty & Mihalik, 1989; Dolinsky & Caputo, 1991; Ennew, Reed, & Binks, 1993; Martilla & James, 1977; Smith & Dattilo, 1989). In recreation and tourism, IP has been applied to evaluations of park facilities (Hollenhorst, Olson, & Fortney, 1992; Mengak, Dottavio, & O'Leary, 1986; O'Leary, Mengak, & Dottavio, 1987), National Park concessionaires (Burns, 1988), marketing (Guadagnolo, 1985), tourism policy (Chon, Weaver, & Kim, 1991; Evans & Chon, 1989), and wildlife planning and management (Dawson & Buerger, 1992, Wright, Backman, & Wicks, 1991). The growth in popularity of IP can be attributed to the increasing emphasis agencies place on service delivery and the need to become more responsive to the demands of different publics.

Importance-performance analyses are concerned with the importance individuals attach to a given set of attributes and how well the organization performs with respect to those attributes. For natural resource tourism, the attributes may represent man-made facilities (e.g., showers and electrical hook-ups in campgrounds), the number and diversity of interpretative programs, the helpfulness of the staff, or the attractiveness of the grounds. Average importance ratings for each of these services are combined with the visitors' evaluations for each service to provide a general indication of where needs are being met and where more attention is necessary. Results are typically plotted on a four quadrant grid to highlight where management actions should concentrate.

For situations involving homogeneous visitors (e.g., similar motivations for visiting), this simple, intuitive, approach is one useful strategy for evaluating the effectiveness of the service delivery. Problems arise, however, when not all users share the same importance attitudes (Beaman & Vaske, in press; Grenier & Beaman, 1993; Stanley & Beaman, 1993). One group, for example, may favor enhanced man-made facilities, while another group may prefer a more natural setting. The optimal agency performance for the first group does not constitute an appropriate solution for the second group.

This paper introduces issues associated with different user groups having different IP ratings, the consequences of determining how to move toward an optimum, and whether the behavior estimation model and research design implicit in IP are adequate. In moving from bivariate analyses of a population to multivariate analyses of subgroups within a population with different objectives, the paper addresses the validity of the simple incremental optimization ideas of IP. To illustrate the consequences of segmentation for IP analyses, a simulated data set was constructed. Although hypothetical, the simulation is supported by previous research (Beaman & Vaske, in press; Greenleaf, 1992; Grenier & Beaman, 1993; Stanley & Beaman, 1993).

SPECIFYING THE RELATION BETWEEN IP DATA AND BEHAVIOR

Critical to examining how IP works as an analysis technique is an understanding of the behavior that IP is being used to optimize. Theory and research in tourism suggest that there is a finite set of possible destinations for a particular type of trip (Louviere & Timmermans, 1990; Woodside & Muhlbacher, 1989). Each destination is characterized by a set of attributes that make it attractive (Uysal, Howard, & Jamrozy, 1991). Included among these dimensions of attraction are: (1) the natural amenities of the setting, (2) the types and number of services offered, and (3) the characteristics of other tourists using the area. The importance attached to each set of factors are often weighted differently by different tourist groups.

To provide a rationale for destination choice, models have been developed to explain how a person selects a single destination from a set of possible destinations (Kim & Fesenmaier, 1990; Perdue, 1986; Stynes & Peterson, 1986; Woodside & Lysonski, 1989). These models generally imply that performance on destination attributes and the importance users assign to these attributes define market shares among destinations with different attributes. From a marketing perspective, IP analyses are intended to assist managers in developing strategies that highlight the potential benefits to users.

As a result of IP research and modeling, however, management decisions may alter the attributes of a destination. The consequences are neither simple nor uniform across all users. Some tourists, for example, may shift their behavior patterns in response to environmental modifications (Robertson & Regula, 1994). Schreyer (1979) suggests that these changes in behavior occur when the individual: (1) perceives that the desired attributes of an experience are no longer available, and (2) does not wish to reemphasize other aspects of that experience. Behavioral changes may involve simply revising the pattern or frequency of participation within a given setting. Some individuals, for example, may choose to visit at only selected times (e.g., off-season). Others who were most attracted to the original attribute set may stop visiting an area entirely when other behavioral or attitudinal adjustments fail to bring about the desired experience. These displaced tourists may seek out a substitutable setting and be replaced with users who perceive the modified attribute set more favorably. Attempts to associate demand for a specific destination with the attributes of that setting have used the displacement hypothesis to explain the lack of a relationship between changes in the environment and satisfaction with the experience (Robertson & Regula, 1994; Shelby, Bregenzer, & Johnson, 1988).

Recognizing these alternative behavioral responses, the simulation model presented here serves as an approximation of reality to illustrate what happens when one attempts to use IP to achieve optima for different user groups who have divergent preferences for selecting a site.

SIMULATION METHODOLOGY AND RESULTS

Assume one has importance-performance data on visitors at a day use beach area. The importance variables might include: (1) the importance attached to beach activities (e.g., swimming, sunbathing), (2) the importance of non-water oriented recreation (e.g., picnicking), and (3) the importance of being close to nature. Multiple attributes were summarized in one scale for each of the three dimensions (i.e., IX, IY, and IZ, respectively). Comparable performance variables were simulated for two management strategies. Table 1 describes these beach conditions *before* (column 1) and *after* (column 2) management action. Although hypothetical, the changes illustrate a strategy of moving from low management presence to one of increasing infrastructure and physical modification; a strategy common to many public natural resource agencies. Following Beaman and Vaske (in press), individual data for the importance variables were simulated with relatively large (1) variable by variable variability and (2) ipsative (individual) factors that influence both the average level of values and the range of an individual's responses across the variables.

Based on an assumed geography and site characteristic preference structure, four hypothetical user groups were simulated to be equal in size for the set of initial conditions given in Table 1. Values for IX, IY, and IZ for 25 people were created for each user segment (Total n = 100). With no random error introduced, the performance measures were specified for the

TABLE 1. Beach Conditions Before and After Management Action

Initial (Before) Conditions	Changed (After) Conditions
The area is accessed by a gravel road off a paved park road. Visitors leave their vehicles in a small unpaved parking lot. A forested area separates the parking lot from a natural grass picnic area and the beach. A nature trail connects the parking area with the recreation area.	The access road and the parking lot are paved. Improvements are made to the nature trail.
The picnic area contains 10 tables and an outhouse for swimmers to change. There is no evidence of any landscaping.	More picnic tables are added and the area is landscaped. The outhouse is replaced with a facility containing flush toilets and unheated showers.
The beach is approximately 20 meters wide and offers nice sand for sunbathing. The beach ends with an area of tall grass and brambles. At one end of the beach, shallow water (under 1) meter extends out 15 meters.	The tall grass and brambles are removed. The shallow area is designated with floating markers. In the deeper water, a floating platform and diving board are installed.

before and after conditions. Performance data were not simulated since they follow a different model than importance. No performance, for example, represents an absolute and unambiguous starting point, while importance does not have such a point.

With the data set just described, one has most of the information necessary to investigate the optimality of the initial IP analysis of the 100 person sample of a population. The performance data (Table 2) were merged into each individual's importance data and a traditional importance-performance analysis was performed. A behavior estimation model was formulated and calibrated to yield participation predictions for the initial conditions. Using the initial estimates, behavior was then predicted using performance ratings of the "improved" beach day use area.

THEORETICAL FOUNDATIONS OF SEGMENTATION

The implicit goal of IP analyses is the optimization of service delivery for clients. Figure 1 depicts the before (i.e., x_b, y_b, z_b) and after (i.e., x_a, y_a,

TABLE 2. Mean Importance-Performance Ratings for Four User Groups

Group	Variable	Mean Importance Ratings	Mean Performance Ratings and Rationale	
			Initial (Before) Situation	Changed (After) Situation
1 Beach Oriented	PX: Swimming	5.0	4 = Unacceptable for beach use	7 = Improved for beach use
	PY: Picnicking	3.9	5 = OK as a picnic area	7 = Improved for picnics
	PZ: Nature	3.9	5 = Not visiting for nature	6 = Acceptable natural setting
2 Nature Oriented	PX: Swimming	3.2	6 = Acceptable natural beach	4 = Unacceptable natural beach
	PY: Picnicking	4.6	6 = Picnic area quite natural	4 = Too much development
	PZ: Nature	5.9	6 = Prefer natural setting	3 = Natural setting disturbed
3 Picnic with amenities	PX: Swimming	3.7	4 = Unacceptable for beach use	7 = Acceptable for beach use
	PY: Picnicking	5.5	4 = Unacceptable for picnics	7 = Acceptable for picnics
	PZ: Nature	3.7	5 = Not visiting for nature	7 = Acceptable natural setting
4 Nature & picnic oriented	PX: Swimming	3.1	6 = OK as a natural beach	6 = OK as a natural beach
	PY: Picnicking	6.0	6 = OK as a picnic area	7 = Improved for picnics
	PZ: Nature	4.2	7 = Prefer natural setting	3 = Natural setting disturbed

z_a) importance-performance ratings for the three variables. Focusing on the initial (before) conditions, an obvious management action is to divert resources associated with z_b which has excellent performance and low importance, to the activity y_b which has high importance and poor performance (Figure 1). This management strategy may be appropriated if all users share common goals for visiting the beach.

When different user groups have different objectives for visiting an area, however, optimizing performance for one group may have negative consequences for another group. To understand how individuals in different subgroups respond to importance-performance issues, a model of how people respond to attitude questions is necessary. Beaman and Vaske (in press) define one such model based on extensive quantitative research conducted by Parks Canada (Grenier & Beaman, 1993; Stanley & Beaman, 1993):

Equation 1: $X_{A,i} = (U_A + u_{A,i}) + (C_A + c_{A,i})P_A + e_{A,i}$

where:

- $X_{A,i}$ is a vector of scores, $[x(1,i), x(2,i), \ldots x(N,i)]$ where A is the social aggregate and i is the individual responding for variables, v, with $v = 1, 2, \ldots, N$.
- U_A is a vector defining the general mean level for a pattern of scores for a social aggregate (e.g., $[U(A), U(A), \ldots U(A)] = [4, 4, \ldots, 4]$)
- $u_{A,i}$ is a vector that defines an individual i's average displacement from U_A (e.g., $[-0.7, -0.7, \ldots, -0.7]$).
- C_A is the "usual" amplitude of a pattern P_A, for a social aggregate A.
- $c_{A,i}$ is a constant that reflects an individual's amplitude in relation to C_A (broader, $c_{A,i} > 0$, or narrower, if $0 > C_{A,i} > -1$).
- P_A is a vector $[P_A(1), P_A(2), \ldots, P_A(n)]$ for an aggregate, A defining an average pattern, centered around U_A, by being orthogonal to it $(\Sigma P_A(i) = 0)$.
- $e_{A,i}$ specifies random variables that defines the variable by variance associated with each pattern variable, $[P(1), P(2), \ldots P(N)]$.

Equation 1 is used here to create realistic aggregates of people who have similar importance profiles, and thus are postulated to display similar behaviors. Following previous research (Cattell, 1944, 1949), the model explicitly recognizes the problems that arise when people respond to a series of importance questions. Some individuals rate higher or lower on average, while others show wider variability in their scoring (Brown & Daniel, 1990; Greenleaf, 1992; Hui & Triandis, 1985). Such differences may be at least partially attributed to ipsative (personal) effects (Beaman & Vaske, in press; Cattell, 1944). Failure to consider these ipsative factors can lead to invalid analysis results (Greenleaf, 1992; Grenier & Beaman, 1993).

Two individual (ipsative) aspects of importance responses can be noted. The first concerns an individual's mean level of high/low rating. The second is amplitude which refers to individual narrow/wide swing patterns. An individual, i, may generally rate below the group's general mean, while another rater, j, in the group rates above the group average. In addition to high and low raters, "extreme raters" and "conservative raters" can be identified.

For a given group, a "typical or average" pattern, P_A, with an average amplitude C_A gives $C_A P_A$. A conservative rater, however, might have a pattern amplitude of $C_A + C_A P_{Aij}$ (e.g., $2 + [-1] = 1$), while an extreme rater may have an amplitude factor of $2 + 1 = 3$. Both share the pattern P_A, but the shared pattern is more easily recognized with a common amplitude of 2 rather than with two different amplitudes. For individual, i, in aggregate A, individual responses on IP questions allow for individual (ipsative) scale variability, $u_{A,i}$, as well as for a generally high/low rater, and an individual (ipsative) scale amplitude variability, $c_{A,i}$. The error term, $e_{A,i}$, for random variable by variable error is treated as additive since IP scales are generally bounded above and below (e.g., Likert type scales).

For the day use beach example, different user segments may visit the area. Table 2 describes 4 such groups in terms of the 3 variables (beach activities, non-water activities [e.g., picnicking], and nature appreciation). Average importance ratings for the 3 variables are presented for each group (column 3). For the beach oriented visitor, water related activities such as swimming are considered important (M = 5.0), while picnicking and nature are less important (M = 3.9). Among the nature oriented visitors, an opposite response profile is evident. This visitor group rates nature appreciation highest (M = 5.9) and water related activities lowest (M = 3.2).

Table 2 also shows mean performance scores for the initial conditions (column 4), as well as after the management changes were implemented (column 5). For the beach oriented visitors (Group 1), and those desiring additional amenities for activities like picnicking (Group 3), implementing the modifications to the physical environment results in increased performance scores on all three variables. Visitors interested in experiencing more natural surroundings (Group 2), however, view the changes negatively.

The consequence of plotting the data for importance-performance analyses for each of the four segments under the initial and changed conditions are presented. The points for user segments 1 and 2 (points with a label beginning with 1x or 2x), show the reversal of emphasis on beach use and nature that reflects the orientation of these groups. For example, 1xa is to the right of 1za while this is reversed for group 2. For segments 3 and 4 where the primary emphasis is on picnicking and related infrastructure but a differing orientation toward nature, there is a reversal of points 3ya and 4ya and of points 3za and 4za.

In terms of the goals of an IP analysis, the optimal solution for the population (Figure 1) is not optimal for *any* or *all* of the particular user groups (Figure 2). Some segments see the change as an improvement, other groups view the modifications negatively. Having information about the importance-performance values for the segments is relevant when considering what kinds of development options to pursue.

A MODEL OF BEHAVIOR OPTIMIZATION

Making a choice to visit is based on what is important, how the area performs, and what alternatives the individual considers as trade-offs. One way to evaluate how segments react to a particular planning option chosen

FIGURE 1. I-P Plot of Overall Means

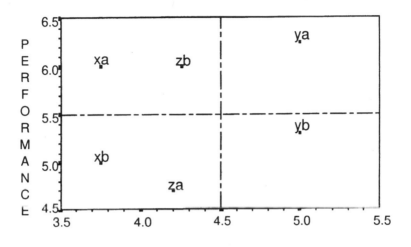

on the basis of an importance-performance analysis for the population is to look at the consequence of introducing the change. The probability of participation can be viewed as manifest in an average use for a given segment. Mathematically, these ratios can be stated as a logistic model:

Equation 2: $\log(R) = C + PX*F(IX-U) + PY*F(IY-U) + PZ*F(IZ-U)$

where:

R   is odds ratio of participating on a sunny summer weekend day as compared to not participating.
F   is a continuous monotone strictly increasing function with constant or strictly increasing slope.

By the logistic form, Equation 2 can be rewritten as a probability of participation:

Equation 3: Probability = $e^{\text{Log}(R)} / (1 + e^{\text{Log}(R)})$

Equation 3 implies that a person's probability of going to a given day use beach on a given sunny summer weekend day depends on the sum of influence of several factors. For each factor, the person's importance measured around his/her personal mean is multiplied times performance to get

FIGURE 2. I-P Plot of Group Means (The Vertical Axis Is Performance)

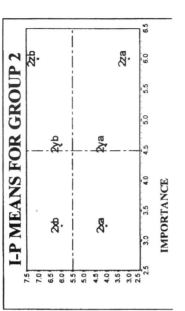

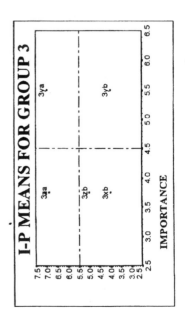

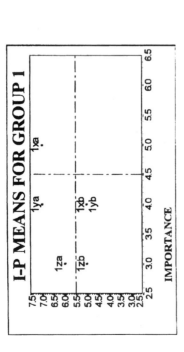

the "relative scores" to sum up. This formulation is similar to a regression model where the PX, PY and PZ are independent variables, and the functions of importance give coefficients that are fixed values for each user group. The equation assumes that importance on something increases from low (negative about the individual's mean) to high. This increase can be more or less rapid and can be non-linear. Unit increase in low importance does not raise the likelihood of participation to the same degree that occurs with a unit increase in high importance except in the special case that F is a linear function. Equations 2 and 3 are consistent with the general "philosophy" of IP that suggests better performance will increase the user's utility and influence how much of something will be consumed. Use is predicted to increase with higher performance.

To illustrate, Table 3 specifies the variables used in the four group beach visitor example. Using Equation 2 with $C = 0$, logs of probabilities were computed to calibrate Equation 3. These logs were ln (.58), ln (.42), ln (.55) and ln (.48) for segments 1 to 4 respectively (ln ( ) is natural log). Based on these, visitation by different segments was modified to make participation by each segment equally probable (i.e., for 10 days 25 trips were predicted by the 25 people in each segment). Each group is thus simulated to have a probability of .1 for making a beach visit on a sunny summer weekend day.

Table 4 shows the overall average and segment by segment behavior before and after the change. Satisfaction has changed as a result of the

TABLE 3. Variables Used to Predict Probability of Participation

1	Segment membership (Cluster 1 to 4)
2	Importance of recreational beach ($0 \leq IX \leq 9$)
3	Importance of picnic area ($0 \leq IY \leq 9$)
4	Importance of nature ($0 \leq IZ \leq 9$)
5	Performance as a beach under initial conditions ($0 \leq IX \leq 9$)
6	Performance as a picnic area under initial conditions ($0 \leq IY \leq 9$)
7	Performance of nature under initial conditions ($0 \leq IZ \leq 9$)
8	Performance as a beach after changes ($0 \leq IX \leq 9$)
9	Performance as a picnic area after changes ($0 \leq IY \leq 9$)
10	Performance of nature after changes ($0 \leq IZ \leq 9$)
11	Initial probability according to Equation 2
12	Probability after change according to Equation 2

TABLE 4. Estimated Relative Participation Rates After Changes to the Beach

	Relative Participation Rates[1]
Overall	1.009
Group 1 – Beach oriented	1.059
Group 2 – Nature oriented	0.883
Group 3 – Picnic with amenities	1.120
Group 4 – Nature and picnic oriented	0.971

[1] Number of visitors after beach changes compared to before modifications
Cell entries are the expected mean participation after the change compared to before the change.

change in performance. The segments favored by the change have become a larger part of the visiting "population" after the change. Since the success of a development option typically involves re-surveying visitors using the same importance-performance questionnaire, Table 4 highlights the types of distortions that may occur. At the aggregate level, satisfaction has shifted in the desired direction (Figure 1). For specific groups, however, examination of the participation probabilities shows that clients who disagree with the management action decrease their use. Such visitors also report lower performance. For Group 3, for example, .883 trips per person were made rather than the norm of 1 before the change. After the change, one can describe such a decrease in participation as displacement of one group by those favoring the new infrastructure. The overall change in performance to 1.009, a 1% increase in use, suggests that the "improved" beach was, at best, only marginally better.

CONCLUSIONS AND DISCUSSION

When importance-performance is applied to a population, a variety of improvements options may be suggested. If the population has segments similar to those simulated here, one arrives at an improvement option that is questionable. For our day use beach example, the IP suggested improvements shifted resources preferred by 2 segments to resources favored by 2 other segments. This occurred because the natural aspects of an area were important to 2 groups, while others placed greater importance on a developed infrastructure.

The beach example illustrates that IP doesn't necessarily optimize. The theorem that IP optimizes is disproved by one counter example. At issue then is the extent to which IP analyses provide misleading or suboptimal results. When answering this question, it is important to recognize that even with a homogeneous group of visitors, IP does not provide information on the trade-offs recreationists will select when management modifies the type of experience offered. Failure to evaluate how visitors will react to management induced changes may have unexpected and negative consequences.

Clearly, how people make importance judgments influences the results of an analysis such as the one presented here. The necessity for the segmentation model is suggested by our own previous research (Beaman & Vaske, in press; Grenier & Beaman, 1993, Stanley & Beaman, 1993), as well as the work of others (Cattell, 1944, 1949; Greenleaf, 1992). These investigations highlight the need to consider ipsative information and the use of an appropriate distance measure (e.g., Pearson r), when attempting to identify distinct clusters of individuals within a population.

The behavioral model (Equations 2 and 3) presented here to predict probable user responses was defined because IP does not provide a theoretical framework for determining visitor responses. Without information on the relative worth of one action compared to another, there is no reason to believe performance will improve.

When management substantially modifies the experience, predictive models such as Equations 2 and 3 are not necessarily linear or additive (Louviere & Timmermans, 1990). Because IP analyses do not consider interaction effects, combinations of IX and IY that are desirable may depend on IZ in a way that differs for different ranges of IZ. Calibrating predictive models based on observed behavior when change is significant poses other problems. For example, the real world yields limited variety in many situations, so coefficients may be both inaccurate and correlated with each other.

Alternatives to IP analyses such as conjoint and choice models are becoming more popular in the literature (Haider & Ewing, 1990; Louviere, 1988; Louviere & Timmermans, 1990; Stynes & Peterson, 1986). Although conjoint models may explicitly incorporate user reactions to specific types of trade-offs under various management scenarios, other problems can arise. First, data collection for conjoint models can be complicated (e.g., nesting, number of levels). Second, conjoint designs do not necessarily include interaction effects (e.g., see Louviere & Timmermans, 1990). Important here, however, is the recognition that when different user segments are present and unrecognized, any technique for identifying more optimal allocation of resources is likely to produce invalid results.

The research presented here was designed to provide a clear example of IP not working when distinct user segments with competing values visit a given resource. The simulation illustrated that IP solutions may result in the displacement of at least some user groups. Methods that fail to consider segments and/or reactions to new options will only be optimal by chance.

LITERATURE CITED

Alberty, S., & Mihalik, B. J. (1989). Use of importance-performance analysis as an evaluative technique in adult education. *Education Review, 13*, 33-44.

Beaman J. G., & Vaske, J. J. (in press). An ipsative clustering model for analyzing attitudinal data. *Journal of Leisure Research*.

Brown, T. C., & Daniel, T. C. (1990). *Scaling of Ratings: Concepts and Methods.* (Res. Pap. RM-293). Fort Collins, CO: U.S. Department of Agriculture, Forest Service, Rocky Mountain Forest and Range Experiment Station.

Burns, T. (1988). Using importance performance to measure the opinions of National Park concessionaires. *Proceedings of the 19th Conference on Tourism Research: Expanding Boundaries.* Montreal: Travel and Tourism Research Association.

Cattell, R. B. (1944). Psychological measurement: normative, ipsative, interactive. *Psychological Review, 51*, 292-303.

Cattell, R. B. (1949). r_p and other coefficients of pattern similarity. *Psychometrika, 14*, 279- 298.

Chon, K. S., Weaver, P. A., & Kim, C. Y. (1991). Marketing your community: Image analysis in Norfolk. *The Cornell H.R.A. Quarterly*, 31-37.

Dawson, C. P., & Buerger, R. B. (1992). Importance-performance analysis: Congruity/disparity between charter boat captains and customers. *Proceedings of the 1992 Northwestern Recreation Research Symposium.* Gail A. Vander Stoep (Ed.). Sarasota Springs, N.Y.: State Parks Management and Research Institute.

Dolinsky, A. L., & Caputo, R. K. (1991). Adding a competitive dimension to importance-performance analysis: An application to traditional health care systems. *Health Marketing Quarterly, 3*, 61-79.

Ennew, C. T., Reed, G. V., & Binks, M. R. (1993). Importance-performance analysis and the measurement of service quality. *European Journal of Marketing, 27*, 59-70.

Evans, M. R., & Chon, K. S. (1989). Formulating and evaluating tourism policy using importance performance analysis. *Hospitality, Education and Research Journal, 13*, 203-213.

Greenleaf, E. A. (1992). Improving rating scale measures by detecting and correcting bias components in some response styles. *Journal of Marketing Research, 29*, 176-188.

Grenier, M., & Beaman, J. G. (1993). *Validity and Robustness of Performance-Importance Analysis Procedures Based on Simulation Model that Emulates Visitor Group Properties Found in Real Data* (CPS-RCB Research Document 93-94-1). Hull, Quebec: Environment Canada.

Guadagnolo, F. (1985). The importance-performance analysis: An evaluation and marketing tool. *Journal of Park and Recreation Administration, 3*, 13-22.

Haider, W., & Ewing, G. (1990). A model of tourist choices of hypothetical Caribbean destinations. *Leisure Sciences, 12*, 33-47.

Hollenhorst, S., Olson, D., & Fortney, R. (1992). Uses of importance-performance analysis to evaluate state park cabins: The case of the West Virginia State Park System. *Journal of Parks and Recreation Administration, 10*, 1-11.

Hui, C. H., & Triandis, H. C. (1985). The instability of response sets. *Public Opinion Quarterly, 49*, 253-260.

Kim, S., & Fesenmaier, D. R. (1990). Evaluating spatial structure effects in recreation travel, *Leisure Sciences, 12*, 367-381.

Louviere, J. (1988). *Analyzing Decision Making: Metric Conjoint Analysis.* Newbury Park: Sage Publications.

Louviere, J., & Timmermans, H..(1990). Stated preference and choice models applied to recreation research: A review. *Leisure Sciences, 12*, 9-32.

Martilla, J., & James, J. (1977). Importance-performance analysis. *Journal of Marketing, 4*, 77-79.

Mengak, K. K., Dottavio, F. D., & O'Leary, J. T. (1986). Use of importance-performance analysis to evaluate a visitor center. *Journal of Interpretation, 11*, 1-13.

O'Leary, J. T., Mengak, K. K., & Dottavio, T. D. (1987). *Importance-Performance Analysis: A Tool for Evaluating Interpretive Services and Facilities.* Washington, DC: National Park Service Research Management Series.

Perdue, R. R. (1986). Traders and nontraders in recreational destination choice. *Journal of Leisure Research, 18*, 12-25.

Robertson, R. A., & Regula, J. A. (1994). Recreational displacement and overall satisfaction: Study of central Iowa's licensed boaters. *Journal of Leisure Research, 26*, 174-181.

Schreyer, R. M. (1979). *Succession and Displacement in River Recreation.* Paper prepared for River Recreation Project. St. Paul, Minnesota: USDA Forest Service, North Central Forest Experiment Station.

Shelby, B., Bregenzer, N. S., & Johnson, R. (1988). Displacement and product shift: Empirical evidence from Oregon rivers. *Journal of Leisure Research, 20*, 274-288.

Smith, R. W., & Dattilo, J. (1989). Importance-performance analysis: Effective evaluation and marketing of sporting events for everyone. *Palaestra, 6*, 8-11, 36.

Stanley, R., & Beaman, J. G. (1993). *Uses of Importance-Performance Measures to Recognize Policy Issues.* Paper presented at the Canadian Congress of Leisure Research, Winnipeg.

Stynes, D. J., & Peterson, G. L. (1986). A review of logit models with implications for modeling recreation choices. *Journal of Leisure Research, 16*, 295-310.

Uysal, M., Howard, G., & Jamrozy, U. (1991). An application of importance-performance analysis to a ski resort: A case study in North Carolina. *Visions in Leisure and Business, 10*, 16-25.

Woodside, A. G., & Lysonski, S. (1989). A general model of traveler destination choice. *Journal of Travel Research*, *27*, 8-14.

Woodside, A. G., & Muhlbacher, H. (1989). Travel destination choices. *Journal of International Consumer Marketing*, *1*, 11-28.

Wright, B. A., Backman, S. J., & Wicks, B. E. (1991). Operating at the "wildlife-human interface": A marketing approach to wildlife planning. In W. R. Mangum (Ed.), *Public policy issues in wildlife management* (pp. 39-52). New York: Greenwood Press.

The Respondent Specific Method:
A New Approach to Conversion Research

Stanley C. Plog

Anne Adams

BACKGROUND OF THE PROBLEM

Conversion studies represent an important and growing area of research for both academicians and researchers in applied fields. A large number of state government tourism departments now have budget items for annual conversion studies, and a number of media companies also periodically conduct such research.

Conversion studies typically sample a group of persons who have answered an ad by filling in a response card in a publication (magazines, newspapers) or by calling an 800 telephone number (for broadcast media, as radio and television) (Woodside, A. G., 1981; Gitelson, R., 1986). The task is to determine how many persons who requested the information about a destination or a travel service (cruise line, airline, tour operator, etc.) plan on taking a trip, or actually took that trip (convert). Of additional interest is how many were actually influenced by the materials they received to choose the specific destination or service offered (Perdue & Petegoff, 1989).

In most magazine conversion studies, respondents are given a long list of advertisers and are requested to indicate the destinations, or other prod-

Stanley C. Plog is Chairman and C.E.O. of Plog Research, Inc., Reseda (Los Angeles), CA. Anne Adams is Vice President and Director of Special Analyses for Plog Research, Inc.

[Haworth co-indexing entry note]: "The Respondent Specific Method: A New Approach to Conversion Research." Plog, Stanley C., and Anne Adams. Co-published simultaneously in *Journal of Travel & Tourism Marketing* (The Haworth Press, Inc.) Vol. 5, No. 3, 1996, pp. 241-252; and *Recent Advances in Tourism Marketing Research* (ed: Daniel R. Fesenmaier, Joseph T. O'Leary, and Muzaffer Uysal) The Haworth Press, Inc., 1996, pp. 241-252. Single or multiple copies of this article are available from The Haworth Document Delivery Service [1-800-342-9678, 9:00 a.m. - 5:00 p.m. (EST). E-mail address: getinfo @ haworth.com].

ucts, for which they had requested information (Woodside, 1981; Ellerbrock, 1981). The destination list includes the one(s) for which they requested information and others about which they presumably had no interest. Then they answer as to whether they took a trip to any of the places they selected, or are planning to take one. Although this is a valid approach, it suffers from an inherent and often overlooked problem (Ronkainen & Woodside, 1987). A number of these individuals may have seen the same ad in a magazine other than the one conducting the study, and requested information from the other magazine. In other words, they may not remember the exact media source that motivated their initial request for information. Thus, magazines may over-represent their effectiveness in motivating their readers to respond since respondents may remember *what* they requested, but may not remember from *where* the prompt originated.

Other problems also become apparent in examining the field. A basic question exists as to the definition of a conversion. If someone has already decided to take a trip and subsequently requests information for that trip, is that a conversion? Most researchers in the field include those instances where a traveler, at some point, is convinced by some source (perhaps a previous similar ad in the same medium) to take the trip as a conversion. This statistic is called the *gross* conversion rate, i.e., a figure that reflects the total number of people responding to an ad who actually took a trip to a destination, or used the travel product. Another important statistic, examined more closely in recent years by persons responsible for tourism advertising budgets, is *net* conversions, i.e., the percent of persons who requested materials, took a trip (or used a service), and were *influenced to take that trip by the materials they received*. Although the influence of advertising materials may appear to be a relatively clear cut dependent variable, it is somewhat difficult to measure and it tends to under-represent total conversions because future trips that occur are not included in the final count.

Other problems also plague researchers in the field. Non-response bias concerns are prevalent in most studies, including tourism advertising evaluation. Additionally, one might question whether those persons who have visited destinations in the past truly can be considered converts. Nevertheless, good research is a necessity, and this area of investigation must press forward.

A limited number of journal articles is available on this topic. Most of the earlier research suggests that conversion studies typically over-estimate the effectiveness of advertising by reporting excessively high rates of conversion (see Ballman, Burke, Blank & Korte, 1984; Burke & Gitelson, 1990; Mok, 1990; and Woodside, 1990). An authoritative statement on the topic is presented by Messmer and Johnson (1993). They review the major findings growing out of previous research, and then use a well designed and controlled study to test several hypotheses and assumptions. They conclude:

> While only a single study, this research strongly suggests that the difficulties of bias in conversion research can be dealt with successfully in a carefully designed and executed survey. Although this study does not convey validity to all conversion research, it serves to demonstrate that valid estimates can be obtained through that approach.
>
> Of broader concern is the translation of conversion research findings into estimates of the impact of advertising on visitation. The trend over recent years has been to narrow the definition of what should constitute the net conversion to advertising. This study suggests that a narrow definition of net conversion provides estimates of advertising's impacts which are far lower than what is realized through an alternative methodology. (p. 21)

The Messmer and Johnson conclusion that conversion studies can be controlled and can, in general, lead to substantiable results, addresses one side of this broad area of research. Their approach can help destinations and other advertisers determine the effectiveness (conversion rates) of their advertising.

Another area of concern relates to the overall effectiveness of various media sources, such as determining conversion rates for individual magazines, specific TV shows, radio programs, city or suburban newspapers, etc. Since most media target specific audiences, it can be assumed that some sources are more effective in motivating (converting) their intended audiences than others. As a result, a growing number of print and broadcast media companies now conduct conversion studies to determine how many of their readers/viewers convert (take trips) after exposure to travel advertising.

A PROPOSED RESEARCH APPROACH

A client request unexpectedly provided an excellent opportunity to develop and test out a new research approach that integrates databasing and publication methodologies. *Endless Vacation* magazine approached Plog Research, Inc. to conduct a conversion study among its readers. The magazine has a large subscription base of 950,000 readers who are members of Resort Condominiums International (RCI), the largest provider of time share exchanges. The magazine features a broad array of travel editorials (articles), supported by a variety of advertisers (airlines, cruise lines, resorts and destinations, tour operators, and destinations offering exchange properties).

When *Endless Vacation* first inquired about conducting a study of this type, a number of problems inherent to magazine conversion research were discussed. The most notable of these is the fact that a questionnaire sent to respondents might have to list 30 or more destinations/services even though an individual respondent may have requested information for only one of these destinations/services. A respondent may have seen, in magazines other than the client's, some of the same ads and be motivated to travel to these destinations. But, they might check the boxes for destinations on the *Endless Vacation* questionnaire "because it's there." Thus, the client's magazine (*Endless Vacation,* in this case) could get credit for conversions for which it had no influence. Glenn Tourville, the Marketing and Sales Manager for *Endless Vacation,* responded immediately with a surprising statement, and without hesitation: "I think we can handle that." Within a few days he called to suggest the following plan:

1. A generic questionnaire would be printed for the study that contains the common elements that all respondents are to answer.
2. An over print would be completed on *each* questionnaire that *customizes the questionnaire for each respondent.* It would print only the specific destinations/services onto a questionnaire that each respondent had requested. No "surplus" (non-requested) destinations would appear on any questionnaire. Thus, there can be no confusion: respondents are reminded of the exact destinations or travel product information they requested and are asked to respond to these alone.
3. Each questionnaire would be further individualized by printing the issue month from which the request had been made.

This approach is made possible because *Endless Vacation* tracks each request by assigning an I.D. number that ties together the person's name, specific advertiser information requested, and the magazine issue from which this request was made. We called this approach to conversion research the Respondent Specific Method (RSM) because it now controls *all* aspects of what the respondent saw in the magazine and requested information about, including the issue in which the ad was seen. Respondents in this study had made from one to twelve requests on the same

"Bingo" card (response reply card), with an average of three requests made per individual.

A research plan was developed in which a total of 5,000 questionnaires were mailed out during the week of April 25th, 1994 using *Endless Vacation* envelopes and letterhead. Self-addressed, postage paid envelopes were enclosed to return the questionnaires to the offices of Plog Research, Inc. A total of 2,891 questionnaires were returned, with 70 "undeliverable," for a response rate of 58.6 percent. Of this number, 2,874 were received by May 16th, the cut-off date for final data entry and, therefore, were included in the results used for this research. By most media research standards, this is a very strong response rate since no additional measures were used to ensure a good return, i.e., no advance post cards to announce an upcoming mailing of the questionnaire or follow-up postcards or telephone calls to encourage participation.

An incentive was used to increase participation. A $1,000 travel certificate, good for airline tickets, a cruise vacation, car rentals or special vacation packages available through RCI Travel, was awarded to a winner chosen at random.

RESULTS OF THE RESEARCH

The results of the study provide some interesting and useful information and conclusions. It is possible to look at characteristics of time share owners, their rates of conversion for various types of advertisers, and ultimately to use this information to determine whether any demographic variables predict conversion.

Characteristics of Time Share Owners

It is useful to review the primary results of the research because they help to explain some of the more relevant findings. These results are consistent with a large (13,500 respondents) syndicated project that Plog Research conducts annually (The American Traveler Survey) that investigates travel behavior and media habits.

Table 1 summarizes the demographic characteristics of persons who requested fulfillment materials from *Endless Vacation* magazine. It indicates that they are well above the norm on most dimensions. Average household income is $65,500 and these persons are extraordinarily well educated. Fifty-three percent have graduated from college and/or gone on to graduate school, and 81 percent have completed at least some college or

TABLE 1. Characteristics of Respondents

	TOTAL
SEX	
Male	50%
Female	50
MARITAL STATUS	
Married	84%
Single	7
Divorced/widowed	9
EDUCATIONAL LEVEL	
Some high school or less	1%
High school grad	18
Some college/trade school	28
College Graduate	26
Post-Graduate	27
ANNUAL HOUSEHOLD INCOME	
Under $24,999	5%
$25,000 - $49,999	32
$50,000 - $74,999	34
$75,000- $99,999	17
$100,000- $149,999	9
$150,000- $199,999	2
$200,000 or more	1

trade school courses. Only one percent failed to graduate from high school. Thus, this is a well educated, affluent audience. The sample consists of an equal number of men and women (50% each) and, as can be seen, a strong majority are married (84%).

Travel Habits and Use of Time Share

Early questions in the study asked about respondents' vacation habits. What is evident from these questions, and also consistent with other studies on time share audiences, is that this group has a considerable amount of vacation time available. They use a large portion of their vacation time away from home (see Table 2). More specifically:

- They have nearly 28 vacation days, on average, available each year, beyond normal holidays and weekends.
- They spend 28 nights away from home; this includes weekends as well as vacation time.
- They typically take nearly seven trips per year, that are wholly or partly for leisure, an extraordinarily large number compared to most population groups.
- A consistent tendency, across all of these data tables, is that the number of vacation days available, nights away from home, and trips taken by air (and/or by car) tend to increase with a the number of time share weeks owned.
- The greater the number of weeks of time share owned, the more vacation days available and the larger the number of leisure trips taken.

Conversion Results

Table 3 summarizes the distribution of questionnaires returned by those making information requests in response to each of *Endless Vacation*'s issues in 1993. Since the study was conducted in April, 1994, it is obvious that a number of these persons would not yet have had an opportunity to take a summer trip, if they requested information from the fall or winter 1993 magazine issues. More will be said about this later.

TABLE 2. Travel Habits and Use of Time Share

		INCOME			NUMBER WEEKS TIME SHARE OWNED		
	Total	Under $50,000	$50K-$74.9K	$75K Plus	One	Two	3 Plus
Number of vacation days available each year (Mean excluding retired).	28	27	27	29	26	29	33
Total number of nights spent away from home on all leisure trips last year.	28	28	27	27	23	30	38
Total leisure trips, air or auto.	5.4	5.2	5.7	5.3	5.0	5.4	6.2
Total business trips with leisure add-on.	1.4	1.0	1.2	2.1	1.3	1.4	1.6
TOTAL LEISURE TRIPS	6.7	6.2	6.9	7.5	6.3	6.7	7.7

TABLE 3. Issues from Which Information Was Requested (1993 Publication Dates)

	Total	INCOME		
		Under $50,000	$50K-74.9K	$75K Plus
January/February	13%	13%	14%	11%
March/April	18	18	17	17
May/June	18	19	16	19
July/August	17	17	18	18
September/October	18	17	18	20
November/December	16	16	17	16

Interesting comparisons can be drawn from other available sources. The Department of Economic Development of the State of Washington publishes an annual survey on the effectiveness of its promotional campaign in various print media (newspapers and magazines). It tracks persons who request tourist information and determines whether they traveled to Washington (gross conversions) and whether the information provided was instrumental in helping them decide to take the trip (net conversions). These data are particularly useful for comparison purposes because the state ranks high on desired destinations, as judged by the annual American Travelers Survey conducted by Plog Research (Plog, 1994). Thus, one would expect to see a relatively high conversion rate for Washington advertisements. In spite of the fact that conversion statistics are measured similarly in both studies, only general comparisons can be made between the two sets of data. The *Endless Vacation* study sampled ads appearing in all issues over a one year period of time. Since data collection occurred in the spring (April), not all persons had an opportunity to take their trip (summer travel is always the heaviest). Washington State completes its research after the summer travel rush on ads that ran in publications during the February through May time period. Also, Washington State does not count planned trips, but these are included in *Endless Vacation* data since a number of the trips could not yet have occurred. Finally, Washington data look at all their media sources; this study only examines results from ads in *Endless Vacation* magazine.

In spite of these differences, it is useful to present some comparative data to provide a feel for the range of scores in conversion research. Table 4 presents these results. It points out:

TABLE 4. Conversion Rates—Washington State and Endless Vacation Magazine (All Data from 1994 Studies)

| | | ENDLESS VACATION MAGAZINE AD CATEGORY | | | | | WASHINGTON STATE |
	TOTAL	CANADA	CRUISE LINES	INTERNATIONAL DESTINATIONS	U.S. DESTINATIONS	MISC. ADS	ALL MEDIA COMBINED
Took a trip/planning trip	75%	71%	70%	68%	77%	62%	43%
Trip decision made after information received	30	23	24	18	31	31	24

- Conversion rates in both studies are very strong, with *Endless Vacation*'s overall total exceeding that of Washington State.
- As would be expected, conversion rates vary by category (see *Endless Vacation* data). Domestic destinations have the highest rates of conversion, probably because of proximity and lower cost of travel. More expensive trips (as international destinations and cruises) have lower scores.
- When only domestic destinations of *Endless Vacation* are compared with the Washington State figures, the difference in favor of *Endless Vacation* is slightly stronger.
- But, it should be remembered that this is not a comparative study since these are not comparable variables. Washington State is an advertiser; *Endless Vacation* is a print medium which presents advertising messages. Additionally, Washington State does not track planned trips that have not yet been taken where as the *Endless Vacation* data accounts for these.

DISCUSSION

A new procedure, called the Respondent Specific Method/RSM, was used to determine conversion rates based on a more controlled process of sophisticated databasing and modern print technologies. The results of this study lead to several conclusions:

1. Conversion research, like other applied research methodologies, needs to move forward and become more focused and precise. The approach (RSM) developed with *Endless Vacation* magazine is a useful step in that direction. Since it eliminates the bias of respondents reacting to ads that they may have seen in other publications, it significantly reduces the possibility of over-estimating the effectiveness of a specific magazine or newspaper.
2. To accomplish the task of improvement suggested here requires not only some specific capabilities by print publishers (sophisticated database management and advanced printing applications) but also considerably more close interaction and cooperation between the client (a magazine or newspaper) and the researcher. More possibilities exist for delays in time schedules, errors in database management, and printing foul-ups. Without good coordination, the questionnaires might not be mailed at the appropriate time to test rates of conversion, or wrong advertisers could be printed on respondent questionnaires, or imprinting of the advertisers could be misaligned

on the questionnaire leading to significant respondent wrong answers or coding errors. Fortunately, *Endless Vacation* controlled all facets of its portion of the research very well.

With the billions of dollars spent on advertising each year, and the tens of millions of parallel dollars devoted to research attempting to measure the effectiveness of this advertising, a constant search exists to find new and better research approaches. Conversion research has one advantage over most of the other research approaches that exist: it is possible to track and follow up on specific individuals who responded to ads. With RSM, *specific individuals* who responded to *specific ads* can be isolated and tracked with greater certainty. Thus, a significant portion of potential research error can be reduced.

What is needed now is the opportunity to compare conversion rates among different print media, with each of them utilizing this research methodology. That may not happen for a period of time, until more publications acquire the necessary skills and capacities. But it should be established as a requirement by advertisers (such as destinations, cruise lines, airlines, etc.) before they agree to an advertising schedule in selected print media. In so doing, they will obtain better information on where their ads achieve the greatest effectiveness. Furthermore they will advance the state of the art for applied research. Destinations promoted by state tourism offices may be in a position to further RSM research. These have a long history of conversion research, and some have regular budgets for such studies. They also have a pressing need to demonstrate to legislative bodies and outside groups that also contribute to their budgets that they are spending advertising dollars wisely. Regardless of where it originates, such research can further help to clarify the issues involved and lead to more significant findings.

REFERENCES

Ballman, G., Burke, J., Blank, U. & Dick Korte (1984). Toward higher quality conversion studies: Refining the numbers game. *Journal of Travel Research*, *26*, 28-32.

Burke, J. F. & Gitelson, R. (1990). Conversion studies: Assumptions, applications, accuracy and abuse. *Journal of Travel Research*, *28*, 46-50.

Ellerbrock, M. J. (1981). Improving coupon conversion studies: A comment. *Journal of Travel Research*, *19*, 37-38.

Gitelson, R. (1986). *1985 North Carolina conversion study: An analysis of those individuals who requested the North Carolina information packet*, North Carolina Division of Tourism.

Messmer, D. J. & Johnson, R. R. (1993). Inquiry conversion and travel advertising effectiveness. *Journal of Travel Research, 31*, 14-21.

Mok, H. M. (1990). A quasi-experimental measure of the effectiveness of destination advertising: Some evidence from Hawaii. *Journal of Travel Research, 24*, 30-34.

Perdue, R. & Pitegoff, B. (1989). Methods of accountability research for destination marketing. *Journal of Travel Research, 28*, 45-49.

Plog Research, Inc. (1994). *The American Traveler Survey.*

Plog, S. C.(1991). *Leisure Travel: Making It a Growth Market . . . Again!* New York, NY: John Wiley & Sons, Inc.

Ronkainen, I. A. & Woodside, A. G. (1987). Advertising conversion studies. In J. R. Brent Ritchie & C. R. Goeldner (Eds.). *Travel Tourism and Hospitality Research* (pp. 481-88). New York: Wiley.

Woodside, A. G. (1981). Measuring the conversion of advertising coupon inquiries into visitors. *Journal of Travel Research, 26*, 38-41.

Woodside, A. G. (1990). Measuring advertising effectiveness in destination marketing strategies. *Journal of Travel Research, 29*, 3-7.

A New Direction

Gordon D. Taylor

INTRODUCTION

Tourism faces new and increasingly complex challenges. That fact is indisputable. How tourism adjusts and reacts to these challenges will determine whether tourism flourishes or withers in the next century. The nature of these challenges and of the initial responses to them are beginning to be identified. This identification process must move ahead rapidly because it is clear that tourism cannot continue to do business as it has in the past. Research must play a key role in this process.

The objectives of this paper are to summarize the ideas and approaches that have been developed for this special issue; to address other important issues that need attention and to provide the basis of an outline for future research. The nature of tourism and the role of research are considered first. Then the research directions suggested in the papers that comprise this edition will be summarized. These ideas will be examined within a total context for tourism research. The need for close cooperation between researchers and users of research will be stressed. A concluding section will attempt to develop an outline of future research needs and to suggest the political and economic environment in which this research will take place.

NATURE OF TOURISM

It is critical that the nature of tourism be thoroughly understood by all players involved in the business. Stewart and Hull refer correctly to Claw-

Dr. Gordon D. Taylor is a Tourism Consultant, Ottawa, Ontario, Canada.

[Haworth co-indexing entry note]: "A New Direction." Taylor, Gordon D. Co-published simultaneously in *Journal of Travel & Tourism Marketing* (The Haworth Press, Inc.) Vol. 5, No. 3, 1996, pp. 253-263; and *Recent Advances in Tourism Marketing Research* (ed: Daniel R. Fesenmaier, Joseph T. O'Leary, and Muzaffer Uysal) The Haworth Press, Inc., 1996, pp. 253-263. Single or multiple copies of this article are available from The Haworth Document Delivery Service [1-800-342-9678, 9:00 a.m. - 5:00 p.m. (EST). E-mail address: getinfo@haworth.com].

253

son and Knetsch's segmentation of the recreation or tourism experience into five trip phases: anticipation, travel to, on-site stay, travel back, and recollection. Each of these phases is different but it is the totality of them that provides the tourist with the experience sought. It is important to note that at each phase of a trip there are a range of different needs and expectations that must be understood and met. The total experience, based on these five components, must become part of any marketing strategy.

In addition to the segmentation by trip phase, there is the much more diverse segmentation of supply which is usually divided into accommodation, transportation, food service, attractions, information, public services and safety. Each of these main divisions can be divided into several types and some of the types can be further subdivided. The result is that the tourism industry is usually seen to be and is recognized as being highly fragmented. The total tourism product, viewed from the perspective of the tourist, is all of the goods and services required to obtain a satisfactory experience from a trip. The role of the various elements in this total product and their relationship to each other is not fully understood.

A major result of the fragmentation of the product is that rarely, if ever, does one supplier have the responsibility for meeting the expectations of a tourist during each trip phase and for the total trip.

The tourists themselves are not homogeneous. They are highly segmented in terms of how they look at travel, how they travel, what benefits or satisfactions they seek from travel, and in the requirements they have for services, attractions and environmental conditions. It is likely that the market segments are becoming increasingly diverse over time. While there may be some universals in these needs, there are also strong indications that they vary by culture.

Thus tourism is an extremely complex phenomenon and one that is changing constantly. If the challenge to tourism marketing lies in selecting the appropriate segments that will be able to satisfy their expectations with the mix of services at a given location and in enticing them to visit that location; the answer to the challenge can only come from a thorough understanding of all of the complexities of tourism.

It is at the local level that the first requirement for cooperation and coordination occurs. All of the suppliers at a given location must realize that they are in the tourism business and that the role of the individual supplier is to provide a part of the total bundle of goods and services that the tourist requires. Each supplier will probably have to meet the needs of a variety of tourist types. These needs likely will be quite divergent in nature. The supplier will have to be knowledgeable about the expectations of different tourist groups and about the services provided by other businesses that are important to his clients.

The failure of one supplier either to deliver a quality item or to direct a client to other necessary services detracts from the ability of the destination to provide a satisfactory experience. One small failure can be a major disaster to the image of the location. Cooperation and coordination amongst all of the suppliers within a destination will ease the difficulties in meeting client expectations caused by the fragmented nature of the industry and the highly segmented character of the market. This will make it easier to deliver better and more satisfying products to the market with the result that there will be a greater number of satisfied customers and the contribution of tourism to the social and economic well being of destinations will be enhanced.

ROLE OF RESEARCH

It is the role of research to be able to develop the ways and means of understanding the complexities of tourism and of translating research findings into information that can be applied directly into policy, marketing and development.

This latter point is crucial to the successful meeting of the challenges. Taylor and Campbell (1993) point out that a large gap exists between the producers and users of research. They described the gap as a near phobia on the part of users in dealing with academics, consultants and researchers. The need to close the gap exists—the problem was how to demystify research. Along the same line, Taylor, Rogers and Stanton (1994) note that while the amount of research developed over the years has grown consistently, the use of this research by many tourism businesses has not. In order to close the gap a high level of cooperation is needed between researchers and users (p. 9). Taylor (1994) later concluded that research reports should not end with just a presentation of the findings, but should include a section that illustrates what data are available in the study, how the data can be used and/or how the potential user can obtain help in applying it for specific needs (p. 3).

The mechanisms for cooperation between researchers and users must have a high priority. They can apply to a specific study or they can be developed on a much wider scale. If this cooperation does not take place much of the research done may be irrelevant to the industry.

The design, execution and analysis of research projects is too important to be left solely in the hands of researchers. Users of the research must be involved at all phases of the process. All too often when examining the history of a research project, the users do not know the details of the information being collected and excuse themselves from any responsibility by saying "It is research's baby." One of the best ways to demystify research is to involve the user right from the start. Successful, useable research requires close involvement of both researchers and users.

Large and valuable data files often lie unused and forgotten after the initial results are released. There is a responsibility incumbent upon the research community to ensure that secondary analysis of their data takes place. Research reports rarely include all of the analysis that could be done; in reality, often only a small fraction of it is initially completed. Too many users, if they do not see anything in the report that interests them, conclude there is nothing in the research of value to their business. Users are not and need not be trained to read and understand questionnaires and to recognize the possibilities of further research. Researchers are not trained, nor should they be, to anticipate the needs of users. But researchers do know how to recognize analytical possibilities and users know what their information needs are. These two groups should work in tandem and not in isolation from one another.

A report (Rogers, 1995) that utilizes the Canadian Travel Survey has just been published. This report demonstrates how complex data sets can be the basis for understandable and useable information for managers. Morrison, Sheauhsing and O'Leary (1994) provide another fine example of the use of an existing data base to develop very useable information. Other similar studies could be mentioned. These studies are two of the most recent to become available.

Thus the role of researchers is to undertake the best research possible. At the same time they should not look on research as their sole prerogative. They must learn how to cooperate with potential users of their findings. They must take the lead in ensuring that the cooperation needed will take place.

SOME RESEARCH DIRECTIONS

The papers included in this special volume develop new and/or improved research methodologies that will greatly assist tourism in achieving a greater understanding of the complexities of tourism. Five basic research themes can be identified as follows:

1. more direct involvement of the tourist in research,
2. improved segmentation analysis,
3. application of sophisticated models,

tem (Room 2E3, Arts Building F Wing)

our campus and a map **of** our campus. PLEASE
the campus map, and there is a $2.00 fee for the
may use the enclosed one-day parking pass and
but a 5-8 minute walk.

- - - - - - - - - - - - - - - - -

nd Environmental Studies
University

PT

April 1996

eography Teachers' Symposium, held on Friday,

4. Importance-performance analysis, and
5. conversion studies.

A brief review of the ideas developed will indicate the directions for research that are being proposed.

1. More Direct Involvement of Tourists in Research

Most tourism market research is based upon quantitative studies that place a high degree of reliability upon recall. Stewart and Hull propose using "Experience Sampling Method" (ESM) that focuses on research taking place in actual recreational situations and requires comparisons between settings by individuals and on individual experiences that differ between situations. In a similar vein, i.e., linking the tourist to a place in time, Dann develops a methodology that will portray the image of a destination from visitors on site. The advantages of ESM over more traditional methods are pointed out, as are some of the qualifications which must be placed around the new methodology. Dann finishes his article with a hope that others will continue in the direction he suggests in order to explore the rich processes which connect the tourist with tourism in space and time. Duke and Persia pursue the same theme in a study of tour users. Their goal is to have issues defined by the tour-goers rather than from a priori theoretical dimensions. Riley moves in a slightly different direction when he makes a case for more qualitative research. He describes a methodology that will explore socially constructed knowledge in order to assist marketing researchers, and hopefully marketers, to better understand why people do what they do.

These four papers place importance on linking tourists and the destination as one focus of research. There is a feeling that research based solely on recall loses part of the flavor of the interaction between tourist and destination.

2. Improved Segmentation Analysis

Two papers recognize the need to identify target groups in order to successfully market tourism products and implement tourism policies. Stemerding, Oppewal, Beckers and Timmermans describe a new and innovative way to segment markets. They use the Dutch initiative of reducing car use for leisure trips as an example. A key point in their paper is that a marketing strategy for each identified market segment is necessary. Carmichael describes a study that segments skiers on the basis of factors influencing ski resort choice. This study tested two different segmentation approaches, the first was based on a hybrid of factor cluster and a priori segmentations, while the second used the a priori approach with segments based on personal characteristics. Her conclusion is that for the purposes of the study, the a priori method worked best.

These two papers illustrate a problem in segmentation research. Large scale national studies may not provide information precise enough for a specific area or activity. Segments developed from small scale studies may produce segments that cannot be generalized. There is a need for work to be done to examine if and how segments produced by studies at vastly different scales can be brought within an overall segmentation scheme.

3. Application of Sophisticated Models

Four papers examined the use of models as an aid to understanding the key factors that help determine the choice of a destination by tourists. Sirakaya, McLellan and Uysal test a multiple criteria decision-making instrument to model the vacation destination choice of individuals based on the factors deemed to be important. The study accentuates the different decision-making characteristics of individual travelers. Their results are keyed to attractiveness, cost and time. Choong-Ki Lee uses an economic model to identify the major determinants of international inbound tourist expenditures in South Korea. Income was found to be the most important contributing determinant. The work uses a regression model with data drawn from existing statistics.

Pyo, Uysal and Warner use an economic model to study international tourism flows between the United States and eight other nations, Canada, Japan, Mexico, The United Kingdom, France, Germany, Italy and The Netherlands. Different factors are found to be important in different countries. Marketing implications have been developed for each country. They recommend additional countries be studied and that micro-data be included in the analysis. Jiann-Ming Jeng and Fesenmaier describe an experiment using artificial neural networks against a conventional conjoint model in order to model individual choice behavior. While the results suggest the neural network to be useful and reliable, many statistical and methodological issues need further research. Models have been a favorite research technique for a long time. These papers show that the need to keep refining and improving methodology is being addressed. The beauty of this type of study is the quantity and quality of available data. The problem becomes what of the available data to use and what is the relationship between the various factors selected.

4. Importance-Performance Analysis

Two papers deal with the topic of importance-performance analysis. Duke and Persia demonstrate how to develop and display information on pre-trip and post-trip expectations and satisfaction and pre- and post-trip importance for escorted tours. They illustrate how to use the data for management decisions and they point out some of the weaknesses of the method. Vaske, Beaman, Stanley and Grenier use a natural resource setting to demonstrate the need to segment clients prior to importance-performance analysis. They also point out some of the problems in the use of this type of analysis.

The results of importance-performance analysis are an excellent way to present critical information to management and, as a result, can have a major impact on decisions. These papers show the rigor required for this work in order to avoid the development and use of misleading information.

5. Conversion Studies

Plog and Adams describe a new approach to conversion research that requires some specific capabilities by print publishers and close interaction between the client and researcher. The Respondent Specific Method allows specific individuals who respond to specific ads to be identified and tracked. The methodology, where it can be adopted, would seem to overcome some of the problems that are present in existing methods.

THE RESEARCH CONTEXT

The ideas developed for this special volume need to be placed within a context of the total role of research for tourism. Many of the issues facing tourism have to do with the total environment within which it operates. Successful marketing of tourism, no matter how sophisticated market research techniques become, will depend to a great extent upon the solution of the larger issues.

The Travel and Tourism Research Association (TTRA) released a report entitled "Agenda for Research for The North American Tourism Industry" in January, 1994 (Smith, 1994). "The agenda identifies the top ten research issues (not in priority order), associated research questions, and resources to assist the interested reader gather more information about each issue" (p. 1). After identifying the top ten issues, the agenda organized them into several broad categories:

1. Social and demographic change,
2. The physical environment,
3. Social and economic aspects of tourism,
4. Human resources,
5. Taxation,
6. Industry structure, and
7. Technology, (p. 3).

The Smith report did not assign any priority order to the issues. All were considered critical for the future. TTRA asked the committee that had worked on the agenda to narrow the range of the top research issues. The original list of 10 was distributed to industry leaders in North America who were asked to identify what in their view were the three most pressing ones. Two key and related issues were identified: environmental and social aspects of tourism. The new report (Smith, b, 1994, p. 2) notes: "The identification of these two related issues as the most important is a mark of the maturation of the North American tourism industry. Although marketing continues to be the premier concern of the industry, the industry also understands the need to be aware of the effects of development and the need to conduct its affairs in such a way to minimize problems and maximize benefits."

Taylor and Stanley (1991) summarized the outline of an initial research agenda for tourism, sustainable development and the environment. They pointed that what was needed was: "Research for management, policy and operations through biophysical, cultural and economic studies carried out at different levels of space and time"(p. 1).

The research issues raised by Taylor and Stanley are compatible with the larger research agenda developed by Smith and his colleagues. For the purposes of this paper, however, sustainable development has been added to the two identified by Smith. Hence three key issues rather than two are used for the purposes of discussion.

Without going into the details of environmental, social and sustainable development research needs and the implications of the results of such research for tourism, it is evident that pressure exists for devoting substantial resources to research other than market research. The key issues for tourism have been identified as a result of a great deal of consultation, discussion and analysis. In the political and economic climate of 1995 the fulfillment of the seemingly ever increasing research needs will have to be met without an increase in research funding. Existing or reduced resource levels will be the norm in both the public and private sectors in North America for the foreseeable future. A way will have to be found to produce more useable and more focused research for less money.

It is essential that future research topics be carefully defined in order to meet the needs of the industry. The issues assigned greatest importance in the research agendas must always be in the forefront of the mind of the research designer. The outcome of any research done on these three key and related issues will have major impacts on the future and the marketing of tourism. It seems clear that market research must become an integral part of any research done on the three key topics. It is equally important that the tourist industry heed the results of such research. It must modify, where necessary, the types of products supplied and the way in which they are marketed.

A LOOK AHEAD

Tourism has the potential to deliver the benefits that its most vocal and sympathetic protagonists proclaim. This delivery cannot take place unless tourism develops a far deeper understanding of itself than it has at the present time. Fitch (1986, p. 65) stated that: "Tourism is arguably the most complex and interactive of all economic activities. In order to service the needs of tourists a broad range of goods and services is required, ranging from agricultural and manufactured products through a wide spectrum of service activities including transport, public utilities and health care."

Fitch only referred to complexity on the supply side from an economic viewpoint. When the complexities of the demand side and the growing need for social and environmental accountability are added in, the full complicated nature of tourism begins to be evident. The many inter-relationships that make up tourism must be identified and understood if it is to be what its proponents claim it is and will be—a vital and growing sector of the world economy.

The challenge to researchers is to realize what the nature of the full challenge is that faces tourism and to insure that in all research done a contribution to the solution of the problems must be made. We have, in the past, studied the extremities of tourism. We must take a more holistic approach.

While research must continue to seek improvements to existing methodologies, as the papers in this volume have done, it must also be prepared to go beyond the comfortable theories and methodologies that have stood it in good stead in the past. New ways of looking at problems must be sought. These new ways may be able to offer assistance in the task of attaining a better understanding of tourism. One such new approach is "The Chaos Theory." It was originally developed by meteorologist, Edward Lorenz, who was attempting to improve weather forecasting. This theory rejects the idea of linear relationships and says that a small event in one place or time can lead to major events in other places or times.

Larson (1994, p. K1) in an introductory popular article noted that "complex systems can be highly sensitive to initial conditions." Larson also notes "while overall patterns can be described, specific events cannot be predicted." Larson also cites Ralph Stacey (1992) who in a recent book concludes "that the business world shows many of the characteristics of the chaotic system." The complex nature of tourism enticingly suggests that the chaos theory may be able, if properly developed, to offer some meaningful insights. These few notes on a relatively new theory seem to strike a chord that is reminiscent of problems in tourism.

In a business where the real mission is to influence thousands, possibly millions, of individual decisions in favor of a particular destination, the appeal of chaos theory should be evident.

DISCUSSION

A public debate on the issues facing tourism is long past due. The questions are simple. What is tourism and how should it operate in order to achieve maximum benefit for people, both visitors and hosts? The answers are far more difficult.

There is a large body of empirical evidence in existence. There are many researchers seeking new challenges in the field, and there are countless businesses looking for useable information to help in the decision-making process. While some excellent work is being done on further analysis of existing data and researchers are seeking out ways to improve their techniques there is no sense of direction available to guide the work. Some guidelines are needed that will enable researchers to obtain maximum benefit from their work and to make an even more substantial contribution to expanding the understanding of tourism. The efforts of the Travel and Tourism Research Association in starting to develop a research agenda should be encouraged and expanded. Tourism journals should encourage contributions that examine the ways and means of bringing a sense of direction to research.

Finally, we need to know what are the stories that are emerging, who needs to know about them, and how do they get used. When all expenditures in public and private agencies are under close scrutiny, tourism must use the information that has been collected in the past and that will be collected in the future to demonstrate that it can work towards the solution of the problems outlined earlier. It must also demonstrate that it can deliver on its promises of increased economic opportunity without damage to the physical and social environment. If these conditions are not met, the research funding may disappear. The consequences of any such disappearance would be catastrophic.

REFERENCES

Fitch, Alan. "The economic impact of tourism on developing countries–Winners or losers?" in Planning for Tourism in Developing Countries, PTRC Summer Annual Meeting, July 1986.

Larson, Peter. (1994) "Managers get insight from chaos theory," The Ottawa Citizen, October 15, K1.

Morrison, Alastair M., & Sheauhsing Hsieh, O'Leary, Joseph T. (1994) "A comparison of the travel arrangement of international travelers from France, Germany and the U. K.", Tourism Management, 15-6, 451-463.

Rogers, Judy. CityScapes and LandScapes–A New Look at Tourism by Canadians, Research Resolutions, 1995.

Smith, Stephen L.J. (a) A Research Agenda for the North American Travel Industry, Wheat Ridge, Co., Travel and Tourism Research Association, January 1994.

Smith, Stephen, L. J. (b) (1994) "Environment, social issues top 1995 agenda concerns," TTRA News, 25-5,. 1-3.

Stacey, Ralph. Managing the Unknowable: Strategic Boundaries Between Order and Chaos in Organizations, Jossey Bass, 1992.

Taylor, Gordon D. and Stanley, Dick. (1992) "An agenda for research: Synthesis of proposals developed at conference workshops," in Reid, L. J. Ed., Conference Proceedings, Travel and Tourism Research Association-Canada, 1991, TTRA Canada Chapter, 1 -2,

Taylor, Gordon D. and Campbell, Bernard F. (1993) "Think tank session on community and cultural tourism issues," in Reid, L..J., ed., Conference Proceedings, Travel and Tourism Research Association-Canada, 1992, TTRA Canada Chapter, 29.

Taylor, Gordon D., & Rogers, Judy, Stanton, Bruce. (1994) "Bridging the research gap between industry and researcher," Journal of Travel Research, XXXII-4, 9-12.

Taylor, Gordon D., How-To-Research Manuals, Ottawa,, Canada Chapter, TTRA, November 1994.

Index

Page numbers followed by f indicate figures; page numbers followed by t indicate tables.

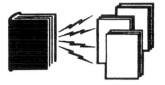

Haworth
DOCUMENT DELIVERY
SERVICE

This valuable service provides a single-article order form for any article from a Haworth journal.

- *Time Saving:* No running around from library to library to find a specific article.
- *Cost Effective:* All costs are kept down to a minimum.
- *Fast Delivery:* Choose from several options, including same-day FAX.
- *No Copyright Hassles:* You will be supplied by the original publisher.
- *Easy Payment:* Choose from several easy payment methods.

Open Accounts Welcome for . . .
- Library Interlibrary Loan Departments
- Library Network/Consortia Wishing to Provide Single-Article Services
- Indexing/Abstracting Services with Single Article Provision Services
- Document Provision Brokers and Freelance Information Service Providers

MAIL or *FAX* THIS ENTIRE ORDER FORM TO:

Haworth Document Delivery Service
The Haworth Press, Inc.
10 Alice Street
Binghamton, NY 13904-1580

or FAX: 1-800-895-0582
or CALL: 1-800-342-9678
9am-5pm EST

PLEASE SEND ME PHOTOCOPIES OF THE FOLLOWING SINGLE ARTICLES:

1) Journal Title: _____

　　Vol/Issue/Year: _____ Starting & Ending Pages: _____

Article Title: _____

_____

2) Journal Title: _____

　　Vol/Issue/Year: _____ Starting & Ending Pages: _____

Article Title: _____

_____

3) Journal Title: _____

　　Vol/Issue/Year: _____ Starting & Ending Pages: _____

Article Title: _____

_____

4) Journal Title: _____

　　Vol/Issue/Year: _____ Starting & Ending Pages: _____

Article Title: _____

_____

(See other side for Costs and Payment Information)

COSTS: Please figure your cost to order quality copies of an article.

1. Set-up charge per article: $8.00
   ($8.00 × number of separate articles)   _____

2. Photocopying charge for each article:

   1-10 pages: $1.00   _____

   11-19 pages: $3.00   _____

   20-29 pages: $5.00   _____

   30+ pages: $2.00/10 pages   _____

3. Flexicover (optional): $2.00/article   _____

4. Postage & Handling: US: $1.00 for the first article/
   $.50 each additional article   _____

   Federal Express: $25.00   _____

   Outside US: $2.00 for first article/
   $.50 each additional article   _____

5. Same-day FAX service: $.35 per page   _____

GRAND TOTAL: _____

METHOD OF PAYMENT: (please check one)

❑ Check enclosed   ❑ Please ship and bill. PO # _____
(sorry we can ship and bill to bookstores only! All others must pre-pay)

❑ Charge to my credit card: ❑ Visa; ❑ MasterCard; ❑ Discover;
   ❑ American Express;

Account Number:_____ Expiration date:_____

Signature: ✗_____

Name: _____ Institution: _____

Address: _____

_____

City: _____ State: _____ Zip:_____

Phone Number: _____ FAX Number: _____

MAIL or *FAX* THIS ENTIRE ORDER FORM TO:

Haworth Document Delivery Service   **or FAX:** 1-800-895-0582
The Haworth Press, Inc.   **or CALL:** 1-800-342-9678
10 Alice Street   9am-5pm EST)
Binghamton, NY 13904-1580